The SCHOOL for QUALITY LEARNING

Managing the School and Classroom the Deming Way

Donna K. Crawford

Richard J. Bodine

Robert G. Hoglund

Research Press
2612 North Mattis Avenue
Champaign, Illinois 61821

Cover design by Jack Davis
Composition by Wadley Graphix Corporation
Printed by Capital City Press

ISBN 0–87822–341–X
Library of Congress Catalog No. 93–84097

To Buck, LaVonne, Cathy, and Barbara
Dawn and Dirk
Terry, Matthew, Daniel, and Timothy

Contents

PART ONE Understanding Quality as the Solution

PART TWO Managing the School for Quality Learning

PART THREE Managing the Classroom for Quality Learning

Figures and Tables

FIGURES

TABLES

Preface

We undertook the creation of this book because we believe that education in America is in crisis. Nearly everyone who looks at education in this country reaches the same conclusion. For years, reports on the crisis in schooling have emanated from panels composed of academicians, school board members, business executives, community leaders, and representatives of national and state professional organizations. Rarely have the people who matter most—principals, teachers, students, and parents—been included or heard. It is significant to us that those who daily work and live in our schools express deep concerns about the viability of our educational system. Educators may offer various reasons for this crisis, express various levels of concern about its severity, and hold various notions of how to cope with it, but few educators would deny that a crisis exists. We believe that the school is a microcosm of our society; the school is not the only institution in crisis. However, as educators, we do not presume to have the expertise to suggest changes beyond the educational system. More important, we refuse to accept the need for change in other elements of society as an excuse to defer action in the realm where we believe we have some expertise—specifically, the nature of schooling.

The crisis in education is not a recent phenomenon. Schools traditionally have required students to accumulate and hold information long enough to pass a test. The primary objective of education, drawn from observing practice rather than accepting the stated purpose, has been to impart knowledge rather than to encourage thinking. Neither the teacher nor the evaluation system has been inclined to determine whether the learner really understands the ideas, the concepts, the meanings of lessons. Learners who have succeeded in school discovered early on that there were two kinds of learning—the kind needed to succeed in school and the kind needed in daily life—and all too often, the two kinds were related only vaguely if at all.

In recent years, the crisis in education has assumed a more national focus. As other countries begin to challenge and even surpass the United States in industrial and economic power, policymakers and the business-industrial complex often cite the failure of the American educational system as a prime cause. As the population in our nation's schools becomes less and less white and more and more impoverished, the lack of success of minority and economically disadvantaged students looms large enough to force recognition of the fact that these groups have never enjoyed success in the American school system. In addition, over at least the past two decades, a growing percentage of students from the nonminority, middle- to upper-class population have refused to buy into a system that requires the learner to delay satisfaction of present personal needs in favor of promised future rewards. This growing group, refusing to continue differentiating between school life and real life, has determined that school life is not need fulfilling and that hard work in school is not justified.

Again, the crisis is not a recent aberration. Simply doing a better job of what schools have been attempting to do all along will not extract the system from crisis. The crisis is a systems problem and, as such, renders fruitless even the most valiant effort toward improvement by modifying or changing specific practices. What is required, we believe, is a radical transformation: not radical in the sense of "far out" or extreme, but radical in the sense of pervasive, fundamental, basic—going to the very root. This radical transformation must be designed and orchestrated collectively by those within the fundamental unit for change, not mandated by those outside it. We believe changing the system is the responsibility of management. Therefore, this book focuses on the management responsibilities of the principal toward the teachers as workers and on the management responsibilities of the teacher toward the learners as workers. The teacher, a key player in the proposed transformations, is both a manager and a worker in the school for quality learning.

We have chosen the school as the unit of change. We recognize that nearly every school is a part of a larger school system: The system must allow the individual school the latitude to implement the changes outlined in this book and must provide the support and encouragement to help the school staff persist through the difficult transition. Whether the process of transferring power and responsibility to the individual school is achieved through site-based management, school autonomy policies, or system decentralization is unimportant; what is required is that the power and responsibility be vested in the principal and staff of the individual school. The school—and ultimately each classroom within the school—is the only entity close enough to the learner to understand and appreciate quality learning and to make a difference for the learner. In this book, building on a sound psychological foundation, we have outlined radical changes in school management and classroom management practices and have challenged principals and teachers to transform schools. We believe that these transformations, if realized, offer each learner a structure that makes possible need-fulfilling experiences that result in quality learning. We believe that these proposed changes will accommodate the ever-increasing diversity of the learner population—offering a true multicultural experience characterized by equal success and quality performance for every learner regardless of race, gender, or socioeconomic status.

This book draws heavily on the psychological teachings of Dr. William Glasser and the management principles of W. Edwards Deming. It calls for an outcome-based approach to education. However, it does not subscribe only to the conservative agenda rigorously advocated by business and industry, and it does not call for more testing. Quite the contrary: The valued outcomes listed in chapter 13 require a broadening of the learning experiences offered in our schools rather than further restriction of those experiences. All segments of the learner population must be invited to participate, given the freedom to feel invested, and provided the support to excel. There are three key evaluative questions: Is what we are doing good for the learner? Are we offering every learner an opportunity for quality learning? and, Are we working hard to ensure that every learner grasps that opportunity?

This book proposes an agenda for transformation by addressing the multiple issues that the school must consider in order to move toward being a school for quality learning. The agenda must be considered in its totality. It is not intended as a menu from which to select isolated items that appeal to the reader. Although many of the ideas may be used independently of others, such a piecemeal approach will not, in our view, result in the system transformation needed to allow quality learning. Each school's staff must design their program to maximize their talents and to address the needs of their learners. We offer this book as an agenda for the transformation to quality. Each issue raised here needs to be addressed collectively by each school staff and independently by each classroom teacher.

This book is for the dedicated educator with the courage to admit that change is needed, even demanded, and with the

energy and desire to take the risks required for the transformations suggested. We believe that you are legion, and we are
hopeful that you will prevail. The mission is a difficult one; the
transformation to quality will not be easy or smooth. We are
optimistic, however. We subscribe to the adage "You are either
part of the solution or part of the problem." We hope that this
book encourages you to join together to become the solution.

We would be remiss if we did not comment on the cost of
the proposed transformations. We believe that education in this
country has been seriously underfunded and is losing ground
rapidly. We believe that providing more money to do what we
have already been doing is not the solution. We believe that the
suggested transformations can be accomplished regardless of the
funding level for education. However, we do believe that if these
transformations are undertaken in good faith, additional funding
will accelerate progress toward the goal of quality learning. We
believe that the goal of quality learning for every learner justifies
additional expenditure. Reducing class size to 15 students per
teacher in every American elementary and secondary classroom
in 1992 would cost 17.4 billion dollars. In 1992, the cost of the
United States defense of northern Norway was 17 billion dollars
("Leading Indicators," 1992). Obviously, there is a political
agenda that we educators and our friends must pursue. But we
cannot wait for the political agenda: We must start now to pursue
an educational agenda toward quality learning.

One final point: Although *quality* is central to our proposals,
we have not specifically defined the term here. We believe that
the definition of quality is the responsibility of each individual
and that the judgment of quality is situational in learning endeavors. We suggest two questions as criteria by which each
may judge quality: Are you doing the best you can do? and,
Are you being the best you can be?

Acknowledgments

Acknowledgments are always difficult because we are the product of many experiences and relationships. We are grateful to all those who have touched our lives and helped influence and create who we are.

In particular, we thank the staff members of Leal School and Washington School in Urbana, Illinois, for their ability to live these ideas enough to show us that the school for quality learning has the potential to be a reality. We truly value their trust and caring.

To Vernessa Gipson, Sharon Hall, Laura Haber, Joe Omo-Osagie, and Bob Shoda, we dedicate chapter 16, which is a synergistic product of our involvement. Their commitment to developing and using these discipline ideas in their daily work with learners who have serious emotional-behavioral problems provided inspiration, hope, and guidance.

To Don Holste, we express our appreciation for sharing our beliefs. We thank Betty LaCrone for her willingness to spend nights and weekends word processing. To Urbana School District 116, we are grateful for the freedom to develop and implement our ideas.

To Dr. William Glasser, we extend our gratitude for his quality work, his support, and the challenge to continue learning.

PART ONE

Understanding Quality as the Solution

CHAPTER 1

Quality: Not the Problem

The United States is experiencing a crisis in education. It may be argued whether the crisis is full-blown or emerging, but few would deny that it exists. Critics, including many practicing educators, state that the system of public education is failing to meet the challenges posed by demographic and societal change. The crisis exists essentially because America has changed but the schools have not. Schools no longer adequately serve the children of this country. Parents, students, educators, and business leaders are concerned about graduates who are unprepared for the workplace; they also worry about the societal impact of numerous high school dropouts. *Agenda: America's Schools for the 21st Century* reports that 82% of incarcerated Americans are dropouts ("Leading Indicators," 1991). The National Center for Education Statistics (1990) has found that the average dropout rate in this country is 25% and approaches 50% in most major cities. Traditionally, dropout percentages are underreported—when the number of students entering high school is compared to the number of high school graduates, the proportion climbs well past 25% and may even approach 50% as a national average.

John O'Neil (1992) describes the effects of our educational shortfall:

> Experts on education and the economy are worried by
> the growing gap between the capabilities of high school

graduates . . . and the skills, knowledge and habits of
mind that employers seek. More than half of our young
people leave school without the knowledge or foundation
required to find and hold a good job, states a recent
report by the U. S. Department of Labor. A recent Harris
poll found that only one-third of employers think that
high school graduates show the ability to read and
understand written and verbal instructions and only one-
fourth say they are "capable of arithmetic functions."
And two-thirds of personnel officers at some of
America's biggest firms say that they must screen more
applicants now than five years ago to find qualified
candidates for entry level jobs, according to another
survey conducted by the alliance of business. (p. 6)

Most public schools today operate under the industrial worldview reflected in a factory mentality. They are designed as institutions in which all students are expected to move through the system simultaneously at the same rate. Those who do not eventually
drop out, either by physically departing or passively accepting
what is offered and meeting only minimal expectations. Teachers
work at separate stations within the "plant," teaching content-
driven curriculum that is seldom connected with that of other subject areas and rarely designed to address the needs of the learner.
Linda M. McNeil, in *Contradictions of Control* (1986), elaborates on
this phenomenon: "The original classroom study of social studies
content found content tightly controlled by teachers, reduced to
simplistic fragments, and treated with little regard for a reference
to resources in the students' experiences or school's references"
(p. 159). Administration follows the traditional mentality of industrial "boss management," where the school is governed from the
top down. McNeil points out that when the school's organization
becomes centered on management by control, teachers and students take school less seriously:

They fall into a ritual of teaching and learning that tends
toward minimal standards and minimum effort. This sets
off a vicious cycle. As students disengage from enthusias-
tic involvement in the learning process, administrators
often see the disengagement as a control problem. They
then increase their attention to managing (by controlling)
students and teachers rather than supporting their
instructional purpose. (p. xvii)

District central offices and state offices of education also contribute to the system's problems by promoting uniformity among schools rather than encouraging the diversity that could address the needs of today's heterogeneous student populations. McNeil argues that

> amid the diverse prescriptions for school improvements, the reforms most likely to be implemented have been those which call for more centralized management controls over factors shaping the curriculum: testing, teacher training and course content . . . and the irony of these reform efforts is that they perpetuate a basic reality that has created the problems in the first place. . . . We assert the purpose of our schools is to increase learning but have organized schools in ways that distort that purpose and even contradict it. (p. xvii)

Although this system may have worked when the United States was the world leader in industrial production, it is not effective in today's complex global marketplace, where a work force capable of creative problem solving and flexibility is needed. This country is moving toward the 21st century with a school system trapped in the 19th century—one designed for a totally different set of economic and social conditions.

The National Association of State Boards of Education (1988) reports on dramatic societal changes that have serious implications for schools. For example:

> During the 1970s and early 1980s, 20 million new jobs were created: 90 percent of them were in services and information industries; only 5 percent of new jobs were in manufacturing.

> The proportion of young people is shrinking. Between 1975 and 1986, the number of youth as a percentage of the total population declined from 21 percent to 18 percent. This trend will continue through the next decade—by 1996 the percentage of young people will decline to 13 percent.

> By the year 2000, one-third of our population will be African-American or Hispanic; these groups currently comprise a disproportionate number of those at the bottom of the educational and occupational ladders.

> The number of children living in single-parent homes has tripled since 1950, from 7 percent to over 21 percent

in 1985. Only 4 percent of today's families are "traditional," consisting of a father, a mother at home, and
two or more school-aged children.

Nearly half of all children living in young families
(those headed by parents under 25) are poor. This is
nearly double the rate of 1973. Overall, one in four
children live in poverty—and regardless of race, young
people from poor families are three to four times more
likely to drop out of school than those from more affluent
families. (p. 2)

Our educational system needs fundamental changes to engage this diverse population in learning. We must focus on the
educational needs—both present and future—of our students. As
young people grow up in an increasingly complex society, it will
become increasingly important for them to continue learning
after they leave school, to adapt to change, and to solve new problems creatively. The abilities to think analytically and strategically
and to communicate ideas are ever more crucial for young people
entering the labor force. Too few of our students are leaving
school equipped with these abilities.

With the changes in American demographics and family
structure, more and more students are in need of diverse instructional methods and strategies to keep them in school and to provide them equal opportunity to be productive citizens. The nation
needs every citizen to be productive if it is to compete in the inter-
national marketplace and be a safe and peaceful place to live.
Peggy Odell Gonder (1991) observes that "in the mid-1990s only
3 citizens will be working for every person on social security,
compared with 17 workers in early 1950. And given advances in
technology, few of those students who drop out of school today, or
who are not well educated, will be productive tomorrow" (p. 2).
If this trend continues, the number of people entitled to social
security benefits will exceed the number productively employed
and paying into the social security system, bankrupting the social
security system in a short time. In addition, the number who are
unemployable and drawing public assistance will increase the demand on the already burdened public welfare system.

Concerned about declining productivity, some school leaders
around the country have looked to the quality management principles of Japanese industry in an effort to meet the challenge of restructuring the public education system. A school's product is the
quality of its students' learning; whether the consumer of that product is a college, an employer, or society at large, a well-educated,

motivated student is desired. Educators can learn much from the industrial restructuring that began in Japan over 30 years ago when Japanese industrial leaders applied the beliefs and strategies of an American, W. Edwards Deming. Deming, author of *Out of the Crisis* (1986), almost single-handedly changed the phrase "made in Japan" from a pejorative to a sign of excellence. Deming brought Japan out of crisis by teaching the Japanese business leaders to transform work processes to bring about a quality revolution. He did this through the commitment to a consistent psychologically based framework for understanding organizational systems. Within this framework, an organization's economic need to focus on purposes and products was aligned with workers' intrinsic needs to have positive influence on those purposes and products.

By modeling organizational change on Deming's quality management principles, schools can become empowered to improve the quality of the education they provide. Such improvement is possible because teachers and administrators have the power to effect system changes. When educators focus on optimizing the learning environment for student engagement, quality learning can be a continual process.

In *The Quality School* (1990) William Glasser explains why Deming's ideas work so well and how these ideas can be applied to the schools

> so that the present elitist system, in which just a few
> students are involved in high quality work, will be re-
> placed by a system in which almost all students have this
> experience. Once they do have this experience, which for
> almost all of them would be a totally new one, students
> will find it highly satisfying. They will no more turn
> down the chance to continue doing this kind of work
> than does the well-managed factory worker . . . students
> are not only the workers in the school, they are also the
> products. Once they see that they themselves are gaining
> in quality, they will make an effort to continue this
> option. (p. 3–4)

Throughout this book, Glasser uses the industrial analogy of workers and managers. He argues that students are the workers of the school and that high-quality work is the difference between success and failure for the organization. Teachers are the first-level managers; administrators are middle- and upper-level managers. As in industry, the school's productivity depends mostly on the skills of those (the teachers) who directly manage the workers (the students). According to Deming, the success of the first-level managers depends almost completely on how well they in turn are managed by those above them.

Deming would see the present school system as a stable system of trouble; in his view, the improvement of quality is the responsibility of management. Deming describes the quality problem this way:

> Folklore has it in America that quality and production are incompatible: that you cannot have both. A plant manager will usually tell you that it is either or. In his experience, if he pushes quality, he falls behind in production. If he pushes production, his quality suffers. This will be his experience when he knows not what quality is nor how to achieve it.
>
> Why is it that productivity increases as quality improves? Less rework.
>
> There is no better answer. Another version often comes forth: Not so much waste.
>
> Quality to the production worker means that his performance satisfies him, provides to him pride of workmanship. Improvement of quality transfers waste of man-hours and of machine-time into the manufacture of good product and better service. The result is a chain reaction—lower cost, better competitive position, happier people on the job, jobs, and more jobs. (1986, pp. 1–2)

In Japan, industrial management observed that the improvement of quality resulted naturally and inevitably in the improvement of productivity. Deming reports that this chain reaction, shown in Figure 1.1, became assimilated in Japan as a way of life; the chain reaction diagram appeared on the blackboard at every meeting with top management from July 1950 onward. Deming further noted that once Japanese management adopted the chain reaction, everyone shared a common aim, that of quality.

A fact of education that gets little real attention or understanding from the current reform movement is that quality, in the long run, does not cost more money. Granted, an initial expenditure may be required to correct ineffective practices, but costs will ultimately decrease when a true focus on quality is achieved. Failure and underachievement ultimately increase the cost of schooling through wasted effort and rework. The situation at Gonzales High School clearly illustrates this point.

Figure 1.1   The Deming Chain Reaction

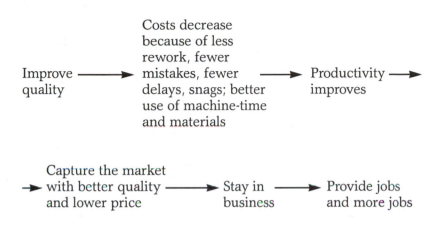

Improve quality ⟶ Costs decrease because of less rework, fewer mistakes, fewer delays, snags; better use of machine-time and materials ⟶ Productivity improves ⟶

⟶ Capture the market with better quality and lower price ⟶ Stay in business ⟶ Provide jobs and more jobs

Note. Reprinted from *Out of the Crisis* (p. 3), by W. Edwards Deming, by permission of MIT and W. Edwards Deming. Published by MIT, Center for Advanced Engineering Study, Cambridge, MA 02139. Copyright 1986 by W. Edwards Deming.

Gonzales is an agriculturally oriented community located in California's Salinas Valley. Upon entering the town, one sees the sign "Welcome to Gonzales—Heart of the Salad Bowl." The enrollment at Gonzales High School is approximately 1,000. More than 80% of the students are Hispanic; slightly more than 90% are considered minorities.

Gonzales High School has begun to move toward quality by examining the system and targeting areas needing improvement. Student learning was one area targeted. School staff learned that the real cost of failing grades was almost 128,000 dollars for one semester (see Table 1.1). Each failed class had to be repeated, if it was required for graduation, or replaced by a different elective class.

What most do not realize is that the cost per pupil remains constant, whether the outcome is success or failure. The 128,000 dollars invested in failing grades represent potential savings that could be an incentive for the school to reduce class size, institute staff training, and provide additional resources to avert failure. Further analysis at Gonzales suggested that student underachievement consumed almost half of the per-course-section expenditure. With the cost per section at 7,000 dollars, with a staffing ratio of 29.65 students per 1.0 staff, the number of sections in

Table 1.1   Grades at Gonzales High School (Spring Semester, 1990)

Grade	Number	Percentage	Grades per student
A's	1,391	24.30	1.46
B's	1,554	27.14	1.63
C's	1,268	22.15	1.33
D's	700	12.23	.73
F's	541	9.45	.57
P's	169	2.95	.18
Other	102	1.78	.11
Totals	5,725	100.00	6.00

A's-B's	51.44%	
C's-below	48.56%	

Grades	Sections	Cost
F's	18	$128,000
C's-below	93	$651,000

Note. From "The Cost of Educational Mediocrity and Failure," by R. G. Hoglund, 1991a, *Journal of Reality Therapy, 11*(1), p. 22. Copyright 1991 by the *Journal of Reality Therapy.* Reprinted by permission.

which students received grades of C or lower was approximately 93. Therefore, 93 sections at 7,000 dollars equals 651,000 dollars for students not making a significant effort to learn. Gonzales High School was paying 779,000 dollars per school semester attempting to educate students who, because of failure or underachievement, would have minimal opportunities to become productive citizens upon leaving school. Unless it made quality the focus, Gonzales High School would continue to have a failure rate greater than 9%, and 48% of student grades would most likely remain C and lower.

Gonzales High School is not unique in this situation. Failures and underachievement consume as much capital in terms of student cost as do grades of A and B. As these defects persist, they continue to necessitate rework and generate added costs.

In education the improvement of quality transforms the waste of human and material resources into increased student learning. When quality is the aim, there are fewer defects, more students are engaged in quality learning, and the system operates more cost effectively, spending money to expand learning opportunities instead of wasting money on rework. Figure 1.2 illustrates Deming's chain reaction as it takes place in education.

Figure 1.2   The Chain Reaction in Education

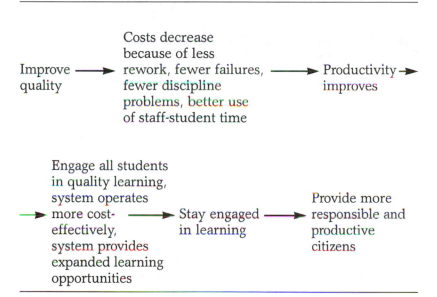

Deming (1986) has enumerated 14 points that managers need to understand and apply if they wish to attain quality and productivity. These 14 points, discussed in detail in chapter 2, evolve from two important principles. The first is the quality principle: Quality is never the problem; rather, it is the solution to the problem. According to this notion, improving the performance of a system of people begins with a concern for the quality of whatever is being done. Improving that quality results in less waste, less cost, more satisfaction for all concerned, greater productivity, and a better product.

The second is the perversity principle: Any attempt to increase productivity and cut costs by imposing quantitative constraints on a system results only in increased costs elsewhere in the system. According to this notion, if a manager attempts to change a system by forcing its members to behave differently, the system will be resistant to management's action—even if the workers say they wish to cooperate. Traditional management theory is the antithesis of the first principle and the embodiment of the second. Table 1.2 contrasts key elements of traditional management theory and Deming's management theory.

The key to the successful application of the quality principle and the avoidance of the results of the perversity principle is an approach called *lead management,* which contrasts with traditional

Table 1.2   Traditional Management Theory Versus Deming's Management Theory

Traditional theory	Deming's theory
Quality is expensive.	Quality leads to lower costs.
Inspection is the key to quality	Inspection occurs too late to prevent defects.
Quality control inspectors can assure quality.	Quality begins with management.
Defects are caused by workers.	Most defects are caused by the system.
Rewarding the best performers and punishing the worst will lead to greater productivity.	Reward and punishment of above- and below-average performance destroy teamwork and creativity.
Profit is the most important indicator of a company's viability.	Profit does not indicate the company's future ability to stay in business.

Note. From *Dr. Deming: The American Who Taught the Japanese About Quality* (pp. 17–18), by Raphael Aguayo. Copyright © 1990 by Raphael Aguayo. Published by arrangement with Carol Publishing Group.

"boss management." Glasser (1990) observes that boss management does not work because it limits both the quality of the work and the productivity of the worker. Glasser defines boss management in terms of four basic elements:

> 1. The boss sets the task and the standards for what the workers are to do, usually without consulting the workers. Bosses do not compromise; the worker has to adjust to the job as the boss defines it.
>
> 2. The boss usually tells, rather than shows, the workers how the work is to be done and rarely asks for their input as to how it might possibly be done better.
>
> 3. The boss, or someone the boss designates, inspects (or grades) the work. Because the boss does not involve the workers in this evaluation, they tend to settle for just enough quality to get by.
>
> 4. When workers resist, the boss uses coercion (usually punishment) almost exclusively to try to make them do as they are told and, in so doing, creates a workplace in which the workers and manager are adversaries. (pp. 25–26)

A lead manager, on the other hand, must communicate a compelling vision of quality and inspire cooperation. According to Glasser, the lead manager devotes his or her time and energy to running the system so that the workers realize that it is to their benefit to do quality work. Table 1.3 shows the difference in focus between boss management and lead management.

Both Glasser and Deming would agree that replacing boss management with lead management in the school and in the classroom is the key to educational reform. Glasser (1990), expanding on Deming's ideas, describes the responsibility of the lead manager:

> 1. A manager is responsible for consistency of purpose and continuity of the organization. The manager is solely responsible to see that there is a future for the workers. (It is our responsibility as a society to manage our schools so that all students get a high quality education.)
>
> 2. The workers work in a system. The manager should work on the system so that it produces the highest quality product at the lowest possible cost. The distinction is

Table 1.3   Differences in Focus Between Management Styles

Boss management focus	Lead management focus
To motivate workers	To remove barriers to motivation
To find out who is wrong	To find out what is wrong
To assign responsibility for defects	To study the process to prevent defects
To fix everyone's attention on productivity	To fix everyone's attention on quality
To call for and reward individual achievement	To call for and recognize group achievement
To give the order "Do your job"	To establish well-defined procedures: "Help me help you do your job"

crucial. They work in the system; the manager works on the system. No one else is responsible for the system as a whole and for improving it. (This means that the administrators, much more than the teachers, are responsible for improving the system.) (p. 31)

Whether we consider lead management of the school (with the administrator as manager and the teacher as worker) or lead management of the classroom (with the teacher as manager and the student as worker), the following elements of lead management described by Glasser (1990) apply:

1. The leader engages the workers in a discussion of the quality of the work to be done and the time needed to do it so that they have a chance to add their input. The leader makes a constant effort to fit the job to the skills and the needs of the workers.

2. The leader (or worker designated by the leader) shows or models the job so that the worker who is to perform

the job can see exactly what the manager expects. At the same time, the workers are continually asked for their input as to what they believe may be a better way.

3. The leader asks the workers to inspect or evaluate their own work for quality, with the understanding that the leader accepts that they know a great deal about how to produce high quality work and will therefore listen to what they say.

4. The leader is a facilitator in that he shows the workers that he has done everything possible to provide them with the best tools and workplace as well as a noncoercive, nonadversarial atmosphere in which to do the job. (pp. 31–32)

What makes lead management work? Deming (1986) credits the power of intrinsic motivation through the creation of joy and pride in work and joy and pride in learning. Glasser (1990) explains this motivation in terms of control theory, which

contends that all human beings are born with five basic needs built into their genetic structure: survival, belonging, power, fun and freedom. All of our lives we must attempt to live in a way that will best satisfy one or more of these needs. (p. 43)

Thus, lead management works because the work place becomes need fulfilling.

Research recognizes the importance of the principal's role in restructuring the school. Management leadership is essential to the implementation of educational change. Lasting change comes from commitment, not authority. When teachers are involved in decisions that affect them, commitment can become a powerful reality. Teachers and administrators who develop a common framework for understanding the interdependence of their work can make the changes that will result in quality learning for students.

Lead management as an approach to school reform is no longer a rare phenomenon. Schools all over the country are experimenting with forms of restructuring in which principals and teachers are becoming involved in school management. This book will help teachers learn to manage students for quality learning and will help administrators learn to manage teachers for quality learning and teaching. Quality is not viewed as the problem for reform; quality is the solution for reform.

This book is designed to familiarize educators—teachers and administrators—with the quality philosophy and with the actions that support the attainment of quality learning. Our aim is to move schools beyond the typical restructuring efforts of the past few years into the critical psychological transformation of school and classroom management. Deming (1986) states that transformation requires directed effort. If a school is to be transformed into a place where quality learning is the product, everyone in the school must be involved in the effort, which begins with the building of a common understanding. To transform is to bring about a radical change or to change into a different form, substance, or state. Transforming the school for quality learning means changing the system—its patterns, methods, and elements. Individuals within the school will be challenged to develop new ways of thinking that depart drastically and fundamentally from conventional beliefs about education. The school for quality learning will require innovations that address the problems of the future. The transformation begins with leadership: It is the responsibility of the lead-manager principal to expect quality learning and to engage the staff in identifying the barriers to quality learning. Once staff members understand the system and realize the need for change, they work together to redesign the system for quality learning. Everyone in the school must work to accomplish the transformation. Deming teaches that transformation is everybody's job.

Becoming a school for quality learning requires processes that can respond to continual change. A school for quality learning never stops improving. Inevitably, needs will change, and the school must be able to address these changing needs through its ability to design and redesign for the future. As the staff embark on the transformation, each individual must develop the proactive habit of creating solutions rather than seeking examples to follow. There exist few examples of schools for quality learning.

Commitment to new learning and a new philosophy is required of any teacher or administrator who seeks transformation. At the same time, any teacher or administrator committed to growth and development has the potential to be a quality educator in the school for quality learning. Our work will never be finished because there is no static state of quality. Our schools will be either improving or declining in quality. The school for quality learning is the one that never stops improving.

CHAPTER 2

Deming's Management Theory: Application in Education

Deming's (1986) theory of management for improvement of quality and productivity calls for the application of 14 points and the elimination of seven "deadly diseases" and some obstacles. Table 2.1 offers a summary of these. Deming notes that his management method can be used anywhere, in small organizations as well as large ones, in service organizations as well as manufacturing plants, and even in a division within a company (and, by extension, a school within a school system). Quality management is holistic and must be adopted in its entirety if it is to be effective. Deming's points, diseases, and obstacles, which will be discussed in depth in this chapter, constitute a broad prescription for reform. Any organization attempting to apply this management theory must work out its own adaptations for its own purposes. Even though this process is never easy, Deming claims that by applying the points and eliminating the diseases and obstacles, management can accomplish much more than it otherwise would. The reform, although difficult, is well worth the effort.

Deming's theory of management, though developed in the business world, can be applied in education. When educators in

Table 2.1   Deming's 14 Points, Deadly Diseases, and Obstacles

The 14 points

1. Create constancy of purpose for improvement of product and service.
2. Adopt the new philosophy.
3. Cease dependence on mass inspection.
4. End the practice of awarding business on price tag alone.
5. Improve constantly and forever the system of production and service.
6. Institute training.
7. Institute leadership.
8. Drive out fear.
9. Break down barriers between staff areas.
10. Eliminate slogans, exhortations, and targets for the work force.
11. Eliminate numerical quotas.
12. Remove barriers to pride of workmanship.
13. Institute a vigorous program of education and self-improvement.
14. Take action to accomplish the transformation.

The seven deadly diseases

1. Lack of constancy of purpose
2. Emphasis on short-term profits
3. Evaluation of performance, merit rating, or annual review
4. Mobility of top management
5. Management based on visible figures alone
6. Excessive medical costs
7. Excessive costs of warranty, fueled by lawyers who work on contingency

Some obstacles

1. Neglecting long-range planning and transformation
2. Relying on technology to solve problems
3. Seeking examples to follow rather than developing solutions
4. Maintaining that "our problems are different"
5. Blaming the work force for the problem

most any school are asked how to improve quality and productivity, the usual answer is "by seeing that everyone does his or her best." Deming reports the same response from the management of most companies. However, he believes that it is not sufficient for people to do their best: They must first know *what* to do. Best efforts, though essential, can do much damage in the absence of guiding principles, including knowledge of mission. Deming (1986) urges, "Think of the chaos that would come if everyone did his best, not knowing what to do" (p. 19). Deming's principles provide the guidance for educational reform. Educators who grasp the principles can transform the schools into a place where quality learning is the product. Following, then, is an analysis of Deming's principles as they apply to the educational system.

THE 14 POINTS

Point 1: Create Constancy of Purpose for the Improvement of Product and Service

According to Deming, management faces two sets of problems— those of today and those of tomorrow. Today's problems in education tend to be viewed by policymakers in terms of disciplining students to work in the existing system and raising achievement test scores. Schools tend to dwell on such matters without attending adequately to the students' future needs. Because teachers have new groups of students each school year, their interests tend to be short-term. Teachers want their students to learn what is in the curriculum prescribed for each grade level and to perform well on achievement tests. However, some students fail to master the prescribed curriculum, and other students are developmentally well beyond that curriculum and underachieve because they are not challenged. The present focus is on fitting a diverse group of students into the existing system without regard to whether or not the system is producing students who are learning.

With school populations growing more and more diverse, educators must question the value of continuing to accept school failure and undereducation as part of the school culture. The same challenge must be posed to schools that are preoccupied with raising test scores by becoming more and more efficient in teaching to the test. What value is there in raising test scores when students do not know how to apply what they have learned and when test-oriented teaching eliminates curricular opportunities for students to explore, create, and discover the changing world around them? If students do not learn in our schools, will they be prepared to be the learners of the future?

Schools, like businesses, need a constancy of purpose that prepares them to address the problems of the future. This constancy of purpose can be thought of as the reason for existence. Deming, deviating from a common assumption, states that the primary purpose of business is not making a profit but staying in business. What is the value of a 30% increase in quarterly dividends to a company that will be out of business in 5 years? For example, eliminating research and development costs may increase the immediate profit margin, but it may soon result in a product that is not marketable because it is no longer state of the art. When the primary focus is on profit, management thinking may be short-term, and long-term success may be the casualty. On the other hand, when the focus is on staying in business, decisions are made in the interest of long-term success.

Likewise, schools' primary purpose is not to produce students who can score well on tests but to prepare students for lifelong learning. Education, like business, must focus on the constant improvement of product (each student's learning) and service (methods for creating that product).

Naisbitt and Aburdene, in their thought-provoking book *Megatrends 2000* (1990), proclaim that by identifying the forces pushing the future rather than those that have contained the past, we possess the power to engage with our reality. The school's reality is to create constancy of purpose for improving students' ability to become—and remain—productive learners and citizens.

Point 2: Adopt the New Philosophy

In Deming's view, quality must become the new mission. Quality means giving the customer what the customer has a right to expect. Business can no longer afford to tolerate mistakes, defects, poor workmanship, bad materials, sullen service, and poorly trained employees. Defects are costly; consumers end up paying for delays and mistakes. The cost of living depends inversely on the goods and services that a given sum of money will buy. Reliable products and services reduce costs, whereas defective products and services increase them. Likewise, the educational system cannot continue to tolerate student dropouts, failure, and underachievement, nor can it tolerate inappropriate curriculum and ineffective teaching methods. Defective products of education usually end up in welfare lines, in prisons, or hopelessly involved in the cultures of crime or poverty. Again, the public pays for these defects.

Schools need a new orientation within which defects are unacceptable. The school must become a place where quality is expected from every student, where every student learns and no student fails. When a school adopts the new philosophy of quality, it will provide what its clientele have a right to expect: quality learning. It is easy to accept a variety of excuses for student failure—for example, "The student is from a dysfunctional family" or "The student is living in poverty." Such statements are often accepted as reasons for the student's inevitable failure in the educational system. What chance does a student have in life if failure is viewed as an inevitable part of the system? Schools must find ways for all students to succeed. Schools must acknowledge that each student is different and that every student can experience quality learning.

Point 3: Cease Dependence on Mass Inspection

According to Deming, inspection of a finished product as it comes off the line, or at key points during production, is too late, ineffective, and unnecessarily expensive. With this type of inspection, the company is paying workers to make defective parts and then to correct the defects. The consumer pays for the duplication of work. This sort of inspection does not improve or guarantee quality because it fails to improve the process that is producing the defects. Deming (1986) says, "Quality comes not from inspection but from the improvement of the process" (p. 29). Inspection the Deming way, then, is a process in which the workers are enlisted and trained to evaluate the quality of their own work.

In education, state and national standardized testing programs do not contribute to the improvement in methods and processes that would lead to quality learning. In fact, the inspection of student achievement through mass testing actually prevents quality learning because teachers spend a significant portion of their instructional time teaching for the purpose of raising test scores. The result is an educational experience that is constricted and contrived. Because instructional time is finite and because preparing students for tests consumes precious instructional time, activities that actually lead to quality learning are most likely to be omitted from the instructional day. Students involved in instruction aimed at test taking usually become disengaged because they see no meaning or relevance in what they are asked to do. The "test" curriculum is unauthentic, and students following it are unmotivated to learn. Quality learning is not the result of students' desire to earn a higher score on a test; rather, quality learning results from the use of instructional methods and processes that engage students in learning activities that draw on knowledge far beyond assorted facts and basic operations. When the inspection process in school becomes a way for students and staff to evaluate what they are doing and plan for ways to improve, the potential for quality learning is greatly increased.

Point 4: End the Practice of Awarding Business on Price Tag Alone

According to Deming, price has no meaning without a measure of the quality being purchased. An example in industry is the practice of purchasing supplies or services from the lowest bidder without careful attention to specifications. This practice can only increase costs elsewhere. When quality becomes the central focus, the practice of buying from the lowest bidder is often abandoned. In education—because most schools are public institutions—the acceptance of the lowest satisfactory bid is usually mandated in the procurement of materials and services. This legal requirement need not be a hindrance to quality; it simply dictates that bid specifications be generated carefully and completely.

In education, the most significant expenditures are in the area of human resources. Class size, defined in terms of teacher-to-student ratio, is often determined solely on the basis of "price tag." In fact, increasing class size is a common way for schools to cut costs. "Cost plus" then becomes the pitfall. Students in large classes who do not receive instruction appropriate to their needs and learning styles either fail those classes and have to repeat them, or they become targeted for special assistance or special education. Special education services and repeated classes are high-cost items. Hence, the cost overruns are likely greater than they would have been if quality, not cost, had been the criterion for determining class size. Would it not be better to pay for smaller classes in the first place, rather than incurring extra costs for special education services and repeat classes? From the student's perspective, being failed and/or disabled by the system is a high price to pay.

Point 5: Improve Constantly and Forever the System of Production and Service

Deming firmly believes that every product should be regarded as one of a kind and that there is only one chance for optimum success. In his view, quality "must be a part of the system, built in at the design stage" (1986, p. 49), and teamwork in design is fundamental to the process. The Shewhart Cycle (Figure 2.1), developed by Walter Shewhart—Deming's mentor for a number of years—is an approach to process analysis and improvement used by Deming.

This cycle involves constantly defining and redefining the customer's needs and wants; it is simultaneously a vehicle for involving every function of the business in these desires of the customer. Thus, the entire organization focuses on the customer and on all parts of the process that affect the stability of the products and services for that customer. Widely known as the PDCA cycle (which stands for Plan–Do–Check–Act), the Shewhart cycle inevitably leads to redesign and improvement. It can be used at every level of decision making from the development of improved methods within a department to the development of a comprehensive strategic plan for the entire system.

Educators often find themselves in the position of "putting out fires" instead of improving quality through systematic changes. As

Figure 2.1   The Shewhart Cycle

Study the results. What did we learn? What can we predict?

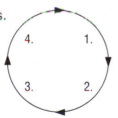

What could be the most important accomplishments of this team? What changes might be desirable? What data are available? Are new observations needed? If yes, plan a change or test. Decide how to use the observations.

Observe the effects of the change or test.

Carry out the change or test decided upon, preferably on a small scale.

Step 5. Repeat Step 1, with knowledge accumulated.
Step 6. Repeat Step 2, and onward.

Note. Reprinted from *Out of the Crisis* (p. 88), by W. Edwards Deming, by permission of MIT and W. Edwards Deming. Published by MIT, Center for Advanced Engineering Study, Cambridge, MA 02139. Copyright 1986 by W. Edwards Deming.

a public institution supported by taxpayers, schools are quick to react to complaints by applying the quick fix. For example, when a school's test scores drop, teachers and students are often blamed. Teachers begin to focus on instruction to raise test scores, and students are worked longer and harder so they will score better on the test. Deming (1986) declares, "Putting out fires is not improvement of the process. Neither is discovery and removal of a special cause detected by a point out of control. This only puts the process back to where it should have been in the first place" (p. 51). What should occur instead is a reevaluation of the system, with educators examining their mission and analyzing the teaching and learning processes.

Educators can use strategic planning in schools to focus on improving the system rather than blaming teachers and students for not working hard enough. Among the quick fixes often proposed when teachers and students are thought not to be working hard enough are a longer school day and more academic requirements. But these changes alone will not solve the system's problems. Everyone involved with a school must continually work to redesign and improve the system. Whether it is a question of designing strategies and methods for an individual student in the classroom or improving a schoolwide service, the PDCA cycle can be applied.

Point 6: Institute Training

Too often in business and industry, workers learn their skills from other workers who have themselves received inadequate training. In education one need only talk to new teachers to realize the necessity for staff development programs. Many teachers have been taught by college instructors who have never taught in an elementary, middle, or high school yet who are purporting to teach teaching. Frequently only one semester of student teaching is required for certification, and the variation in quality and competency of supervising teachers exacerbates the problem. The supervising teacher is usually also a product of inadequate training, with experiences very similar to those afforded the prospective teacher. If the supervising teacher is truly superior, that expertise is most likely the result of good personal instincts plus appropriate inservice training, on-the-job experience, and mentorship of a highly skilled colleague. It is very difficult to erase improper training. Sadly, often neither the supervising teacher nor the student teacher knows what it takes to help all students achieve quality learning.

To develop a school for quality learning, administrators and teachers must understand the psychological framework for quality and develop the skills necessary to promote it. They must establish a staff development program to build a common foundation of knowledge for all staff members. Further, administrators and teachers must develop skills in addition to those required for basic effectiveness in their professions. (Those skills will be described in chapters 12 and 18.) The staff development program in a school for quality learning must embody the same principles and practices as the quality program for student learners. It must be designed to meet the varied needs of staff members with different concerns and styles. A staff development program that attempts to fit all participants into a single mold will certainly send the wrong message about the design of a quality learning program.

Point 7: Institute Leadership

Lead management plays a crucial role in the realization of quality. In Deming's view, the aim of leadership is to help people do a better job. The leader is the primary agent for improvement of the system. Leaders must understand the overall system and know how they and the groups they facilitate fit with the aims of the organization.

Lead managers do not judge their workers and rank individual performances. Instead, they judge their own performance as they observe the workers and determine what they need to do to foster improvement. The lead manager builds trust and encourages everyone to improve, creating an environment where the workers can experience pride in their work. A lead manager's efforts are devoted to cultivating each worker so that all workers can perform to their greatest potential and, at the same time, in a manner consistent with the organization's aim.

In education as in business, the antithesis of lead management is boss management. Boss managers set standards, tell rather than show how, and rely heavily on reward and coercion to motivate and control workers (students and staff). In a boss-managed system, workers do not realize their greatest potential. They rarely experience joy and pride in their work, and they have little commitment to the aim of the organization. Lead management in the school means that the principal must create an environment where teachers can feel pride in their work; lead management in the classroom means that the teacher must create an environment where students can feel pride in their learning.

Pride, an internal sense of one's own dignity and self-worth, is indispensable to quality learning. The lead manager's responsibility, to keep everyone working toward the common goal of quality, is an impossible mission unless individuals can experience pride in their work. If the sense of pride is absent, there is something wrong with the system. It is the responsibility of management to discover the barriers to pride and to modify the system so that everyone can do quality work.

Point 8: Drive Out Fear

Coercion, or managing through fear, is the most destructive element in a workplace. It impedes productivity and interferes with quality work. Workers who fear their bosses or supervisors may produce enough to meet minimal standards, but they will never achieve quality. Administrators and teachers who work in an atmosphere of coercion and fear will never elicit respect and loyalty from those under their management, nor will they improve the quality of the work being produced.

Deming writes that people cannot perform at their best unless they feel secure—that is, without fear, not afraid to express ideas or to ask questions. Deming believes that a consequence of fear in any form is loss of quality due to impaired performance. It is interesting to note that the idea of driving out fear was not a part of Deming's initial management concepts developed in Japan. The Japanese managers did not have to be counseled to eliminate fear: The workers were eager to pull together to build their nation after the war; they regarded their employers not with suspicion and distrust but as benefactors. All belonged to a family working toward the same goal. Only later, through experience in working with American companies that stressed boss-management systems, did Deming incorporate driving out fear into his 14 points.

Fear takes a devastating toll in education. Management by fear, whether it means the principal managing teachers or teachers managing students, prevents people from thinking. It deprives them of pride in their work and thus destroys intrinsic motivation. Through fear, the thinking and creative potential of students and teachers alike is suppressed. Most educators who rely on fear believe that individuals need to be controlled—that they cannot be trusted and will not work if they are not threatened with some external consequence. This view eventually becomes a self-fulfilling prophecy.

Fear in education takes the form of performance appraisals, evaluations, grades, punishments, reprimands, and competitive reward systems. Until educators accept the fact that fear and quality work are incompatible, there can be no real improvements in the quality of the educational system. To eliminate fear, principals and teachers must strive to create an environment where intrinsic motivation is understood, is valued, and is the inspiration for learning. They can do this through self-evaluation, an internal assessment process that actuates intrinsic motivation to improve quality. (Self-evaluation will be discussed further in chapters 6 and 17.)

Point 9: Break Down Barriers Between Staff Areas

Breaking down barriers between staff areas is really a matter of teamwork. To illustrate this point, Deming cites a not atypical example in which people in a company's design department work with people in sales and engineering to design a new product. The eager salespeople begin showing prototypes of the product to wholesalers, eliciting advance orders. Unfortunately, the manufacturing department cannot produce the item economically as it was designed; small changes in style and specification are necessary. These changes cause production delays, forcing the salespeople to return and communicate the changes to the wholesalers who have placed the orders. The result is loss of time and loss of sales, losses that could have been prevented through initial teamwork with the manufacturing people. Deming constitutes teams of people in design, engineering, production, and sales. These teams, called QC (quality control) circles, combine their resources to develop designs for the future and to improve the quality of products and services.

In schools, the most significant barriers between staff areas arise from the segregated and segmented subject matter approach to curriculum. The teacher teaches a content area in isolation from all other content areas. Students use structured textbooks containing drills and exercises that reinforce content that they often perceive as having no connection to the world outside the classroom. Learning is viewed as an individual activity, and students are discouraged from collaborating with one another.

If students are to be actively engaged in learning, they must view the curriculum as meaningful and relevant. Integrating curriculum and employing cooperative learning can break down the barriers to relevance. Integrating curriculum requires teamwork among teachers with expertise in various content areas. They combine their information and teaching resources to develop learning experiences and opportunities that keep students continually engaged in learning. Cooperative learning requires teamwork among students as they complete learning activities. With the barriers gone, teachers have the opportunity to learn from one another, students have the opportunity to learn from their peers, and teachers and students can learn from one another as well. The result is quality teaching and quality learning.

In addition to breaking down the barriers created by the segregation of curriculum, management must eliminate the barriers that prevent teamwork. A combined effort is necessary if the school is to become a place for quality learning. Individual staff members must cooperate to meet the students' needs and address the school's improvement priorities. Secretaries, custodians, clerks, teacher aides, librarians, special educators, counselors, teachers, and administrators all affect one another's ability to work consistently with the quality philosophy. When everyone in the school is pursuing the aim of quality learning for each student, services can be focused on the learner and designed, coordinated, and delivered by the team. It is the principal's responsibility as lead manager to break down barriers that have been built by years of tradition and to help staff members work together—in other words, to facilitate teamwork.

Point 10: Eliminate Slogans, Exhortations, and Targets for the Work Force

At first glance, posters in offices and factories urging workers on to higher quality or targeting some quantitative measure of production seem relatively harmless. According to Deming, the problem with such slogans, exhortations, and targets is that they are directed at the wrong people, generally implying that the desired improvement depends on additional efforts of individual employees rather than on a well-functioning system. Because most causes of low quality and low productivity are systemic, the power to effect improvement lies beyond the work force. Workers alone can do little to change the system; the burden of improvement rests with management. Slogans, exhortations, and targets frequently generate frustration and resentment. They advertise to the workers that management is unaware of the barriers to pride in workmanship, thus creating adversarial relationships.

In the schools, "excellence in education" has been a popular slogan for a number of years. Some schools have based their whole system of management on this exhortation, which suggests that teachers and students could do better if they would strive harder for excellence. Unfortunately, the slogan has had no long-term effect and in some cases has even backfired: Many schools embraced the "excellence" target only to find themselves several years later with even more students underachieving or dropping out. The slogan backfired because excellence was interpreted to mean more rigid graduation requirements, more arduous expectations for existing curriculum, and more strict and uncompromising discipline policies. These standards tend only to increase the number of students who fail, underachieve, drop out, or create discipline problems. There are at least three explanations for this phenomenon. First, while the original standards prevailed, a number of students were working hard and achieving marginal success. As standards were tightened, those students' efforts no longer resulted in a success experience. Without recognition of at least marginal success, the students no longer chose to expend the effort. Second, another contingent of students may have seen the old standards as irrelevant yet chose to work hard enough to achieve success in school because they recognized such success as prerequisite to future opportunities. The increased standards, however, exceeded their tolerance for the absurd. In their view, the school experience shifted from being tolerably irrelevant to being totally alien to their lives and goals. Third, the study opportunities or courses that students most desired—for example, home economics, industrial arts, music, art, and so on—were no longer accessible because the school day or term was totally consumed by courses needed to satisfy graduation requirements.

The schools that promoted the slogan "excellence in education" made the mistake of believing the problem—a lack of quality learning—to be within the power of the workers (teachers and students) to change instead of undertaking much-needed system modification. The slogan implies that the system itself is working and that the lack of productivity is due to inadequate effort on the part of learners, teachers, or both. In reality, the system is not working—for students and teachers alike.

Point 11: Eliminate Numerical Quotas

Deming maintains that quotas and other work standards such as those used in management by objectives interfere with quality, perhaps more than any other working condition. The problem with quotas and management by objectives is that they can function only as well as the system permits. They focus on the end goal rather than on the process. Management by objectives and quota systems, according to Deming, usually do not include "any trace of a system by which to help anyone do a better job" (1986, p. 71).

Deming cites the case of an airline reservation clerk who was required to answer 25 calls an hour while being courteous and not rushing callers. Because that figure did not allow for unforeseen circumstances such as computer down time and the need to look up additional information, the clerk was unable to meet the quota. What was the employee supposed to do in this situation: satisfy the customer or make the quota? If management eliminated the quota and concentrated on system changes that would increase productivity (number of calls) and quality (customer satisfaction), the reservation clerk might even exceed 25 calls per hour with satisfied customers. In any case, satisfied customers must be the goal.

When quotas are based on the average output of a group, the outcome will be mediocrity, with half the workers producing above and half below the quota. Peer pressure often will hold the upper half to the average, and those below will be unable to meet the standards. In any event, half of the workers will be below average with little opportunity for improvement because the system remains the same; the result is a waste of human resources. The problem is to improve the system and find out who is having trouble. Changing the system so that all workers can succeed is the only way to achieve quality results.

In education, there is great pressure for teachers to raise achievement test scores and for students to earn higher grades. These demands run counter to quality learning because the focus becomes the grade or the standardized test score, not the learning process or even a meaningful product of learning. The problem is exacerbated because much less attention and instructional time are devoted to skills that cannot be evaluated in terms of a standardized score. Quality learning is not average learning or minimal learning; it is learning that cannot be based on the average output of the class or the school. When 50% of students are performing at or below average, is quality schooling taking place?

Point 12: Remove Barriers to Pride of Workmanship

When Deming works with a company or conducts a seminar, he frequently asks participants to name obstacles that prevent them from experiencing pride in their work. Often, the responses include the following:

1. Conflicting or unclear goals

2. Arbitrary decisions by supervisor

3. Lack of time, resources, and direction

4. Devaluation of efforts

5. Fear of mistakes or failure

6. Insufficient information and training

7. Little feedback on performance

Often managers do not understand the problem because they do not focus on the human processes behind the product or service. Faced with problems that concern people, managers sometimes establish employee involvement or participation programs. These programs often disintegrate through frustration because management fails to act on employees' suggestions for improvement, and the employees believe that management does not value their effort or ability. Employees in this situation cannot feel pride in their work. On the other hand, when management understands the human processes, works with the people to develop a plan of action for improvement, and institutes the improvement, pride of workmanship is strengthened.

In education, barriers to pride of workmanship exist when teachers are excluded from decision making about the school and students are excluded in decision making about their instructional programs. Most teachers and students want to do a good job and are distressed when no one seems able to help them do it. In Deming's work we see that, 85% of the time, the problem lies with the system and not with the worker. Administrators will not be able to help teachers do quality work unless they collaborate to identify the system's problems and find effective solutions; the same holds true for teachers and their students. Whether principals are working with teachers or teachers are working with students, removing the barriers to pride in workmanship empowers people to manage themselves for quality. They become responsible for their actions and committed to the goal of quality learning.

Point 13: Institute a Vigorous Program of Education and Self-Improvement

Although this point is similar to Point 6 (institute training), there is a distinction. The purpose of training is to build a foundation of common knowledge; Point 13 is concerned with instituting a comprehensive continuing education program that not only builds the skills needed for workers' current jobs but also encourages them to acquire new knowledge and understanding in preparation for future challenges.

Deming's views on retraining and education stem from his conviction that workers' self-improvement is linked directly to a company's ability to improve its system. He considers the company responsible for offering continuing educational opportunities and holds that motivation comes from pride in learning and self-improvement. It is not enough for an organization to have talented and skilled people; those people must continually acquire the new knowledge and skills required to deal with new materials and methods of production.

Self-improvement and retraining are crucial for educators. The skills and knowledge of the principal and the teacher have a direct impact on the quality of the students' learning. No two students are alike; each one brings a uniqueness to the learning environment. This fact alone underscores the need for vigorous education and retraining. A heterogeneous group of students with diverse learning styles, skills, knowledge bases, and talents require a teacher who can call on a variety of strategies and methods to meet the needs of each individual in the classroom. Teachers need to acquire skills in a number of areas, such as learning styles, cooperative learning, whole-language instruction, integrated learning, and responsibility education—not to mention keeping abreast of overall developments in the profession.

Management training is needed as well so that administrators can function as lead managers in the school and teachers can be lead managers in the classroom. Lead managers must not only understand the processes of quality teaching and learning, they must also be skilled in communication, team building, decision making, problem analysis, reality therapy, and conflict resolution. Vigorous training in these skills will equip staff to create a school environment where all students experience quality learning. (Chapter 12 treats these managerial skills in detail.)

Point 14: Take Action to Accomplish the Transformation

"A journey of a thousand miles begins with the first step." This ancient Chinese proverb summarizes Deming's final principle. According to Deming, the first milestone on a company's road to quality is passed when a critical mass of the employees understand the 14 points and become active participants in the process of transformation.

Following are the actions that lead to Deming's transformation:

1. People in the organization come together to understand the 14 points and decide how to apply them. They will agree on what the points mean and how to use them, and they will agree to carry out the new philosophy of quality. Deming stresses that if this step is omitted individuals will go off in different directions, well-meaning but misguided, diluting their efforts and sometimes working at cross-purposes.

2. Managers analyze the need for change and affirm the desire to transform their style of management. The word *transformation* is used because most people in an organization find Deming's ideas vastly different from what they initially learned; now they must change not only their perceptions but also their actions, to make them consistent with that thinking. Before managers can commit to this transformation, they must feel frustration and dissatisfaction with past performance. They must realize that the old system is not producing quality and find the courage to break with tradition.

3. Through seminars and other means, management helps a critical mass of employees understand why change is necessary and realize that change will involve everybody. Enough people must understand the 14 points to put them into practice. This training process builds a foundation of knowledge as well as a basis for teamwork.

4. Every activity and every job is analyzed for improvement. Everyone belongs on a team working in the PDCA (Shewhart) cycle to address specific issues such as constancy of purpose, improvement of product and service, purchase of materials, removal of ratings, and removal of barriers to pride in workmanship. Application of the PDCA cycle, Deming says, will lead to continual improvement of methods and procedures. It can be applied to any process.

Educators can take these same actions in their schools and classrooms. The school for quality learning is a product of lead management in the school and in the classroom. When principals and teachers agree on their mission and institutionalize Deming's 14 points, the quality of each student's learning will improve.

The 14 points constitute Deming's theory of management. Their application has the potential to transform the traditional boss-management style into lead management. Deming also writes of seven deadly diseases and some obstacles that can stand in the way of transformation. The distinction between the diseases and the obstacles is based partly on the difficulty of eradication and partly on the severity of the damage they cause. Deming views the diseases as more serious than the obstacles because traditional management suffers deeply from them and they are potentially fatal unless corrected. In reading the following section, note that the diseases and obstacles are not only closely linked with the 14 points, they are also linked with one another.

THE SEVEN DEADLY DISEASES

1. Lack of Constancy of Purpose

If constancy of purpose (Point 1) is essential for a company to stay in business, its absence means devastation. A company without constancy of purpose does not think beyond quarterly profits and has no long-range plan to survive. Deming advocates protecting investment by working continually toward the improvement of processes—and thus products and services—that will bring the customer back again and again.

In education, the focus on compartmentalized content-driven curriculum, test scores, and grades severely limits opportunities for quality learning. A lack of constancy of purpose underlies the focus on these short-term issues; in the long term, the student is prevented from becoming a lifelong learner. This situation prevails despite the profession of nearly every school that its mission is to develop lifelong learners.

2. Emphasis on Short-Term Profits

Deming says that the pursuit of quarterly dividends and short-term profits defeats constancy of purpose and long-term growth. His comparison of America to Japan helps define the problem: "Most American executives think they are in business to make money, rather than products and service. . . . The Japanese corporate credo, on the other hand, is that a company should become the world's most efficient provider of whatever product and service it offers. Once it becomes the world leader and continues to offer good products, profits follow" (1986, p. 99).

Just as American industry's relentless drive for short-term profit diverts attention and resources from the job of forming the productive base, the drive within the American educational system to increase national test scores diverts attention and resources from the job of creating lifelong learners who will become the productive citizens of the future.

3. Evaluation of Performance, Merit Rating, or Annual Review

Deming reports that many companies and government agencies in the United States have systems in which employees receive annual ratings from their superiors. He charges that such systems represent management by fear and considers them devastating for a number of reasons. Evaluation of performance, merit rating, or annual review encourages short-term performance at the expense of long-term planning, discourages risk taking, builds fear, undermines teamwork, and pits people against one another in competition for the same rewards. The result is people working for themselves, not for the company. Rewards and punishments do not motivate people to do their best; in fact, they do exactly the opposite, and pride in workmanship is lost. Managers, in effect, are managers of defects, and the organization becomes the loser.

In education, test scores, grades, merit pay systems, and annual teacher ratings are symptoms of this disease. With the disease spreading, teachers manage more and more defective students, and principals manage more and more defective teachers. The results in education are the same as the results in business: unmotivated workers with little pride in workmanship.

4. Mobility of Top Management

When people cannot take pride in their work, they look for other jobs. Deming observes that it is difficult for workers to remain committed to policy or achieve long-term improvement when they know that their manager's tenure is likely to be short. The job of management is inseparable from the welfare of the company. Mobility undermines teamwork; workers become disillusioned when forced to endure a succession of new managers and new programs for improvement. If individuals are to work jointly toward a common end, they require time to build trust and synergy. Teamwork—along with team effectiveness—develops over time.

It is folklore—and probably very close to actual fact—among school board associations and educational leadership associations that a school superintendent holds a position for 3 years on the average. It is no wonder that the school reform movement is progressing so slowly. It is nearly impossible for a superintendent to develop the quality of administrative teamwork needed to transform a school system in just 3 years.

In the classroom, the teacher is considered the top manager. The lock-step practice of moving children to a new classroom and a new teacher each school year provides little opportunity for the teacher to effect true long-term improvement in the student's ability to do quality learning. Students will do quality work when they value their relationships with their teachers and when the teachers truly understand the individual student's needs. These relationships and this understanding take time to develop; for this reason, students should remain with their teachers for more than a single year.

5. Management Based on Visible Figures Alone

Deming says that a company cannot claim success on visible figures alone. He believes that the most important figures needed for management are unknown or unknowable. Paradoxically, even though figures may be unknown or unknowable, they must be taken into account. Deming cites an example in which the visible figures of a company's credit department indicated success in retaining most customers who paid promptly. The credit department had performed well on its assigned job, which it perceived as obtaining prompt payments. Eventually, the not-so-visible figures showed that the credit department had driven some of the company's better customers to the competition. Even though these customers were not paying promptly, they were purchasing in large quantities and were responsible for their payments, albeit sometimes late. Management accounted too late for the invisible figures. It would have been better for the company to work out a long-term payment plan with these major customers than to lose their business by demanding prompt payments.

Deming warns that the potential gains from application of his management methods cannot be quantified year by year in terms of dollars. People should know before they start that they will be able to quantify only a minor portion of the gain. For example, how does one quantify a happy customer's multiplying effect on sales—or the opposite effect from an unhappy customer?

In education, leaders make budget cuts that, in their view, will not cause major harm to "basic" educational programs. Some school systems delay the purchase of supplies and equipment;

some cut back funding of athletics, extracurricular activities, and academic programs outside the "basics"; some eliminate administrative positions and rewrite job descriptions so that those remaining have more responsibility and more work; and some increase class size to reduce the number of teachers employed. In such school districts the quality of education is no longer the focus. The schools are run on visible figures alone. Costs of a "basic" education are plainly visible, but they do not tell the story about quality. Perhaps this is one reason that public school students are no longer engaged in learning.

6. Excessive Medical Costs

For some companies, according to Deming, medical costs represent the largest single expenditure. Excessive medical costs take many forms. For example, employer-provided health insurance benefits pay for counseling of employees who may be depressed from dissatisfaction with work, for treatment of employees whose performance is impaired by alcohol or drugs, or for general health care. These medical costs have a multiplier effect for any company because they are embedded in the costs of the products and services of every other firm with which it does business.

Excessive medical costs in education—in the form of health insurance benefits and, especially, in excessive use of sick leave—equal less money available for improvement of programs for students. Employees who find the work situation personally fulfilling are likely to have better attendance patterns.

7. Excessive Costs of Warranty, Fueled by Lawyers Who Work on Contingency

Deming calls the United States the most litigious country in the world. Fear of being sued raises costs. Liability insurance costs and legal fees cost both the company and the consumer because the businesses build these costs into the prices of their products and services.

Education is not immune from these costs. In fact, litigation in the area of special education burdens school systems not only with their own attorneys' fees; they also pay the attorneys' fees of parents when parents prevail in court. Liability insurance and attorneys' fees are paid with tax dollars, again at the expense of educational programs.

SOME OBSTACLES

In addition to the deadly diseases, Deming identifies a number of obstacles that significantly limit an organization's effectiveness in reaching quality. Following are the obstacles he cites.

1. Neglecting Long-Range Planning and Transformation

Long-range plans are crucial to a company's survival. However, management may entirely neglect the development of such plans. Even when long-range plans do exist, they are frequently ignored because of so-called emergencies. Managers spend their time and energy dealing with immediate crises and do not analyze the organization for possible transformations that could prevent these short-term crises and offer potential for future growth.

Deming also uses the example of company policies that are essentially frivolous—for instance, concerning attendance and punctuality—that consume management time. Managers spend large amounts of time enforcing these policies and disciplining employees when rules are broken. In a climate of lead management, these matters would not be issues because employees would be committed to quality and have an environment where they could experience joy and pride in their work. Lead management requires long-range planning and transformation.

In a school for quality learning, the lead-manager principal is not concerned about staff attendance, number of hours worked, or punctuality. Lead-manager teachers do not spend much time disciplining learners. These issues are not prominent because the teacher "worker" and the learner "worker" see the school as need fulfilling. Everyone understands the mission of quality. Thus, all are engaged in the continual transformation of the system.

2. Relying on Technology to Solve Problems

Deming criticizes the supposition that technology (computers, modern machinery, and tools) will resolve deep-seated quality and productivity issues. The fact is that technology cannot transform a company; only lead management can transform a company. Technology as a resource can contribute to quality, but it is only a resource. In education, transformation to quality can occur with or without technology.

3. Seeking Examples to Follow Rather Than Developing Solutions

Deming notes that companies facing problems tend to look for solutions already used elsewhere. He warns against this because examples by themselves teach nothing; it is necessary to know why a practice succeeds or fails. This obstacle is represented as a key point in the United States Department of Education's America 2000 plan, designed to create new schools across the nation that will serve as models to be broadly replicated. John I. Goodlad (1991), Director of the University of Washington's Center for Educational Renewal, rejects the search for example:

> It is unrealistic and dysfunctional to propose to replicate in one setting schools that work in another. It is possible, however, to seek to implement broadly some principles and concepts characteristic of good schools, such as small size, a close relationship between home and school, small teams of teachers staying with groups of students over a period of years, diagnosis of children's progress, mixed age groups. (p. 12)

Deming would likely suggest that to improve quality in schools through implementation of the principles and concepts suggested by Goodlad, one would first need to understand why these ideas succeed and why their opposites have failed.

4. Maintaining That "Our Problems Are Different"

"Our problems are different" is a common complaint that afflicts management and government administration the world over. "They are different, to be sure, but the principles that will help to improve quality of product and service are universal in nature" (Deming, 1986, p. 130). In education, this obstacle is often presented as an excuse for not making the transformation necessary to improve quality.

5. Blaming the Work Force for the Problem

Deming states that workers represent only 15% of the problem and that the system is responsible for the other 85%. The system is the responsibility of management. Instead of blaming the production and service problems on the work force and demanding that workers work harder to do their jobs in the way they were taught, management should scrutinize the system and work to transform it. The essence of quality management is the ability to treat problems of the system and of the people simultaneously.

In education, workers are not the problem, and they should not be blamed for the problem. If lead managers in the school and in the classroom transform the system, students will begin to achieve quality learning and become quality learners. They will no longer be disabled by the system.

CHAPTER 3

Psychological Framework of Quality

Understanding the psychological framework that defines and undergirds Deming's (1986) management method is essential to the achievement of quality and the efforts to constantly improve. According to Deming, no one will do quality work who feels threatened or coerced; when work is rewarded or punished, people tend to do the minimum expected and are not as creative as they would otherwise be.

The traditional boss-management approach is based on stimulus-response psychology focusing on extrinsic motivation through rewards and punishments. Much of what takes place in schools emerges from a set of assumptions about human nature based on stimulus-response psychology. These assumptions can be observed not only in the way students are disciplined but also in the fact that attempts to control their actions are viewed as discipline; not only in the way students are graded but also in the fact that grades are regarded as a way to improve achievement; not only in teachers' orders to students not to interact during work time but also in the fact that student interaction is seen as extraneous to the learning process. These extrinsically motivated management system practices—*extrinsic* meaning not part of the essential nature of the individual—rest on the theory that humans can be controlled through external rewards and punishments.

By contrast, lead-management methods are derived from an understanding of intrinsic motivation, which comes from within each individual. It is part of one's internal system, and it is essential to the individual's nature. Deming notes that people are born with a need for relationships with others and a need to be loved and esteemed by others, emphasizing that the needs for self-esteem and for respect are innate. If people are denied dignity and self-esteem, intrinsic motivation becomes suppressed. Deming's management theory recognizes that extrinsic motivation is a submission to external forces that neutralize intrinsic motivation. Deming's ranking of evaluation by performance, merit rating, and annual review among one of the seven deadly diseases that rob people of pride and innovation demonstrates his commitment to management that restores power to the individual instead of overpowering the individual by extrinsic force. In schools relying on extrinsic forms of motivation (e.g., gold stars, tokens, or grades), the joy of learning becomes suppressed. The student who focuses on working for the grade or the star consequently is divested of the intrinsic joy and pride that can come from learning itself. Figure 3.1 illustrates Deming's view of the way in which intrinsic motivation is gradually destroyed by extrinsic systems.

Glasser (1990) explains that, in schools, boss management is the major reason why so few students are doing quality work. He believes that the problem is the boss manager's view of motivation: that people can be motivated from the outside. Boss managers fail to understand that all motivation comes from within. Consequently, they interact with people in a manner that implies that the people can be controlled through external rewards and punishments. Glasser's analysis of motivation, based on control theory, provides the foundation of knowledge everyone in the school for quality learning must possess. In the school for quality learning, not only does *extrinsic motivation* become an oxymoron, *intrinsic motivation* is a redundancy. Motivation is defined as something that causes a given action. The lead-manager principal and the lead-manager teacher know that motivation comes only from within the individual and that each individual's behavior can be driven only by his or her internal system. Thus, motivation can only be intrinsic, and only the individual chooses and has control over his or her actions. When boss managers attempt to control workers' behavior through extrinsic methods, they destroy what they are attempting to cultivate: motivated workers.

Understanding true motivation is crucial to becoming a lead-manager principal or teacher. Efforts to transform a school will

Figure 3.1   The Forces of Destruction

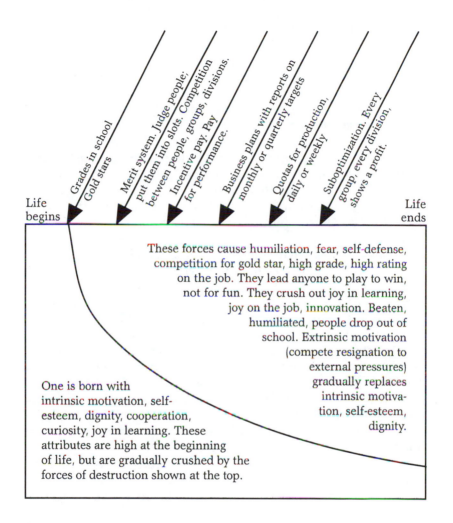

Grades in school
Gold stars
Merit system. Judge people; put them into slots. Competition between people, groups, divisions.
Incentive pay. Pay for performance.
Business plans with reports on monthly or quarterly targets
Quotas for production, daily or weekly
Suboptimization. Every group, every division, shows a profit.

Life begins

Life ends

These forces cause humiliation, fear, self-defense, competition for gold star, high grade, high rating on the job. They lead anyone to play to win, not for fun. They crush out joy in learning, joy on the job, innovation. Beaten, humiliated, people drop out of school. Extrinsic motivation (compete resignation to external pressures) gradually replaces intrinsic motivation, self-esteem, dignity.

One is born with intrinsic motivation, self-esteem, dignity, cooperation, curiosity, joy in learning. These attributes are high at the beginning of life, but are gradually crushed by the forces of destruction shown at the top.

Note. Reprinted from *The New Economics for Industry, Government, Education* (p. 215), by W. Edwards Deming, by permission of MIT and W. Edwards Deming. Published by MIT, Center for Advanced Engineering Study, Cambridge, MA 02139. Copyright 1993 by W. Edwards Deming.

fail unless the principal and the staff fully understand and internalize the psychological framework for quality. The staff must then have the opportunity to develop the skills that will allow them to align their actions with the theory.

The remainder of this chapter is devoted to the contributions of Dr. William Glasser, specifically his work in control theory and reality therapy. Glasser's books are essential reading for those striving to create a school for quality learning.

Control theory, according to Glasser (1984), explains why (and to a great extent how), all living organisms behave. Under this theory, everything we do in life is behavior; all of our behavior is purposeful, and the purpose is always to attempt to satisfy basic needs that are built into our genetic structure. The theory is called control theory because all behavior is our best attempt at the moment to control ourselves (so that we can control the world around us) as we continually try to satisfy one or more of these basic needs.

Reality therapy (Glasser, 1965) is a method of counseling based on control theory and aimed at helping individuals gain more effective control over their own lives. Individuals can also use it to improve their own effectiveness. This process has been proven effective in education, parenting, leadership, and management; it lends itself to any situation where people need to learn how to satisfy their needs in responsible ways. Reality therapy is based on the belief that we all choose what we do with our lives and that we are responsible for the choices. Responsibility is defined as learning to choose behaviors that satisfy our needs and, at the same time, do not deprive others of a chance to do the same. Practitioners of reality therapy persuade individuals to look honestly both at what they want and what they are doing to get what they want. An individual who is frustrated, or is frustrating others, is taught to evaluate what he or she is doing and, from this evaluation, learns about and puts into practice more effective (need-satisfying) behaviors.

In the school for quality learning, the lead-manager principal applies reality therapy in facilitating group decision making with the faculty, conducting individualized staff development and evaluation, and implementing discipline and responsibility education. Likewise, the lead-manager teacher uses reality therapy in evaluating student work, planning group and individualized learning experiences, and managing behavior. Reality therapy is a skill the entire faculty can learn. It is a flowing and adaptable communication process that allows the lead-manager principal and teacher to create a supportive environment in which individuals are freed to do quality learning.

CONTROL THEORY

Control theory is based on the assumption that all behavior represents the individual's constant attempt to satisfy one or more of five basic inborn needs. In other words, no behavior is caused by any situation or person outside of the individual. Accepting this idea requires a paradigm shift on the part of those who view life according to stimulus-response theory. According to the stimulus-response paradigm, we answer the telephone because it rings and stop the car because the traffic light is red; students stop running down the hall because we tell them to walk. From the stimulus-response perspective, behavior is caused by someone or something (the stimulus) outside the individual; the action following is a response to that stimulus.

According to the control theory paradigm, people or events outside us never stimulate us to do anything. Rather, our behavior always represents the choice to do what most satisfies our need at the time. From this perspective, we follow the rules of a game to achieve a meaningful outcome. We answer the phone because we choose to do so in order to communicate, not because we react to the ring. We stop at a red light because we choose to avoid risking a traffic ticket or an accident, not because the light turned red. Likewise, if the students stop running down the hall it is because they choose to walk in the belief that walking is more need fulfilling at the moment. When we repeat a choice that is consistently satisfying, we exercise less and less deliberation in making that choice. Even a quick action is chosen and not automatic.

Basic Needs

All individuals are driven by genetically transmitted needs that serve as instructions for attempting to live their lives. The needs are equally important, and all must be reasonably satisfied if individuals are to fulfill their biological destiny. These basic needs are (a) the need to survive, (b) the need to belong, (c) the need to gain power, (d) the need to be free, and (e) the need to have fun. The individual has no choice but to feel pain when a need is frustrated and pleasure when it is satisfied. When any need goes unsatisfied, there is a continual urge to behave. This urge is as much a part of human genetic instructions as is eye color. Instructions related to survival—such as hunger, thirst, and sexual desire—are relatively distinct. Individuals quickly learn that the particular discomfort is attached to this need, and it is plain what they must do to satisfy the survival instructions. The nonsurvival, or psychological, needs are challenging because it is often less clear what an individual must do to satisfy them. Psychological needs, like biological needs, have their source in the genes, even though they are much less tangible and the behaviors that fulfill them are more complex than the physical behaviors used to fulfill the survival needs. Glasser (1984) holds that we are essentially biological beings, and the fact that we follow some of our genetic instructions psychologically rather than physically makes neither the instructions less urgent nor the source less biological.

The ways in which we fulfill psychological needs can be summarized as follows:

1. We fulfill the need to belong by loving, sharing, and cooperating with others.

2. We fulfill the need for power by achieving, accomplishing, and being recognized and respected.

3. We fulfill the need for freedom by making choices in our lives.

4. We fulfill the need for fun by laughing and playing.

Even though individuals may not be fully aware of their basic needs, they learn that there are some general circumstances that strongly relate to the way they feel. For example, people behave lovingly with their parents because it feels good; they realize that when people pay attention to their words or actions they feel powerful; by making choices they feel the importance of freedom; and through laughter they learn about fun.

Even though human needs are essentially the same for everyone, the behaviors through which individuals choose to satisfy those needs may be quite different. Beginning at birth, individuals have unique experiences that feel either pleasurable or painful. Through these experiences, individuals learn how to satisfy their needs. Because individuals have different experiences, the things they learn to do to satisfy their needs will be different as well. Each individual has memories of need-fulfilling behaviors specific to his or her unique life experiences. These pleasurable memories constitute the individual's *quality world* and become the most important part of the person's life. For most people, this quality world is composed of pictures (or, more accurately, perceptions) representing what they have most enjoyed in life. These perceptions become the standard for behavioral choices. Unlike the basic survival needs, which are the same for everyone, the

perceptions in each person's quality world are very specific and completely individual. Individuals choose to behave in different ways to fulfill their needs because their quality worlds are different. To be in effective control of one's life means integrating this knowledge into the way one deals with others.

Total Behavior

To satisfy the basic needs, a person must behave. This means acting, thinking, feeling, and involving the body, all of which are components of the *total behavior* generated in the effort to get what is wanted. Whenever there is a discrepancy between what one wants and what one has, the internal behavioral system is activated. This is because all humans function as control systems: Their motivation is always to control, not only for present needs but, after those are satisfied, for future needs. People innately reject being controlled by others because they are capable of fulfilling only their own needs—indeed, that is the purpose of the control system. Loss of control to another is dysfunctional and runs counter to the fulfillment of needs.

To satisfy needs, people must be able to sense what is going on both around them and within them, and then be able to act on that information. When we sense a discrepancy between what we have and what we want, we behave by acting upon the world and upon ourselves as a part of the world. If we examine this behavior, it may seem to be composed of four different behaviors, but these are actually four components of what is always a total behavior. These four components, which always occur synchronously, are as follows:

1. Doing (e.g., walking, talking)

2. Thinking (e.g., reasoning, fantasizing)

3. Feeling (e.g., angering, depressing)

4. Physiology (e.g., sweating, headaching)

The feeling component of behavior is typically the most obvious. However, the more a person can recognize that feelings are just one component of total behavior, the more the person will be in control of his or her life. Glasser (1984) explains that, as individuals learn control theory, they stop using nouns (like *depression*) that describe only the feeling component of total behavior

and begin to use verbs that more accurately describe total behavior. Thus, verbs like *depressing, anxietying,* and *headaching* replace nouns like *depression, anxiety,* and *headache.*

The value in learning about total behavior is that it enables people to control their behavior to satisfy their needs more effectively. Glasser (1984) illustrates total behavior by relating how he might deal with a frustrating situation—failure to pass an important examination:

> When I went into the test, the dominant picture in my head was of passing, but now all my senses are busy informing me of the bad news that I flunked. Because I still want to pass, I will begin to generate some mostly sensible (at least to me) behaviors that I believe will help me to regain control of this unsatisfactory situation.
>
> In this case, what makes immediate sense to me to *do* is to go home, sit in my chair, drink a few beers, and avoid my classmates, most of whom I believe passed the examination. What I may *think* is sensible is to condemn myself for not studying hard enough, wish that I had passed, wonder what to do now, and hope it was all a mistake—a whole series of thoughts that are my immediate best attempts to both deal with and rationalize what happened. I will also generate a variety of *feelings* that also make good sense to me right now. Probably I'll be depressed, irritated, somewhat resentful, despondent, anxious, tense, and fearful—a whole series of emotions that seem to me appropriate to this failure. I also may be "suffering" from a headache or diarrhea, which added to what I am doing, thinking, and feeling, comprises my total behavior in this situation. (pp. 47–48)

In most situations, people are more tuned in to their feelings than their actions, thoughts, or physiology. It is unlikely that an individual would mention all the components described in this passage if asked how he or she was doing after failing an examination; most likely the person would talk about the feeling component—being upset or depressed about the situation. When people are asked to talk about a complex situation, they tend to describe the most obvious or recognizable factor. Glasser (1984) says that most people are much more aware of one component of behavior than of others and, hence, tend to view it as a discrete behavior, not as part of a total behavior. By recognizing that the feeling component is just one of four that make up total behavior, people can be more in control of their lives.

When people begin to think in terms of total behaviors, they can see that they choose these behaviors and have the option to change them. The way to change a total behavior is to change the behavior's doing and thinking components. We have almost total control over the doing component of behavior and some control over the thinking component; we have less control over the feeling component and very little control over physiological phenomena. Behavior in its totality ultimately gives us control over all components. When we change what we are doing, we will notice that our thoughts, feelings, and physiological responses change as well.

Returning to Glasser's (1984) narrative, we see that he deals with the disappointment of the failed exam by changing the doing and thinking components of behavior and, thus, the total behavior:

> I do not have to sit huddled in my chair depressing;
> I can, regardless of how I feel, call a friend and arrange
> a game of tennis. When we begin to play, I may still
> complain of how bad I feel, say I'm sorry I got him out
> on such a "bad" day, and, between games, tell him over
> and over how bad I feel and that, educationally, I'm
> doomed. I may not play my best, but I still can play.
>
> As I play, however, invariably I will notice that I
> begin to think different thoughts, feel different feelings,
> and experience a different physiology. My headaching
> or stomachaching clears up, my depressing seems to go
> away, and I start to think more about winning the match
> than failing the test.
>
> All of us have had experiences like this, and from
> them there is a very important lesson to be learned:
> *Because we always have control over the doing component*
> *of our behavior, if we markedly change that component, we*
> *cannot avoid changing the thinking, feeling, and physiological*
> *components as well.* The more we get involved in an active
> doing behavior that is markedly different from what we
> were doing when choosing a misery, like depressing or
> headaching, the more we will also change what we
> think, feel, and experience from our bodies. And if what
> we do gives us greater control, it will be accompanied by
> better feelings, more pleasant thoughts, and greater
> physical comfort. (p. 51)

The message is that, because people always have control over the doing component of behavior, if they change that component, they cannot avoid changing the thinking, feeling, and physiological components as well. A choice of action that results in greater control will be accompanied by better feelings, more pleasant thoughts, and greater physical comfort. To get their needs met effectively, people must realize that they always have control over the doing component and can choose to do something more effective than being miserable.

REALITY THERAPY

Reality therapy helps people learn to be in effective control of their lives. It is a noncoercive method of communicating that enhances people's ability to make effective, need-fulfilling choices. Reality therapy is an ongoing process with two major components: (a) the counseling environment and (b) specific procedures that lead to changes in behavior. The art of reality therapy is to join these components in ways that lead people to evaluate their lives and decide to move in better directions.

The Counseling Environment

Reality therapy requires a supportive environment within which individuals can begin to make changes in their lives. Following are guidelines for creating this environment.

1. Be friendly and listen to the person.

2. Do not allow the person to focus on past events unless those events relate easily to the present situation.

3. Avoid discussing feelings or physiological responses as though they were separate from total behavior; always relate feelings and physiology to concurrent actions and thoughts over which the person has more direct control.

4. Accept no excuses for irresponsible behavior, particularly when a person fails to do what he or she has expressed an intention to do.

5. Avoid punishing, criticizing, or attempting to protect the person from the reasonable consequences of behavior.

Crucial to the counseling environment is involvement characterized by mutual trust and caring. In the absence of involvement, people will not be willing to risk making changes in their lives.

Procedures Leading to Change

To encourage change through reality therapy, the counselor has specific procedures to follow—not necessarily in the order presented here, but rather entwined in a holistic manner appropriate to the person and the circumstance.

1. Focus on the person's total behavior—the way he or she is acting, thinking, and feeling now. Help the person learn the difficult lesson that all total behavior is chosen, however painful and self-destructive it may be.

2. Ask the person what he or she wants now—look at the present pictures of the quality world. Then expand the question to the direction he or she would like to take in life. If the answer is "I don't know," continue to focus on what the person is doing now (total behavior) to reinforce the understanding that the present direction is the result of choice.

3. Ask the person to make the following evaluation: "Does your present behavior have a reasonable chance of getting you what you want now, and will it take you in the direction you want to go?"

4. If the answer is no (meaning that the desired direction is reasonable but the present behavior will not take the person there), help the person plan new behavior.

5. If the answer is no but the person seems unable to get what he or she wants no matter how much effort is made, suggest changing directions. In this case, the focus is more on changing what the person wants than on the behavior itself.

6. If the answer is yes (meaning that the person sees nothing wrong with the present behavior or desired direction), focus on the present behavior and keep repeating the evaluative question in a variety of ways.

7. Agree upon a plan that has a good chance to succeed and ask the person for a commitment to follow through with it. A written plan and commitment are generally most effective.

8. Do not give up on the person's ability to achieve a more responsible life, even if the person makes little effort to follow through on the plan. Giving up tends to confirm the belief that no one cares enough to help.

In following the procedures for change, it is important to keep in mind that people choose their total behaviors even though one or more of the individual components may not be chosen. Also, remember as well that, however ineffective or self-destructive a behavior may appear, it is always the best that the person believes he or she can do. In that sense, the behavior is "effective" for the individual. A person will not make a change in behavior until the following two prerequisites are met: (a) using his or her own evaluation, an individual must decide that present behavior will either not attain what is desired or take the person in the desired direction and (b) an individual must believe that he or she has available another behavior that will permit his or her needs to be satisfied reasonably well.

Reality therapy teaches that people can live their lives most successfully when they acknowledge and accept responsibility for their chosen behaviors. The practitioner of reality therapy should never doubt that people are able to choose more responsible and effective behaviors. It is up to the practitioner to help the individual avoid excuses and accept this responsibility and to provide opportunities for the individual to learn and test new and more effective behavioral choices.

CONCLUSION

Deming's management theory works because application of the 14 points creates a need-fulfilling work environment. In that environment the worker's natural inclination to learn and be innovative is nurtured and preserved. Lead management understands that true motivation is intrinsic and results in joy and pride in work. When workers are motivated, quality becomes their goal. Table 3.1 contrasts total behaviors of workers under Deming's style of management and under traditional boss management.

This comparison shows in psychological terms why workers managed the Deming way are more capable of achieving and improving quality than workers under boss management. Is a worker who is complaining, avoiding, fearing, headaching, or daydreaming going to do quality work?

When the work environment is need fulfilling, the choices available to meet workers' basic needs create opportunities to develop a number of effective, need-fulfilling behaviors that are part of their quality worlds. Traditional boss management, by contrast, offers workers few opportunities to build a repertoire of

Table 3.1   Total Behaviors of Workers Under Different Management Styles

	Workers' behavior	
	Under Deming management	**Under boss management**
Doing	Cooperating Accomplishing Contributing Delivering	Withdrawing Complaining Avoiding Punishing
Thinking	Wondering Evaluating	Daydreaming Judging
Feeling	Priding Trusting	Fearing Depressing
Physiology	Energizing Normal heartbeating	Tiring Headaching

need-fulfilling behaviors (see Table 3.2). In fact, traditional management perpetuates workers' use of ineffective, unfulfilling behaviors. For workers who are boss managed, work is rarely a part of the quality world.

Whether the worker is the employee in the factory, the student in the classroom, or the teacher in the school, the psychological effects of boss management are the same: It deprives the individual of innate motivation, self-esteem, and dignity while cultivating fear and defensiveness. The result is loss of motivation to do quality work.

Parts 2 and 3 of this book will explain how the lead manager in the school and in the classroom applies the knowledge of control theory and the skills of reality therapy in developing the school for quality learning.

Table 3.2   Choices for Workers Under Different Management Styles

Basic needs	Workers' choices	
	Workers' choices under lead management	Workers' choices under boss management
Belonging	To share and cooperate with others	To work alone and compete with others
	To contribute to welfare of organization	To work for welfare of self
	To see goodness in self and others	To isolate self and mistrust others
Power	To make action plans to achieve	To anger, criticize, and punish to control others
	To take risks and learn new skills	To play it safe
	To think win-win	To think win-lose
	To be more into process than outcome	To be more into outcome than process
Freedom	To brainstorm alternatives to problems	To blame others for problems
	To take action	To make excuses
	To create opportunities	To complain about limits
Fun	To view work as pleasurable	To view work as boring
	To initiate fun activities	To find no time or energy for fun

PART TWO

Managing the School for Quality Learning

CHAPTER 4

Overview: The School for Quality Learning

Constancy of purpose (Deming's, 1986, Point 1) is present when the school staff reaches a common understanding of the purpose of school and learning. In developing a school for quality learning, creating constancy of purpose means embracing a new philosophy (Deming's Point 2), the philosophy of quality. The following reflections on the attributes of a school for quality learning offer a paradigm for transformation.

First and foremost, a school for quality learning is a good place—a gratifying place for both adults and children. The school is no more and no less than the human interactions among its inhabitants. The school environment must be designed with great care so those interactions will be as good as possible. An atmosphere of sharing and caring must be established. All individuals must know that they have a place in the school, that others care, that they themselves must care—and that the environment is incomplete when they are not present.

The adults in the school must be environmentalists. They must design, maintain, and constantly strive to improve an environment that is flexible enough to accommodate everyone. That environment must provide opportunities for the development of individual responsibility and self-directed behavior. It must provide opportunities for everyone to experience success and avoid failure. The environment must foster positive self-concepts for all involved. The adults must ultimately be judged according to whether they consistently model constructive and inspiring human interactions within the school environment. Modeling requires one not only to behave but also to behave visibly, and one can consistently model only that which one believes.

The school in its totality—the environment and the interactions within it—must bear out the notion that each learner is capable of quality learning and, further, that each has unique talents. The school must provide opportunities for those talents to emerge and grow. All members of the school community must be encouraged to believe that they can, should, and will learn—and moreover that they can learn from their own thoughts and behavior as well as from the thoughts and behavior of others. It must be clear that everyone in the environment is a learner and a facilitator of learning.

Teachers and other learning facilitators must ensure that the environment affords a variety of activities that will foster critical thinking. Learners must be challenged to use convergent, divergent, and evaluative thinking processes. There must be a balanced offering of opportunities, and the learners must have the chance to make balanced choices from among the offerings and even to generate their own learning experiences. Learning activities must provide sufficient practice in the basic skills of data collection, data processing, and application of knowledge. The activities must be varied to support and develop varied learning styles; they must be meaningful, purposeful, and relevant to the learners' lives.

The total environment and the various interactions within it must be supportive of what each person has done and is doing. Furthermore, the environment and the interactions must challenge each one to do better and different things. The environment must support and encourage, even demand, individual creativity, curiosity, and inquiry; at the same time, it must demand and promote cooperation.

The school must constantly strive to provide the ultimate in humane, individualized learning and living experiences. It must not only tolerate but encourage and celebrate differences. It must provide choices based on alternatives. The school staff, especially its professional members, must constantly monitor the school's performance and be alert for new ways to perform. The school must be open to new ideas and involvements. It must always look for additional resources to enhance existing learning activities, and it must allow learners to develop personal learning activities.

Just as no two people in the school will be the same, no single approach to education will enable the school to fulfill its mission. Above all, whatever the school's characteristics, it must be judged on whether or not it is a good place—a place where people feel good and capable, where learning is possible and where the humanity of each individual is accepted, respected, and guarded.

How does a school carry out these charges and achieve an atmosphere conducive to quality learning? The key to the transformation is management behavior. In considering management in the school for quality learning, we will focus on the building administrator (the principal) as the noncoercive lead manager of the school and on the teacher as the noncoercive lead manager of the classroom. Lead-manager behavior is a significant and necessary departure from the boss-manager behavior that prevails widely among principals and teachers.

One theme that emerges consistently from the literature on school effectiveness is that schools judged effective have effective principals and that the principal is a key determinant of a school's effectiveness. It is possible for a boss-manager principal to succeed in developing some of the essential characteristics of an effective school. When such success occurs, policymakers and educators will likely judge the school effective because it has improved on its own previous record or appears better than other schools. Nevertheless, a high percentage of the students in that school—now judged effective—may not be engaged in quality work. Glasser (1990) argues that even in the best schools, only about half of the students are engaged in quality work some of the time.

A school judged effective is not necessarily a school for quality learning. Quality work and quality learning are different; one can produce a quality product (work) by repeating the same activity many times, whereas quality learning means being engaged in growth activities and aspiring to do all things well—new and old alike.

In the school for quality learning, the expectation is that each student will participate fully in quality learning, not merely that the student body as a whole will perform at a higher level. Only a lead-manager principal can lead a school toward quality learning for each student. An effective boss manager may improve a school's effectiveness, but even the best boss manager will not create a school for quality learning.

In Part 2, we will examine closely the role of the principal as lead manager and the relationship between the principal and the teacher as worker. This relationship is crucial for two reasons: First, the principal provides a powerful model for the teacher as lead manager in the classroom; second, the organization that the lead-manager principal establishes in the school recognizes the teacher's authority and gives the teacher the freedom to organize the classroom for quality learning.

The relationship between principal and teacher is so important to quality learning that no organizational barriers must exist between them. That is, there must be no chain of command or line and staff organization—whether in the school or the school system—in which other individuals are interposed between the teacher and the principal in areas of important philosophical and operational decisions required to organize the classroom for quality learning. If middle positions do exist for the purported management of curriculum, instruction, student discipline, budgeting, evaluation, or staff development, those positions should be redefined to facilitate direct involvement between principal and teacher in all these critical areas. This requirement is consistent with Deming's Point 9 (break down barriers between staff areas). The middle managers in question may be within the school and under the supervision of the principal, or they may occupy district level positions and have the authority to direct the principal's actions and/or dictate policy or practice directly to the teacher. District level positions may be redefined as support positions to provide assistance to the principal and the teachers regarding identified problems or concerns. If the middle management positions are within the school, the school is probably too large to produce quality learning. In that case, the school may be reorganized into smaller units (schools within a school), each headed by an autonomous lead manager. Another alternative is to eliminate the middle management positions in favor of additional teacher positions. System change and reorganization are discussed further in chapter 11.

Whatever form the reorganization takes, middle management positions in the school or district must be removed as possible barriers, either real or perceived, to the formulation of the relationship between the lead-manager principal and the teacher. One of Deming's obstacles to quality is blaming the work force for problems. He asserts that workers are responsible for only 15% of the problems. The other 85%—system problems—are the responsibility of management. In the view of the school as a system, the principal is management and the teachers are workers. To address problems and design strategies for developing quality, the principal and the teachers need an unbroken chain of communication.

The principal's primary mission is to facilitate the teachers' efforts to organize the classroom for quality learning. In the simplest terms, the lead-manager principal's behavior makes clear that the principal has the ultimate responsibility for quality learning but has no authority to dictate procedures or processes to the teachers. The lead-manager principal opens communication with the teachers and strives to develop a relationship of mutual trust with each one. The principal believes that each teacher is deeply committed to providing the best possible learning opportunity for each student and is doing the best that he or she knows how to do at any moment. A crucial responsibility of the principal is to communicate high expectations to each staff member. The lead-manager principal's expectation is that each teacher will grow in the ability to facilitate quality learning in the classroom. Teachers who are actively engaged in such growth are performing satisfactorily and deserve full support.

Another important responsibility of the principal is to exercise leadership in the development of a positive and healthy school climate. *School climate* is a rather fluid concept. That climate is an aggregate of certain properties of the school environment that (a) distinguish the school from other schools, (b) are relatively enduring over time, (c) are experienced by everyone involved with the school, and (d) influence school participants' attitudes toward outcomes and strategies for achieving those outcomes.

A healthy school climate is characterized by a problem-solving approach that rests on the participants' sense of common purpose, personal satisfaction, and mutual trust. In the literature on effective schools, a healthy school climate is consistently cited as a factor that distinguishes effective schools from others. The literature strongly suggests that the principal is most influential in the establishment of the climate.

It is through behavior that the principal exerts the most influence on school climate. Because the lead-manager principal expects all staff members to interact with one another and with the learners in a positive, caring manner, the principal must be seen consistently interacting with others in that way. Because the lead-manager principal expects staff members to manage learners without coercion, the principal must set a consistent example, especially in those recurrent situations where the principal is called on to help with a discipline problem. Because the lead-manager principal expects staff members to be accessible to parents and students, he or she must also be seen as consistently accessible. Because the lead-manager principal expects staff members to provide mutual support, the principal must be seen consistently offering support and encouragement. The lead-manager principal will also seek involvement with students who are doing quality learning, rather than limiting interactions to the traditional involvement with students who are behaving unacceptably. This positive involvement is spontaneous and immediate, rather than being reserved for an awards function remote from daily activities of the school.

The lead-manager principal clearly understands that, although appropriate organizational measures are important to the development of a healthy school climate, that climate depends mostly on the behavior of the participants—especially the behavior of the adults and of the principal in particular. Kelley (1980) states that the principal's leadership in determining school climate consists of skills in responding to concerns, expectations, and existing conditions, as well as skills in establishing new expectations and conditions. The lead-manager principal demonstrates these skills.

In the remaining chapters of Part 2, we will examine some of the principal's traditional major areas of responsibility and see how a lead-manager principal fulfills those responsibilities in developing a school for quality learning. These areas of responsibility actually constitute action plans for helping teachers develop the classroom for quality learning and for fostering a healthy school climate. Although considered independently, these responsibilities are in reality interdependent.

Consensus decision making yields a school mission and certain agreed-upon guiding principles and strategies for accomplishing that mission. The organization that expands the individual teacher's responsibility to make decisions affecting the classroom increases the likelihood of satisfaction as well. A major goal of the evaluation plan is the creation of an atmosphere of mutual trust between the principal and each staff member. Decision-making forums and the evaluation system enable the lead-manager principal to communicate high expectations for each staff member (the principal included) in a positive manner.

Responsibility education is crucial to school climate, and family involvement is crucial to the school's mission. The classroom teacher relies heavily on available support services in striving to provide quality learning experiences for all students.

Finally, the school is a part of the total system and must take that reality into account. The lead-manager principal is central in all of these dimensions. Until the system transformations suggested in Part 2 are undertaken, transformations that directly affect the learner (suggested in Part 3) will not be realized.

CHAPTER 5

Decision Making

Developing a school for quality learning entails a significant system change. Educational change has been well researched. The most important notion to emerge from that research is that unless the people ultimately responsible for implementing the change are heavily invested in it, the change will not be permanent. The literature is replete with examples of educational change efforts that were well intentioned and well designed but that did not survive the test of time because they were imposed from the top down.

An organization has inherent mechanisms that maintain the status quo. The traditional organizational structure reflecting the industrial worldview is a formidable foe of the kinds of changes needed in a school for quality learning. (The traditional structure will be addressed in detail in chapter 11.) The school system, and each school within it, represents a traditional structure. The only way to alter the organization successfully is to bring about change at the lowest level of the hierarchy and to create channels of communication to let information from this level flow upward through the organizational structure. In the school for quality learning, the lead-manager classroom teacher plays the most critical role in sustaining the school's transformation. Therefore, the teacher must be invested in every stage of the transformation.

The principal's success in organizing a structure for making decisions about the school's mission and the strategies for accomplishing that mission are of critical importance. The purpose of a decision-making structure is to ensure that every staff member is invested in the change and committed to the common goal—in this case, quality learning. The guiding axiom is that only those staff members affected by a decision should be involved in making that decision and, conversely, that all those affected by a decision must be involved in the decision.

This axiom is a radical departure from the decision-making practices in nearly all schools. However, it is consistent with the notion that the lead-manager principal (in contrast to the boss-manager principal) has total responsibility but must not exercise total authority. This axiom, to be fully applied, requires decision making by consensus. Because consensus decision making is difficult and time-consuming, decisions that affect everyone and therefore require global participation should be chosen carefully. Few decisions in a school fall in this category. The most important of these global decisions concern the school's mission and philosophy. To create constancy of purpose (Deming's, 1986, Point 1) and adopt a new philosophy (Point 2), all staff must be involved in these decisions and reach a consensus. Most of the other decisions requiring full staff participation and total consensus concern schoolwide strategies to implement the mission. If quality learning is to flourish, many decisions traditionally made by management must be entrusted to individual teachers.

Although the idea of entrusting more decision-making power to teachers may seem radical and contrary to quality control, it is consistent with control theory and the Deming management method. Teachers are decision makers; to deny this premise is to deny their professionalism. Denial of professionalism, particularly formal and informal organizational efforts to limit or control the teacher's decision making, suppresses initiative and motivation.

Herzberg, Mausner, and Snyderman (1959) spoke eloquently to this point in their pioneering work on sources of satisfaction and dissatisfaction in the workplace. According to Herzberg et al., once the sources of workplace dissatisfaction—such as concerns about working conditions, fair wages, reasonable supervision, job security, and peer relations—are addressed, the worker will likely be committed to remaining in the workplace. Free of dissatisfaction, the worker can concentrate on higher level concerns that, when resolved, will yield satisfaction. In the Deming model, the teacher as worker seeks responsibility, autonomy, recognition, and the freedom to cultivate a personal teaching style; these are the higher level concerns that lead to teacher satisfaction. The vehicle for addressing these concerns is the authority to make instructional decisions. This authority is critical to the school for quality learning. In educational practice, the denial of this decision-making authority comes primarily though standardized curricula. The commonly stated purpose of a curriculum, whether locally developed or driven by adopted textbooks, is to ensure quality control by exposing all learners to common information and skills. The actual outcome, however, is the stifling of teacher creativity, initiative, and motivation, leading directly to a lack of quality teaching and, therefore, a lack of quality learning. (In Part 3, we will examine curriculum organization and the curricular changes needed in the school for quality learning.)

To confirm the fact that teachers are decision makers, one need only observe a classroom. The more individualized the classroom, the more encompassing and detailed the teacher's decision making. The ability to think well on one's feet distinguishes the master teacher from the average one. The lead-manager teacher is a learning facilitator, a role that requires considerable decision making for and with each learner. To best serve the learner, the teacher needs the freedom to decide. This is not a radical idea in actual practice: Teachers do make decisions based on their judgment of the situation or the learner. The recognition and sanctioning of teacher decision making will free teachers to exercise the power that they already have but to do so without being subversive. It will also free teachers to discuss decisions and results with others in the school. Open discussion of such matters is fundamental to professional exchange and mutual growth. Deming's Point 8 (drive out fear) addresses this issue directly. Teachers refrain from open communication with administrators and even with colleagues because they fear that others will discover what they are actually doing in their classrooms. This fear prevents teachers from sharing successes that could enhance the quality of teaching throughout a school and also keeps them from obtaining the assistance they need to grow and improve.

In a school for quality learning, the individual teacher has broad discretion in decisions related to curriculum. At the very least, the teacher should be free to choose the materials and strategies for teaching the curriculum. Further, to the extent possible, the teacher should choose what to teach. These decisions are basic to the design of quality learning experiences. They can only be made by someone who knows the learners and considers their individual needs and wants. In the school for quality learning, both broad curriculum reform and the transfer of curriculum-related decisions to the classroom teacher are essential.

Each teacher should be responsible for a classroom budget, deciding what resources are needed for his or her classroom and what the budget will allow. Money is power. By delegating budgetary decisions to the teacher, the principal is sending a strong message of trust. The money legitimizes other responsibilities vested in the teacher. If the teacher is free to choose teaching strategies and materials, some vehicle must exist for exercising that freedom; a classroom or program budget serves this purpose.

In the decision-making process, small groups with common interests and concerns may naturally develop. A small group might include people with similar jobs—such as the primary teachers, the kindergarten teachers, the mathematics teachers, and so on—or it might be an interdisciplinary teaching team whose members are linked by an integrated curriculum and a common group of learners. In any event, the small groups are formed because their members determine that cooperation facilitates the development and improvement of their programs. They may see an advantage in combining budgets for greater purchasing power or in pooling materials for certain learning activities. They may be facing a decision that affects all members of the small group but not the school at large. These smaller groups, which form naturally from the demands on their members and from a desire to collaborate, can develop when there are no barriers between staff areas (Deming's Point 9—break down barriers between staff areas).

Once formed and functioning, these small groups can be a strong force in the development of the school for quality learning because they provide an atmosphere for mutual sharing and learning, they advance the integration of curriculum, and they foster the collaborative consultation model for supportive service delivery. Deming would call these groups *QC circles* (quality control) because they combine resources to contribute to designs for the future and to improve the quality of products and services. These groups can use the PDCA cycle (also called the Shewhart cycle; see Figure 2.1) to facilitate decision making. Deming uses this cycle in process analysis and improvement.

The lead-manager principal establishes decision-making structures with the aims of (a) transferring maximum decision-making power to the individual classroom teacher and (b) involving every staff member in determining the school's mission and the strategies for accomplishing it. Fundamental to the development of a school for quality learning are the design of a decision-making model and the determination of what represents a consensus. Both will vary from school to school. Decisions about these matters are perhaps the first important decisions. The lead-manager principal involves all staff members in the deliberations, using a consensus-building process that ensures commitment to the design.

Before the group embarks on the decision-making process, it is sometimes helpful to examine various cooperative decision-making strategies because some staff members may have no experience with group decision making. Table 5.1 presents some common strategies; the group decision-making activity, an exercise in various aspects of group decision making, may provide useful preparation.

Table 5.1   Common Decision-Making Strategies

Decision by	Process	Outcome
Majority	More than half of the group makes the decision.	The decision fails to meet the concerns of the minority.
Averaging of individual opinions	The most extreme solutions are eliminated and the middle-of-the-road option is chosen.	The decision fails to meet the interests of all and sometimes fails to resolve the real problem; it may provide a choice without real support.
Authority after group input	The group leader makes the decision after members have discussed the problem.	The process, typical in hierarchical groups, fails to elicit a strong commitment to a solution.
Compromise	Each member sacrifices in order to find a solution.	The decision fails to meet the concerns of most group members.
Consensus	All group members agree on a solution to a problem.	All concerns are considered and solutions that combine the interests of all are created.

GROUP DECISION-MAKING ACTIVITY

Goal

To compare the processes and outcomes of five common decision-making strategies

Group Size

Five to seven participants (several groups can work simultaneously in the same room)

Time Required

Approximately 1 1/2 hours

Materials Needed

Cryonics Decision Exercise Instruction Sheet
Cryonics Individual and Group Decision Score Sheet
Newsprint and markers

Process

1. Participants sit in a circle, and the facilitator randomly designates a group leader.

2. Each group member receives an instruction sheet and a score sheet, as shown. The facilitator explains the instructions and gives participants time to read them and ask questions.

3. After the small groups complete the activity, the facilitator brings them together to report their choices and to discuss the outcomes. The following questions can be used to stimulate discussion.

   - Which process took the most time?

   - Which process took the least time?

   - What are the disadvantages of each strategy?

   - What are the advantages of each strategy?

   - Which process would you most favor using to make decisions about the operations of the school? Why?

   - Which process would you least favor using to make decisions about the operations of the school? Why?

- What did you learn about decision making from this activity?

CRYONICS DECISION EXERCISE INSTRUCTION SHEET

Situation

You are cryonics researchers at a large university hospital. Your research team must make a very important decision for a landmark study. Six individuals have volunteered to be frozen for the 10-year experimental period. All volunteers have been approved by the hospital board and the Food and Drug Administration as appropriate candidates for this study. Approval has been given for *only one* candidate to be frozen. Which volunteer will be selected to be frozen?

Volunteers

1. An 18-year-old genius with HIV, female, college graduate, white

2. A 25-year-old minister and peace activist, male, married, no children, white

3. A 42-year-old scientist close to discovering a cure for cancer, female, single, Hispanic

4. A 34-year-old teacher and author, male, two children, black

5. A 31-year-old environmentalist respected for having an impact on public policy and a vision for the solutions to global environmental problems, male, married, two children, Asian

6. A 50-year-old former Olympic gold medalist who still runs 6 miles a day, female, married, four grown children, three grandchildren, white

Instructions

1. Each group member independently rank orders the volunteers on the basis of personal opinion.

2. The group leader calls for a majority vote, with each member voting for one volunteer. The volunteer with the most votes is the group's choice. (Record the choice on the score sheet.)

3. The group leader averages individual opinions. Each member reports his or her rank order, and the leader totals the numbers for each volunteer. The two volunteers with the highest and lowest scores are eliminated. The group then ranks the four remaining volunteers. These scores are totaled, and again the volunteers with the highest and lowest scores are eliminated. The process is repeated until only one choice remains. The volunteer with the average (mean) score is the group's choice.

4. The group leader makes an authority decision after group input. Members are asked their individual opinions and the reasons behind them, then the leader makes the decision for the group.

5. The group leader asks all members to sacrifice in order to achieve a solution. The volunteer is chosen by compromise after everyone has made concessions.

6. The group leader facilitates consensus decision making by conducting the following activities:

   a. Each time a group member makes a statement, the statement is clarified and summarized by another member (facilitates active listening).

   b. The group establishes criteria for evaluating possible solutions.

   c. The group lists on a large sheet of newsprint pros and cons of each alternative.

   d. The group evaluates the alternatives according to the established criteria.

e. From time to time, the group leader polls the members to see how close the group is to agreement and identifies and clarifies areas of continuing disagreement.

f. The group continues discussing the alternatives and makes a decision that takes into account the concerns and interests of all members.

CRYONICS INDIVIDUAL AND GROUP DECISION SCORE SHEET

Individual Opinion Rank Order

1. _____
2. _____
3. _____
4. _____
5. _____
6. _____

Group Decisions

Volunteers	Majority	Average of individual opinions	Authority after group input	Compromise	Consensus
18-year-old genius with HIV					
25-year-old minister and prominent peace activist					
42-year-old scientist					
34-year-old teacher and author					
31-year-old environmentalist					
50-year-old former Olympic gold medalist					

Conclude the decision-making activity by considering what decision-making strategies would be best for the school. Following are important issues to raise:

1. How important is decision making to the school's day-to-day operation?

2. How important is decision making to the school's future success?

3. If some group members are not satisfied with a decision, will working with them to gain their support or to discourage sabotage move us in the direction we want to go?

4. Will seeking an alternative solution that all group members support move us in the direction we want to go?

DEVELOPING A DECISION-MAKING MODEL

The goal of establishing a group decision-making model is cooperation. The model empowers the group to develop a set of shared values and commitments that bond the members in a common cause. The decision-making model emerges as the group finds acceptable answers to such questions as the following.

Membership

- Who will the members of the decision-making group be?
- What will be the relative status (power) of different job classifications within the decision-making group?
- Who may vote?
- Is there a proxy provision?

Input

- What are the procedures for providing input to the decision-making group? From insiders? From outsiders?

Decision Making

- What constitutes consensus?
- How is a decision made?
- What is the responsibility of dissenting members?

- What does silence signify?
- What is the responsibility of a member who abstains?
- How can a decision be reversed?

Areas for Decision Making

- What decisions will the group consider?

Procedures

- How are decision-making meetings conducted?

The example group decision-making model was developed by the staff of Leal School in Urbana, Illinois. It is used in all regular faculty meetings involving decisions falling in category A or B under the heading "Areas for Decision Making."

EXAMPLE GROUP DECISION-MAKING MODEL

Membership

Membership includes all Leal School personnel whose responsibilities require certification. To participate in the decision process, the member must be present at the meetings.

Weight

All members shall be accorded the weight of one.

Input

Input to the group may be made by any employee or parent of Leal School or by any invited guests. The decision-making group shall conduct discussion in a circle. An item brought for discussion may be tabled (further action to be determined) if, of those present, more than two

Note. From *Leal School Staff Handbook,* by R. J. Bodine, unpublished manuscript, n.d., Leal School, Urbana, Illinois.

members object to the item on the basis of inappropriateness. An agenda will be published at least a day before the meeting. Members will make every effort to have included on the agenda those items they wish to bring before the group. Nonmembers must clear agenda items with the principal's office. Agenda items will usually appear as proposals for discussion. Any member of the group may call for a vote on a proposal.

Decision Making

A decision shall be made by the group when a vote is called unless, of those present, more than two members dissent. Silence or not voting is considered a dissention or an abstention. Dissenting members are obligated to state a reason for their dissention but are not required to offer an alternate proposal. A member may abstain provided a reason is stated for the abstention. A decision may not be recorded unless a simple majority of those present vote. Voting will be done by show of hands, for and against.

Decision Reversal

A decision once made may be reversed if, at some subsequent meeting of the decision-making group, the majority of those present vote to cancel the decision.

Areas for Decision Making

The decision-making group will make decisions in two major dimensions:

A. Decisions concerning the total operation of Leal School Educational Program and all that directly affects the operation of that total program.

B. Decisions concerning how other decisions may be delegated and to whom decisions may be delegated. (This specifically includes those items tabled.)

Conduct of the Meeting

The member who calls for the vote shall tally the vote and obtain reasons for dissensions and abstinence. The principal shall serve as the agenda manager unless another member volunteers to so serve. Volunteers are encouraged. Attendance at meetings is optional.

A DECISION-MAKING PROCESS FOR ADOPTING THE DEMING POINTS AND ELIMINATING DISEASES AND OBSTACLES

Adopting Deming's 14 points and eliminating the seven deadly diseases and the obstacles are essential measures in the creation of a school for quality learning. A school must make a number of significant decisions in proceeding with those measures. Strategic planning will facilitate the decision making. All staff members must embrace the quality management principles in both theory and practice if the school is to become a school for quality learning. Before the strategic planning process is begun, the school staff must have in place a decision-making model such as the Leal School model. This model will be used throughout every stage of strategic planning.

Building a foundation of understanding about quality management is prerequisite to effective planning. By reading this book and discussing it chapter by chapter, staff members can begin to lay that foundation. (See Appendixes A and B for discussion guides.) It is essential that the principal demonstrate lead management consistently during this crucial initial stage. Staff involvement must be sought without coercion. Participation cannot be mandated; rather, it must come from a desire to grow and advance toward the consensus goals of the decision-making group.

Strategic Planning

Every faculty member is encouraged to participate in a strategic planning process as described in the following pages. Full participation will ensure understanding, commitment, and involvement in the creation of a school for quality learning.

Beliefs

The planning process begins with a listing of beliefs—a formal expression of the school's philosophy. These beliefs embody the fundamental values that influence faculty members to com-

mit to a specific mission. These beliefs, simple and easily understood, establish moral and ethical priorities that guide all policies
and activities of the school. In the school for quality learning, the
beliefs reflect the quality management principles and an understanding of their psychological framework. The following are
sample belief statements:

1. All learners are capable of quality learning.

2. A fundamental responsibility of the educational
   process is to create lifelong learners.

3. All individuals learn in different ways, and each way
   must be understood, respected, and valued.

4. Motivation comes only from within each individual.

To develop the listing of beliefs, faculty members begin by
brainstorming in small groups to produce six to eight belief statements that everyone in the group can support. There are two
phases to the brainstorming process: The first involves generating
the list of beliefs; the second involves selecting from the list. It is
important to separate the two parts of the process. Each phase has
simple but explicit rules:

Phase 1: Generate belief statements

1. Designate one person to record ideas.

2. Expect controversial or far-fetched ideas.

3. Say any idea that comes to mind.

4. Record every idea.

5. Do not evaluate ideas.

Phase 2: Select beliefs

1. Evaluate the statements:

   • Combine those that are similar.

   • Circle those that everyone agrees are significant.

   • Eliminate those that do not represent strong convictions.

2. Improve upon the resulting belief statements.

3. By consensus, choose six to eight belief statements to bring to the large group.

4. Record the selected belief statements on newsprint and post them.

Each group then presents its listing of beliefs to the large group, which applies the selection phase of brainstorming and the staff decision-making model to select the belief statements for the school.

Mission Statement

The mission statement is a one-sentence expression of the school's purpose and function, a bold declaration of what the school will be. The mission statement reflects the vision of the school, emphasizing its uniqueness and primary focus. It is the foundation for the school's entire plan. In practice, the mission statement serves to focus everyone's energies on a common purpose; this is the constancy of purpose called for in Deming's Point 1. The mission statement in a school for quality learning might be as follows:

> Our mission in the school for quality learning is to provide a people-focused, supportive, and challenging environment within which every learner (meaning both staff and students) vigorously pursues quality in both behavior and learning, becoming a lifelong self-evaluating, productive, caring, and responsible member of the diverse and constantly changing world.

The mission statement is developed through the process outlined for the belief statements, with faculty first working in small groups and then coming together for a final decision.

Strategic Policies

Policies in the school for quality learning are not traditional school board policies nor routine administrative rules and procedures. They are not laws or regulations handed down from the state. In short, they are not restrictions imposed either externally or internally on the school. Rather, policies in the school for quality learning are the parameters within which the school will operate in fulfilling its mission, the imperatives that keep the organization true to itself. Following are examples of policies of a school for quality learning:

1. Only programs and decisions that comply with Deming's 14 points will be instituted.

2. No individual will be denied access to the pursuit of quality behavior and learning.

3. Every individual in the school will use a self-evaluation process.

The strategic policy statements are developed through the process used to develop the belief statements, initially by small groups that then come together. Any policy developed should be comprehensible and manageable, definitive in its terms, and practical.

Plan of Action

The development of a plan of action is a dynamic and ongoing process in the school for quality learning. The plan is conceived and written from an operational point of view and is constantly improved. It ensures that Deming's 14 points are applied and the seven deadly diseases and the obstacles are eliminated. The development of a plan includes four phases.

Phase 1: Identify needs and wants

1. Identify needs and wants.

2. Explore the reasons each need or want should have priority in the development of the school.

3. Order the needs and wants according to their impact on the development of the school.

Phase 2: Identify strategies

1. Identify possible strategies to address the needs and wants.

2. Evaluate the potential success of each strategy in addressing priorities established in Phase 1.

3. Improve strategies where possible.

Phase 3: Select strategies and implement activities

1. Prioritize and select strategies.

2. Develop an action plan for implementing the strategies (specifying who, what, when, where, and how).

3. Implement the plan.

Phase 4: Evaluate the plan

1. Is the plan taking the school in the direction that we want it to go?

2. What are we doing? Is it helping?

3. Could the plan be strengthened?

4. What is needed to strengthen the plan?

Like the belief statements, mission statement, and policies, the plan of action is developed through the small-group/large-group process.

Full realization of the school for quality learning will take a number of years. The strategic plan provides the staff with a process focused on the attainment of that goal. The belief statements, the mission statements, and the strategic policies combine to provide the school philosophy. The remainder of this book outlines various components of the plan of action.

CHAPTER 6

Staff Development: Evaluation and Training

Traditionally, the school principal has been charged with the improvement of instruction. Most agree that staff evaluation is an important aspect of this responsibility. For the lead-manager principal, staff evaluation is even more important—arguably the single most important responsibility. The responsibility for and the effects of evaluation relate directly to seven of Deming's (1986) management points and indirectly to the remaining seven. The following points are directly related:

- Point 3: Cease dependence on mass inspection.

- Point 5: Improve constantly and forever the system of production and service.

- Point 6: Institute training.

- Point 8: Drive out fear.

- Point 11: Eliminate numerical quotas.

- Point 12: Remove barriers to pride in workmanship.

- Point 13: Institute a vigorous program of education and self-improvement.

Personnel evaluation has historically addressed two objectives: improving performance and bringing about dismissal of workers judged inadequate or nonproductive. These two purposes are in conflict. When the threat of dismissal is a possible outcome of evaluation, improvement is thwarted and the worker's sense of security is eroded. Despite the broad protection of tenure laws, experienced teachers are intimidated by the possibility of dismissal. Herzberg et al. (1959) noted that a lack of security is a major source of dissatisfaction in the workplace. Deming acknowledges the detrimental effects of fear in his Point 8. An insecure worker will not seek assistance from others, particularly from a supervisor who possesses the power of dismissal. The worker fears that a request for assistance will be viewed as an admission of weakness. In teaching, this problem is compounded by the nature of the job and by the relatively vague definitions of acceptable performance. Teachers are frequently unsure what is expected and what constitutes fulfillment of those expectations. Even a teacher whose performance is satisfactory or exemplary may harbor self-doubts.

A climate of fear undermines quality in many ways. Behavioral change occurs only when the owner of the behavior decides change is needed. If the system intimidates the teacher to the extent that he or she cannot seek assistance to change, improvement (if any) must depend on the personal resources of the teacher. Sharing and cooperation are stymied. A teacher with a good idea will guard it closely because that good idea may be reflected in a better evaluation for that teacher than for his or her colleagues. The school would be better served if teachers helped one another and shared their good ideas. Similarly, in a competitive system, a strong teacher might choose not to cooperate with colleagues for fear that cooperation would elevate others to a similar level of performance and thus reflect negatively in his or her own evaluation. Therefore, dismissal as a goal of evaluation has no place in the school for quality learning.

We do not mean to imply that dismissal may never be necessary; rather, the two purposes of evaluation must remain distinct, and the teacher should never have any doubt about which purpose underlies an evaluation. Dismissal is rare in education. In the school for quality learning, the fear of dismissal must be eliminated for the vast majority of teachers who are performing satisfactorily. The evaluation system should reflect the expectation that each teacher will be trying to improve and grow. Teachers need to know that, although they may not be perfect, the principal has no concerns about their performance that would warrant dismissal. The occasional employee at risk of dismissal must be well aware of that fact. The evaluator is responsible for clearly informing the employee that dismissal procedures are being undertaken. These procedures are specifically outlined in law; dismissal is a legal procedure, not an educational one.

The lead-manager principal defines the purpose of evaluation as personal and professional growth toward improved performance. The principal acts as a facilitator for each teacher, just as the lead-manager teacher serves as a facilitator for learners in the classroom. The principal makes clear that evaluation is designed to lead to improved performance and that the principal may do much to facilitate that improvement.

The most important element of effective evaluation for personal improvement, especially in a social profession like teaching, is self-evaluation. Self-evaluation is vital for a teacher because another person cannot observe the scope and nature of the teacher's performance often enough to document total classroom interactions and because there is no valid and reliable way to measure the totality of student learning. Teacher self-evaluation is especially vital in the school for quality learning because the lead-manager teacher is in turn responsible for involving the learners in self-evaluation.

The lead-manager principal approaches personnel evaluation with two broad goals in mind. The first is to cause each staff member to develop the skills for, and to engage in, a continual self-evaluation leading to personal and professional growth. Any staff member unable or unwilling to engage in this process will not be an effective participant in the school for quality learning. The second goal is to prepare each teacher to develop self-evaluation capabilities in the learners. The self-evaluation process is the same, whether directed toward quality teaching or toward quality learning.

The school for quality learning must have an effective and humane system of personnel evaluation. Such a system is grounded in the following basic beliefs about human nature and about the individual's potential as a satisfied, productive employee:

1. Individuals have a continual desire to learn, search, and inquire, and they are by nature goal striving and improvement seeking.

2. Growth occurs only when one is free to experiment with new or modified behaviors. One will experiment and take risks only when one is free of fear.

3. To help others grow and thus fulfill the school's mission, one must be actively involved in one's own growth.

4. Demonstrating respect for an individual as someone with innate human worth and dignity rather than solely, or even primarily, as someone who has worth because of what he or she does enables that individual to respect the worth and dignity of others.

5. An individual's incentive to grow and contribute to the excellence of the school comes from recognition of that individual's strengths and accomplishments.

6. Individual strengths and weaknesses in job performance in part define the uniqueness of each person's contribution to the school. To promote growth for each individual while maintaining this uniqueness, and to encourage diversity among school employees, management should view individual strengths rather than weaknesses as the foundation for growth.

7. Individual responsibility, developed through participation in determining both personal and school goals, increases motivation to achieve and produces greater satisfaction.

8. Sharing of responsibility, in the work situation and in the evaluation process, leads to more imaginative and creative involvement on the part of each staff member.

McGregor (1961) describes two vastly different views of human nature, called theory X and theory Y, influencing manager behaviors. The theory Y view is based on the following assumptions:

1. The expenditure of physical and mental effort in work is as natural as play or rest.

2. External control and the threat of punishment are not the only means of bringing about effort toward organizational objectives. People will exercise self-direction and self-control in the service of objectives to which they are committed.

3. Commitment to objectives is a function of the rewards associated with their achievement.

4. Human beings learn, under proper conditions, not only to accept but also to seek responsibility.

5. The capacity to exercise a high degree of imagination, ingenuity, and creativity in the solution of organizational problems is widely, not narrowly, distributed in the population.

6. Under the conditions of modern life, human intellectual potential is only partially utilized.

More traditional and widely held is the theory X view, based on the following assumptions:

1. Human beings have an inherent dislike of work and will avoid it whenever possible.

2. Because of this inherent aversion to work, most people must be coerced, controlled, directed, and threatened with punishment if they are to put forth effort adequate to the achievement of organizational objectives.

3. Human beings prefer to be directed, wish to avoid responsibility, have relatively little ambition, and want security above all.

Theory X management style, based on the theory X view of human nature, is the predominant management style in American school systems. This observation applies to the management of the school district by the superintendent, the management of the school by the principal, and the management of the classroom by the teacher. The theory X view supports boss-manager behavior.

The decision-making structure described in chapter 5 and the facilitative evaluation system advocated here correspond to McGregor's theory Y view. A principal who subscribes to theory X will not be a lead-manager principal. A facilitative evaluation system is the driving force for school improvement. It is the main vehicle for communication between the principal and each teacher. Through this process, principal and teacher develop a relationship of trust, cooperation, and respect. The evaluation system is formative, never summative. Checklists, labels, rankings, or comparisons—other than comparisons with one's own previous behavior—have no place in facilitative evaluation. The teacher's self-assessment of performance, strengths and weaknesses, and potential is extremely important, more important than the principal's assessment.

The continuing effort to make the school a place of quality learning for all learners requires each staff member to be immersed in a personal growth plan in which the principal has a key part. The principal establishes a process for in-depth dialogue with each teacher about classroom life, learning activities, and individual students. In this evaluation dialogue, the principal discovers the teacher's concerns and successes, and the teacher hears the principal's feedback, be it a reflection of success or a question about a concern. Through this dialogue, through direct classroom observation, and, it is hoped, through involvement with the student learners in the classroom, the principal comes to know what the teacher is actually doing. It is the dialogue, however, that allows the principal to understand the teacher's decisions and allows the principal and teacher to determine whether the classroom activities are consistent with the school mission. During the evaluation dialogue, the principal is responsible for offering suggestions, expressing concerns, and challenging the teacher to build on specific strengths or seek improvement in specific areas of weakness.

The evaluation dialogue is not associated with a particular time but rather continues throughout the school year and from one school year to the next. Initially, principal and teacher confer to discuss the teacher's responsibilities and jointly to determine personal and professional growth goals for the teacher. Figure 6.1 shows a sample form that can be used to record goals as well as activities related to those goals.

Figure 6.1   Sample Staff Development Form

Name _____ School year _____

Conference dates _____

Fall goal-setting conference _____

Spring evaluation conference _____

Professional and/or personal growth goals	Means of accomplishment: Major activities related to stated goals

Both parties can suggest needs that should be addressed in the growth plan. However, the lead-manager principal, understanding control theory and the psychology of behavior change, knows that the teacher will be the one to select the actual growth targets. If the teacher decides not to address an area of concern identified by the principal, the lead-manager principal accepts that decision, knowing the teacher is doing the best he or she knows how to do at that moment. The principal continues throughout the school year to facilitate the teacher's self-evaluation process and seeks other opportunities in that dialogue to persuade the teacher to address the concern. It is highly unlikely that a teacher and a principal in a trust relationship would continue to ignore each other's concerns or suggestions. Indeed, if that occurs, it indicates that trust is lacking. The nature of the goals selected by the teacher offers a clue about the trust relationship. If the goals are superficial and trivial, the teacher does not trust the principal. The teacher whose goals are to organize a filing system or upgrade the bulletin boards is sending a clear message of distrust.

The goal-setting conference is followed by frequent observations and conferences throughout the year, some very brief and some in-depth. These contacts will normally not concern overall progress toward all goals; rather, each encounter will address a specific issue. Frequent contact provides the principal ample opportunity to give the teacher feedback, to become familiar with his or her program, and to assess how well that classroom corresponds to the mission of the school. Moreover, by keeping the principal current on the teacher's perceived needs, frequent contact enables him or her to support the teacher to the extent possible. If the trust relationship with a teacher is lacking, the lead-manager principal uses these encounters to build a helping relationship and to reveal the principal's true agenda: to involve each staff member in an active plan for becoming a facilitator of quality learning.

Near the end of each school year, the principal and the teacher will confer to assess the outcome of the growth plan and to establish tentative goals for the next year. Summer staff development opportunities may figure significantly in this discussion. It is not unusual for a teacher to restate a goal for the following year. This is, in fact, desirable in many situations: Such a goal is usually an important one. The teacher may make progress—perhaps even extraordinary progress—but may challenge himself or herself to grow and improve further in the same area. For example, a middle-grade elementary teacher's goal to "totally convert the classroom reading program to a children's literature–based

..oach emphasizing increased comprehension by each reader" unlikely to be achieved in 9 months. The same is true for a multidisciplinary secondary school teaching team whose goal is total curriculum integration.

Throughout the personnel evaluation process, the lead-manager principal listens, analyzes what is said and observed, and asks clarifying questions. The principal refrains from telling or ordering but instead attempts to clarify, extend the discussion, and challenge the teacher with questions such as these:

1. Which of the learners in your classroom are you most concerned about?

2. What is the nature of the concern?

3. What do you want those learners to do?

4. What are you doing with those learners?

5. Is what you are doing working? Helping?

6. How might you address your concerns?

7. Do you have a plan?

8. What assistance do you foresee that you might need?

9. Where would you get that assistance?

10. How will you know if you are making progress in addressing your concerns?

11. Do you believe the learners' concerns are the same as yours?

12. If not, do you have a strategy for channeling the learners' interest toward your concerns?

13. Can you address the learners' concerns? Will you?

14. What has been your biggest success so far with this class?

15. Tell me about an example of quality learning that you have witnessed with this class.

16. What are your plans to further integrate the curriculum?

17. How will you begin?

18. If you could change only one thing, what would you try to change?

19. How would you evaluate success in that endeavor?

20. What is frustrating you the most at this time?

21. What could you do to relieve some of that frustration?

22. Can I help? How?

23. Is there other assistance that you would find appropriate?

24. On the basis of your assessment of the needs of the learners in your class, what do you see as your biggest challenge?

25. If you could do over anything you have done so far with your class, what would that be?

26. How would this make a difference?

27. Can you do something now that will accomplish this same result?

28. What aspect of your work that you consider high quality would you like me to notice?

29. Are you planning to do anything different with the responsibility education program?

30. What plan do you have for family involvement? For providing information to families?

31. What questions do you find most effective in challenging learners to self-evaluate behavior? Learning?

32. How do you see learners' collaborative efforts fitting into your classroom program?

33. What formal training programs are you planning to become involved in this year?

Because this approach to personnel evaluation, like all communication between the lead-manager principal and the teacher, relies heavily on trust, it is important to consider the disposition of evaluation results, reports, or data. The principal has no need for such information other than for his or her "extension of memory" file—a separate file for each teacher containing information about the principal-teacher interaction. This file is solely a record for the principal's personal review. The lead-manager principal provides all evaluation results, reports, and data to the teacher in the understanding that those materials are the teacher's sole property. The teacher decides with whom, if anyone, to share the information and what information, if any, to place in the personnel record maintained by the school or the district. This gesture is the principal's ultimate statement of trust; it closes the book on the teacher's fear of dismissal relative to the evaluation process.

The lead-manager principal must have staff development resources for individualized training opportunities based on teachers' assessed needs. Deming speaks to this issue with his Point 6 (institute training) and Point 13 (institute a vigorous program of education and self-improvement). The staff development program for teachers must be individualized, as is the quality learning program for students, to be described in Part 3.

The lead-manager principal recognizes that the promotion of collegial relationships is a powerful tool for staff development. Cooperation and sharing are hallmarks of a school for quality learning. It is especially important that the school's staff members enjoy such relationships because they collectively represent a major resource. There are few schools for quality learning and probably fewer staff training programs. A teacher is more likely to obtain assistance from fellow staff members than from resources outside the school. Collegiality is an essential element of a school for quality learning. Because consensus decision making demands extraordinary communication, the drive to accomplish the school's mission will not succeed without strong mutual commitment borne out by cooperative, caring behavior. The decision-making group of people with similar jobs is an excellent vehicle for promoting collegiality. Other, less obvious, groupings may grow out of common interests or concerns. For example, a group might form for those concerned with better integration of computers in the classroom, those interested in children's literature as the basis for a reading program, those looking into cooperative learning strategies, those concerned with restructuring the mathematics curriculum, and so on. The lead-manager principal has an overview of teachers' interests and concerns and is in a position to link teachers who are likely to help one another. In most schools a teacher rarely, if ever, sees another teacher performing in the classroom. A teacher rarely, if ever, has an opportunity to obtain feedback about classroom performance from another teacher. The lead-manager principal will promote such exchanges.

CHAPTER 7

Selection of Staff

The selection of new or replacement staff in the school for quality learning is a critical area of responsibility. Because the school has developed a mission, identified strategies to accomplish the mission, and designed structures for the school's operation—all through the full participation and consensus of the entire staff—the selection and integration of new staff members requires extreme care. The school must have the responsibility for recommending prospective employees to the governing board. Only those who are closely identified with the school's mission and are familiar with the school's ongoing development can truly know what is needed from new staff members.

The lead-manager principal understands that the school has the opportunity to enlarge its pool of expertise and talent by recruiting an individual with experiences and skills that complement those of current employees. The principal also appreciates the importance of the match between the prospective employee's personal philosophy and the stated philosophy and mission of the school for quality learning. The selection process must ensure that a new staff member wholeheartedly believes in and supports the school's mission and has the potential to make a unique contribution to the total effort.

The lead-manager principal will involve teachers in interviewing and selecting new staff members. This broad involvement of other staff will likely improve the selection process. Participation in the process also has a positive impact on teachers. First, it further affirms the principal's trust in them. Second, it provides a forum for teachers to share concerns and issues and to

learn more about one another. It is not unusual for the staff selection process to strengthen individual teachers' beliefs or to yield
ideas they can use in the classroom; some of the ideas come from
the candidates for employment, some from the other interviewers. Third, and perhaps most important, teachers involved in the
process learn of their colleagues' expectations, not only for the
prospective employees but for their own teaching and for the
school as a whole.

Glasser (1990) contends that effective teaching may be the
hardest job there is. This observation, which we will discuss further in Part 3, unquestionably applies to the lead-manager teacher
in the school for quality learning. A new teacher in a school for
quality learning faces extraordinary and, possibly, overwhelming
challenge, even if he or she is experienced in the profession.
Every teacher in the school for quality learning needs support
from the others; none, however, needs it more than the new
arrival. A major benefit of involving teachers in the hiring process
is that it gives them a stake in the new employee's success. All
participants in the consensus choice want the individual to succeed because that success validates their collective judgment; further, they want the individual to succeed because that success
contributes to the school's progress toward fulfillment of its mission. From the outset, the new teacher has a support group among
colleagues already encountered in the interview process, colleagues who have an investment in the new teacher's growth and
development. Having met several staff members, the new teacher
already has some idea whom to turn to for assistance.

When a new teacher is to be hired, the lead-manager principal first invites a representative group of teachers to assist in the
selection process. This group should include teachers with whom
the new employee would work most closely—for instance, those
who teach a similar age group at the elementary level or a similar
subject at the secondary level. The group should also include a
sampling of other teachers. If teachers are working as an instructional team, all team members should be included, along with
other staff members for variety and broader representation. The
principal meets with the group to discuss the position to be filled
and the expectations for the candidate. From this discussion, the
group generates a list of criteria for evaluating potential candidates. The most useful criteria relate to knowledge or training,
qualifications, proficiency in desired teaching strategies, and personality traits. For example, the following criteria might guide the
search for an intermediate-level elementary school teacher:

1. Experience working with 10- to 12-year-old children, whether in a school or nonschool setting

2. A strong background in mathematics and science

3. Training in and experience with cooperative learning and conflict resolution strategies

4. Experience working as a team member

5. Training in the teaching of reading through the use of children's literature

The foregoing are specialized criteria related to subject and grade level. They are secondary to the following criteria, which are applied in every search:

1. Personal philosophy consistent with the philosophy and mission of the school for quality learning

2. Acceptance of and commitment to the mission and philosophy of the school for quality learning

3. Certification for the position

4. High energy level

5. Highly developed oral and written communication skills

6. Propensity and skills for self-evaluation

7. A positive self-concept

8. Possession of effective strategies for fulfilling own needs

9. Possession of effective strategies for facilitating others' need fulfillment

10. People orientation

The specialized criteria drawn up by the group give the principal or the human resources department a basis for screening applications and selecting candidates to interview. The interview is the most critical stage in determining how well the candidate will meet both the specialized and general criteria. The interview lets the principal and the interviewing teachers gather information that is personally meaningful, in contrast to the information in the application file (which reflects the applicant's view or the opinion of the person providing the reference). Both of these sources provide valuable information, but neither the applicant nor the reference source is likely to know the individual school; thus, neither can predict how well the applicant will meet the school's particular expectations.

The interview must be designed to discover as much as possible about the applicant. The interviewers will try to learn about the candidate's commitment to the profession, life experiences and view of self, beliefs about learning and learners, personal and professional strengths and weaknesses, aspirations including personal and professional growth interests, expectations of the job and of colleagues, and personal strategies for assessing the impact of his or her own behavior. The interview questions should be open-ended. The following is a sampling of questions and statements, in no particular order, to which a candidate might be asked to respond:

1. What were some factors that influenced your decision to become a teacher?

2. Tell about a person who influenced your life.

3. Describe a significant event in your life.

4. Tell about a child you know.

5. What qualities do you possess that make you a good friend?

6. What quality do you see in others that you wish you could develop more fully in yourself?

7. What is your most prized possession?

8. What are the standards by which you judge your life to be successful or less than successful?

9. What are the purposes of education?

10. If I visit your classroom, what will I see that will be a clear demonstration of your beliefs about teaching and learning?

11. How do children learn?

12. What should a learner be able to demonstrate if he or she has successfully completed schooling in a school for quality learning?

13. When you are teaching, how are you behaving? What can you be observed doing?

14. How would you help a learner form and maintain an enabling self-concept?

15. Assume that you have complete freedom to organize your classroom. Tell about a typical day for one of the students in your classroom.

16. Confronted with a learner who you believe has high potential but who is doing very little if any quality work, what would you do?

17. How would you evaluate a learner?

18. If you could change one thing about education, what would you change?

19. Where in this school do you think you might go for help?

20. What assistance do you anticipate you would appreciate and find helpful?

21. Describe an incident that might occur in your classroom that would give you great joy. What about great despair?

22. What do you do for yourself when you feel overwhelmed or discouraged?

23. What staff development programs or ideas seem attractive to you?

24. What strategies or programs do you propose to use to foster creativity and critical thinking?

25. Describe your philosophy of teaching for (*subject area*). What is important? How do you present that to the learner?

26. What does "integrated curriculum" mean to you?

27. What directions would you expect from the principal relative to your teaching job?

28. What do you plan to tell parents about your program? About their children?

29. What are your behavioral expectations for the learners in your classroom?

30. Describe your plan to help learners display appropriate behaviors in the learning environment.

31. What makes you the best candidate for this position?

Because the information elicited in an interview is so important, the interview process is necessarily time-consuming and intense. There is merit in conducting more than one interview with a potential candidate. One strategy is to divide the interview responsibilities between the principal and the teacher interview group. The principal conducts the initial interviews of all candidates selected through the screening of the applications and then refers a number of potential candidates who seem to meet the established criteria to the group of teachers for a second interview. When all candidates have been interviewed, the principal and the teachers meet to share their findings. If the principal and the teacher group have a consensus choice, that candidate would be recommended for employment. If there is no consensus choice, more interviews would be conducted: Additional candidates could be brought in for the initial interview; the teachers might interview candidates already interviewed by the principal but not originally referred to them; or the principal, the teachers, or both could interview a candidate again. The process is repeated until a consensus choice evolves and the recommendation for employment is made.

Occasionally, an untimely vacancy will occur, necessitating an almost immediate replacement. In such a circumstance, it is far better to employ an interim replacement and free the search process from time constraints than to attempt to hurry the process.

CHAPTER 8

Responsibility Education: The Discipline Policy

A fundamental component of school climate involves behavioral expectations for students. In a school for quality learning, each student is expected to be fully engaged in quality learning activities. When the school attains that lofty goal, there will likely be little concern about behavior and about the effects of students on one another. Each student will be highly productive, and the total school experience will be satisfying. The student worker will not seek other avenues to satisfy the needs for belonging, power, freedom, and fun. The activities of the learning environment will ensure need satisfaction.

Glasser (1990) distinguishes lead managers from boss managers by their view and establishment of rules. Boss managers depend on rules, and rules proliferate with each new problem. These rules are sacred and often become more important than the problem they were designed to solve. Lead managers also have rules, but they do not depend on rules to solve every problem. The lead manager designs the total operation so that hard work will produce need-satisfying results. The only reason to have a rule is to facilitate the operation of a very complex system. In the school for quality learning, the lead-manager principal will keep the rules few and simple.

The philosophy of the school for quality learning stresses certain behavioral conventions for the entire school that require consistent implementation by each staff member. Still, in the school for quality learning, each classroom is unique. The rules for behavior and the conventions for learning will vary from one classroom to another. At the same time, no classroom is totally isolated. A student worker may be in several different classrooms in a single day. Even in the essentially self-contained classroom structure found in many elementary schools, students interact at various times and through various functions with students from outside the self-contained classroom. Moreover, a school does not become a school for quality learning at a specific point; rather, it is engaged in a continuing journey toward that goal. Most schools start far back on the road to quality and will not soon attain the state where nearly all learners are fully engaged in need-satisfying, quality learning activities. For these reasons, some attention to behavioral expectations of students is warranted.

The lead-manager principal knows that the rules must be few and that they must be seen as sensible by those who must follow them. Rules designed to ensure the safety of all and to guarantee the preservation of each person's basic human rights are understandable to students of every age, provided they are discussed and explained in age-appropriate ways. Glasser (1990) suggests that the rules create an atmosphere in which courtesy prevails. The purpose of the rules is to clearly define what behavior is acceptable.

The document entitled "Leal Rights and Responsibilities" shows how one school, Leal Elementary School in Urbana, Illinois, stated its behavioral expectations. In the context of our democratic culture, the notion of rights and related responsibilities makes sense to everyone. The behavioral expectations apply to all members of the school environment, be they adults or children, teachers or learners, and so on.

The lead-manager principal facilitates a consensus agreement among the staff regarding standards for acceptable student behavior and strategies for helping students to display acceptable behavior. In the school for quality learning, student behavior is managed without coercion. Each student is doing the best he or she knows how to do to meet basic psychological needs for belonging, power, freedom, and fun. If, in the judgment of the school's adults, the student's behavior is unacceptable, the adults' responsibility is to help the student choose an acceptable behavior through the self-evaluation/planning process of reality therapy.

In the school for quality learning, once the basic rules are agreed upon, strategies are developed to inform the students of the rules and to help each one understand them. These strategies

LEAL RIGHTS AND RESPONSIBILITIES

My rights

I have a right to be happy and to be treated with compassion in this school. This means that no one will laugh at me or hurt my feelings.

I have the right to be myself in this school: This means that no one will treat me unfairly because I am black or white . . .
fat or thin
tall or short
boy or girl
adult or child.

I have a right to be safe in this school: This means that no one will . . .
hit me
kick me
push me
pinch me
threaten me
hurt me.

I have the right to expect my property to be safe in this school.

I have the right to hear and be heard in this school: This means that no one will . . .
yell
scream
shout
make loud noises
or otherwise disturb me.

My responsibilities

I have the responsibility to treat others with compassion: This means that I will not laugh at others, tease others, or try to hurt the feelings of others.

I have the responsibility to respect others as individuals and not to treat others unfairly because they are black or white . . .
fat or thin
tall or short
boy or girl
adult or child.

I have the responsibility to make the school safe by not . . .
hitting anyone
kicking anyone
pushing anyone
pinching anyone
threatening anyone
hurting anyone.

I have the responsibility not to take or destroy the property of others.

I have the responsibility to help maintain a calm and quiet school: This means that I will not . . .
yell
scream
shout
make loud noises
or otherwise disturb others.

Note. From *Leal School Staff Handbook,* by R. J. Bodine, unpublished manuscript, n.d., Leal School, Urbana, Illinois.

I have the right to learn about myself and others in this school: This means that I will be free to express my feelings and opinions without being interrupted or punished.	I have the responsibility to learn about myself and others in this school: This means that I will be free to express my feelings and opinions without being interrupted or punished, and I will not interrupt or punish others who express their feelings and opinions.
I have the right to be helped to learn self-control in this school: This means that no one will silently stand by while I abuse my rights.	I have the responsibility to learn self-control in this school: This means that I will strive to exercise my rights without denying the same rights to others, and I will expect to be corrected when I do abuse the rights of others as they shall be corrected if my rights are abused.
I have the right to expect that all these rights will be mine in all circumstances so long as I am exercising my full responsibilities.	I have the responsibility to protect my rights and the rights of others by exercising my full responsibilities in all circumstances.

will involve interactions both with groups of students (perhaps in class discussions) and with individual students who need extra assistance in choosing new behaviors. These interactions, especially the group discussions, are scheduled regularly and constitute the most important element of the responsibility education program of the school for quality learning. Their purpose is to help the learners understand their own behaviors and the effects of those behaviors on others. The learners are also exposed to alternative behaviors. Glasser (1969) maintains that because such discussions are open-ended and address the learners' own concerns, the learners are involved, see the discussions as relevant, and engage in thinking. Failure of the school to devote adequate time to social education will result in discipline problems, which will be largely the result of individuals attempting to do the best they know how to do in a situation where they are unsure what is expected.

Parents also need to be informed about the school rules, as do all support staff who work in the school, including volunteers.

The excerpt entitled "The Staff's Commitment" expresses an entire staff's support for responsibility education. The communication entitled "Parent Notice," along with a copy of the Leal Rights and Responsibilities, is mailed to each student's household before the start of each school year.

THE STAFF'S COMMITMENT

The document entitled "Leal Rights and Responsibilities" is the basic concept of governance for all of Leal School. *A total commitment by all staff members is vital in assuring the success of this program.* Each teacher has the responsibility to consistently engage his or her students in discussions and activities designed to enable the students to understand the concepts of "Rights and Responsibilities" and how the rules of the school reflect these concepts. It is agreed by staff consensus that this is a top-priority concern and that each classroom will devote a specific time each week to a class activity designed to assist students to develop social responsibility and a positive self-concept. *Each teacher is responsible for establishing rules and procedures for his or her classroom or area of assignment that are consistent with and supportive of "Leal Rights and Responsibilities."* Each teacher is responsible for helping each of his or her students learn responsible behavior through individual counseling and by seeking appropriate assistance from the principal, special services personnel, and other staff members. Every staff member is responsible for referring rule violations to the appropriate teacher—the teacher most involved with the rule violator. Each teacher is responsible for guaranteeing that each person at Leal accepts his or her responsibilities and exercises his or her rights. Each teacher is responsible for involving parents to help students learn desirable behaviors.

Note. From *Leal School Staff Handbook,* by R. J. Bodine, unpublished manuscript, n.d., Leal School, Urbana, Illinois.

In addition, the following specific provisions shall apply:

1. Any fight between students, no matter how small, will be called to the attention of the principal. The principal, in addition to the teacher, will counsel with the involved parties. At a minimum, parents will be called by the principal upon the second incident of fighting.

2. Any incident in which a student is caught stealing will be called to the attention of the principal. The principal will counsel with the student(s) involved, restitution will be enforced, and the parents will be advised of the problem.

3. Any act of physical aggression (or extreme defiance) toward a staff member will be called to the attention of the principal. The principal will counsel with the student, and the parents will be advised of the problem.

4. Any act of destruction of school property or vandalism will be called to the attention of the principal. In the case of property destruction, the parents will be contacted, and restitution for damage, either by work repair or by payment, will be demanded. The guilty student will clean up the mess.

5. Each classroom teacher will maintain a log of contacts with parents regarding discipline/behavior incidents.

Further, in order to generally improve the atmosphere of the school, the staff will make concerted efforts to develop an appreciation for the building and the property therein by the following means:

1. Not permitting students to write on the furniture, walls, and so on, in the classroom. Anyone found doing so shall wash off the writing.

2. Insisting that classrooms be cleaned—paper picked up, furniture straightened, and so on—at least twice daily (before lunch and before dismissal).

3. Ensuring that lockers are cleaned out periodically.

4. Demanding respect for displays and bulletin boards throughout the school.

5. Implementing other appropriate activities.

   Also, each classroom teacher will take whatever action is needed to ensure that his or her class does not disrupt other classes during school time—for example, by

1. Impressing upon all students that, as a courtesy to others, reasonable quiet in the halls during school time is essential.

2. Using some measure of control to guarantee that a very limited number of students would be in relatively unsupervised activities, such as using the bathrooms, getting a drink, or otherwise being out of the classroom, at any one time.

3. Making sure the class is together and under reasonable supervision when moving as a class to the library, to the playground, to the labs, to the gym, or to other areas of the building.

PARENT NOTICE

At the back of the *Leal School Parent/Student Handbook* is a one-page document . . . entitled "Leal Rights and Responsibilities." This document was developed by a group of teachers, parents, students, and the principal several years ago. It was developed to provide a consistent basis for our effort toward our general goal: to make Leal School "a good place for children and adults." The "Leal Rights and Responsibilities," safety considerations, and the need to maintain a learning environment serve as the foundation for all school rules and discipline procedures.

   Each classroom teacher assumes the responsibility to consistently and continually engage his or her students in discussions and activities designed to enable the students to understand the concepts of "Rights and Responsibilities" and how the rules of the school reflect these. The classroom teacher is responsible for helping each of his or her students learn responsible behavior through individual counseling and by seeking appropriate assistance from the principal, special services personnel, and other staff members. If the student continues to exhibit unacceptable behavior, the teacher is responsible for contacting the parents for assistance.

As a total staff, we are dedicated to this program. The development of social responsibility in each of our students is a top priority at Leal. It is our intention to continually strive to improve the total climate of the school and to minimize the number of disruptions to the learning activities in each of our classrooms. We feel that we have been successful but that this focus should continue as a top priority each year.

Additionally, we continue our concern about four specific and highly undesirable behaviors: fighting and/or verbal abuse of others, stealing and/or property damage, intimidation and/or extortion, and defiance and/or acts of aggression toward staff members. It is the consensus of the staff that these behaviors cannot be tolerated in the school environment and that we and the parents have the responsibility to help students learn desirable behaviors. We are prepared to deal consistently and firmly with these undesirable behaviors. If your child exhibits any of these behaviors, we will seek your assistance in helping your child develop more acceptable behavior.

We need your help. This effort toward the development of desired behaviors, exemplified by the point where each person is exercising fully his or her responsibilities and enjoying his or her rights, will be a major focus at Leal again this year. Please discuss the "Leal Rights and Responsibilities" in your family. Please do so at fairly regular intervals. Ask questions of your children regarding the discussions about rights and responsibilities at school. Perhaps you can even talk about rights and responsibilities in the home.

We believe that a consistent effort on the part of the staff at school, with the support of the parent at home, will result in growth in social responsibility in each of our students.

Using the overall school rules for expected behavior—the behavioral constitution of the school for quality learning—each classroom teacher develops the specific rules for his or her classroom. The lead-manager teacher understands that those rules, like the school rules, must be few and simple and must be viewed by the learners as sensible. Rules for the school and the classroom are the rules for success in any life venture. Helping learners make this connection is the ultimate aim of the responsibility education program. Classroom programs and strategies are further addressed in chapter 16.

CHAPTER 9

Family Involvement

Parents' perceptions of a school have a significant impact on school climate. Parents are an important component of the school community. Greater parental involvement is one battle cry of the school reform movement. Clearly, the school for quality learning requires parental support and involvement. The school must be perceived as open and inviting by parents and other family members significant in the student's life. It is the principal's responsibility to foster good school-family relations.

The lead-manager principal understands the school's responsibility to families and knows that they have a right to be informed about the school and its mission. The principal accepts that responsibility proactively, exercising leadership in promoting parental knowledge of and involvement in the school. A student progress reporting system that features face-to-face parent-teacher communication, classroom-level parent meetings, and joint parent-child activities is a proven strategy for increasing parental involvement. A school newsletter is a good way to tell families about the school's mission and strategies for accomplishing it.

The involvement of family members in addition to parents is a significant long-term investment in the quality of student learning. Family volunteers are encouraged to assist in the daily operation of the school. Family visitors are welcomed at all times. Family involvement in school governance issues is sought through the formation of ad hoc committees seeking solutions to particular school problems. Organized parent groups are allies in the effort to develop the school for quality learning. The lead-manager principal will obtain staff consensus on schoolwide strategies for increasing family involvement.

FAMILY INVOLVEMENT STRATEGIES

The tradition of family involvement in early childhood education yields quality strategies that can be extended to elementary and secondary levels. The following description of family involvement strategies was developed by the staff at the Washington School Early Childhood Education Program in Urbana, Illinois. This is a public school prekindergarten program serving approximately 400 children aged 3 through 5 and their families.

WASHINGTON SCHOOL FAMILY INVOLVEMENT

Family involvement is an integral part of the Urbana School District #116 Early Childhood Program. The family support programs serve parents, children, and families in differing ways and in a variety of settings. In general the family involvement component is designed to:

- Focus on prevention

- Build on the family's strengths

- Deal with parents as partners and as the primary teachers of their children

- Enhance the capacity of parents to foster the optimal development of their children

- Provide services to help parents deal with natural parental concerns and cope with the stresses encountered in parenting

- Support parents in seeking opportunities which will allow them to achieve their potential

Note. From *Washington School Staff Handbook* and Urbana School District #116 early childhood education grant proposals, by D. K. Crawford, unpublished materials, n.d., Urbana, Illinois.

- Respect the integrity of the child's family unit, be it two parents, single parent, foster parent, grandparents, or significant others

- Foster cultural, ethnic, and religious sensitivity

- Provide linkages within the community to other systems of services and support

- Build self-esteem in children, in parents, and in families

The Family Center is a place in the school especially for parents, children, and family activities. The Family Center provides:

- A comfortable setting for parent groups and workshops

- An area for parents and children to interact

- A family resource, toy, and book lending library

- A warm environment in which parents can discuss family issues

- A space for G.E.D., literacy, and other adult education classes

- Opportunities for parents to socialize with and learn from one another

- A place for parents to have a cup of coffee or tea

- A place for parents to spend quiet time

The Family Center Advisory Board, composed of parents, other family members, community members, and representatives of the Washington School Staff, meets quarterly to plan and to develop the Family Center programs and activities. The board provides opportunity for involvement in developing supportive services for families.

Involvement Options

Family members may become involved with a variety of activities in the school. Families determine how they want to become involved and have a variety of options from which to choose. These options include but are not limited to the following.

Family-Teacher Conferences

Formal conferences are routinely scheduled in both daytime and evening each semester. Informal conferences are scheduled throughout the school year as requested by parents and by teachers.

Home Visits

Teachers may visit the children and their families at home in order to support the education program. Home intervention services to address the individualized needs of families will be provided by the support service staff as needed. Home visits may be requested by either families or school staff.

Family-Teacher Volunteers

Family members are encouraged to assist in their child's classroom at regularly scheduled times either daily, weekly, or monthly. A family member who becomes a Family-Teacher will be provided a T-shirt to wear when volunteering in the classroom.

Classroom Involvement

Families are encouraged to visit classrooms at any time. Families are invited to attend field trips, send in special treats, and share interests such as music, crafts, art, and storytelling. Families are encouraged to share their cultures through photographs, art, cooking activities, music, stories, projects, and so on.

EC Newsletter—"The Early Word"

Through the monthly school newsletter, the family is able to learn more about their child's educational program as well as learn new ideas that can enable them to support the educational program at home. Family members are also invited to contribute their own ideas and articles each month.

Family Groups and Workshops

Support groups and other workshops specifically designed to meet the needs of individual parents will be offered. These support groups and workshops will be developed according to interest survey results obtained by the Family Advisory Board.

Child's Backpack

Each child is asked to carry a backpack to and from school every day. Teachers and families use these backpacks to send notes, messages, and the like. The backpack is viewed as an important communication link between the school and the home.

Family Events

Special family events and celebrations are scheduled throughout the school year. These events are designed to support the development of a sense of belonging within the school community and to provide opportunities for families to experience playful and enjoyable times together.

The Washington School material characterizes a school that is "family-friendly." Although the Washington School options for family involvement were designed with very young students in mind, they could be adapted and built upon for older students and their families. A section of any school library could be set aside as a family resource area; perhaps a parent lounge could be provided in the school. The school for quality learning would certainly develop a number of resources and activities for families.

PARENTAL CHOICE

Parental choice of an educational program for the child is another important vehicle for increasing family involvement in the school. The school is operated in a manner that offers students a variety of program options or alternatives. Each program is consistent with the school mission and philosophy, and the programs will likely exhibit far more common characteristics than differences, but the differences are made clear so that parents and students can indicate their preferences. At the elementary level, a program might be differentiated by the age of the students, by the nature of the teaching assignment organization, by the teaching style to be employed, and so on. The following passages from Leal School handbooks describe two examples of choice utilized at that school. The first example concerns choice based on an age level grouping plan and on teaching assignment organization. The second example concerns choice based on teaching style and on teaching assignment organization.

EXAMPLES OF CHOICE AT LEAL SCHOOL

We at Leal School are committed to provide a quality individualized learning program for every child. In so doing, we each subscribe to the following school philosophy statement.

Leal School Philosophy

Leal School subscribes to and attempts to implement a philosophy of "continuous student progress," an educational strategy in which the ability of the student to achieve determines the level of instruction and instructional materials introduced. An individual must be allowed to work according to his or her own abilities. Students are as diverse intellectually as they are physically; they have different backgrounds and experiences, feelings, ways of thinking, personalities, and ways of working and learning. In order to be effective, a school must allow and encourage students to work at their own rate, to develop their own unique style of learning, and to develop a respect for differences between individuals. Each child is a worthy individual and has rights, responsibilities, and

Note. From *Leal School Parent and Student Handbook,* by R. J. Bodine, unpublished manuscript, n.d., Urbana, Illinois. Portions of the lettered list have been adapted from *Position on the Teaching of English: Assumptions and Practices,* by the National Council of Teachers of English, 1991, Urbana, IL: Author.

privileges; the school should help the child acquire a sense of self-direction and social responsibility. Education should be based upon the individual's strong, inherent desire to learn and to make sense of his or her environment. Desire to learn is accentuated when the experiences are stimulating and nonthreatening. Learning about things is a natural part of a child's life, and in the process of growing up the better part of learning is done independently.

The development of an individual's thought processes should be primary; rote learning of facts should be de-emphasized; facts should become the building blocks for generalities and processes. The ability to solve problems, whether social or academic, must be given preference. School experiences must relate to the world beyond school. The environment within which students are encouraged to learn must be expanded; the total culture surrounding each individual should become the learning environment.

A student must be accepted as a person whose feelings and values deserve consideration and development. The school must assume an active role in helping each individual to develop or evolve a set of personal values which will be most meaningful in helping her or him to meet the challenges of life as a student and later as an adult. All persons need success to prosper; youths are no exception. A continual series of failures, if experienced in the school, can lead to a negative self-image, loss of desire to continue to participate, and an urge to seek this needed success outside of the school situation. A school should be flexible and divergent enough to allow each student to find some measure of success. We must seek to individualize our expectations of a student's progress as we strive to provide learning experiences for each student.

Students should be encouraged to develop a sense of responsibility. The student's school should be "his" or "her" school, one to be proud of and one in which the student is actively involved. The attitude of belonging and being an important contributor can do much toward establishing a spirit of cooperation and respect. This sense of responsibility should be further developed to include peers and adults. It is vital that each student realize that every other person is an individual with unique feelings, with unique ideas, with strengths and weaknesses, and with his or her own problems. A sense of responsibility and respect for the individuality of each person is necessary for better understanding and cooperation.

Being consistent with the Leal School philosophy and in an effort to provide the best possible educational environment for achieving the goals of the philosophy, the following basic beliefs are reflected in all Leal classrooms:

A. Every person is a learner. It is the nature of everyone to learn: to grow and change through interacting with others and responding to experiences. Learning is not confined to school times. Learning is ongoing and limited only by the sensory and reflective powers of the learner.

B. Teachers and students are a community of learners. Learning is a collaborative effort. Teachers are learners—from self and others. Learners are teachers—of self and others. Teachers respond to students in ways that enable them to explore options, make choices, and participate in meaning-making experiences. Teachers not only bring their expertise and authority to interactions with students, they also precipitate change by challenging and questioning to stimulate thinking and enable students to ask their own questions and seek answers.

C. Learners have diverse backgrounds, which reflect a mosaic of cultural heritages. They bring to their classrooms their different language proficiencies, their learning styles, and their own authority and expertise. The community of learners appreciates these diversities of cultural heritage and socioeconomic background, validating and challenging learners' representations of the world. Every language, culture, and experience is a resource in the classroom.

D. Learning comes from active response, evaluation of ideas and events, interactions with materials, discussion with others, and construction of knowledge. In a learning environment, students are given time to articulate and revise what they know. Teachers structure classrooms so that experiences address their own as well as students' interests. Support for risk taking requires acceptance of error as a part of learning.

E. The classroom setting contributes to the climate of the learning. The class schedule provides opportunity to reflect. Uninterrupted time blocks allow for learning, not "just covering." Freedom to use time in a flexible way helps students to become committed to the tasks at hand. The pace of the classroom is determined partly in response to the development and inquiry of the students. The variety of materials available reflects the diversity of the students. Students have easy access to learning materials of all types, which are organized and accessible to entice and accommodate students. Students are expected to choose materials, work in a variety of situations, and interact with all class members in an environment that is predictable but not static, exciting but not chaotic, disciplined but not restrictive. Assessment reflects what is valued in education. The classroom uses diverse kinds of assessment, including self-assessment, as opportunities for reflection on individual growth and change. Beyond simple recall of facts, assessment, which is always limited, grows naturally from classroom learning and is an extension of that learning.

F. Knowing is active and ongoing, a process of interactive learning. The classroom is a place where knowledge is socially constructed through interaction among teachers, students, and materials. Knowledge is not neutral but political, enabling the knower to make choices among conflicting sources. Knowledge is not just information, yet it requires information. Because the world's diverse information base is expanding at a rapid rate, teachers cannot limit their classes to narrow lists of information or sets of readings. Although students use certain resources, they must also know that a much larger body of resources exists and that they can gain access to these resources. Individualized, learner-based pedagogy requires that students have access to a variety of materials through libraries and other sources. Knowledge is more than a mastery of facts and processes. It includes understanding and use of these facts and processes in historical, social, political, and personal contexts. Students bring substantial knowledge to the classroom. Teachers build on that information.

Each classroom at Leal will be characterized by the following practices:

- All classrooms will stress the acquisition and development of basic skills and will promote the development of critical thinking and problem-solving skills and strategies.

- All classrooms will be student success oriented and will have instructional activities tailored to meet the needs of each student.

- All classrooms will employ a variety of learning experiences, including direct instruction in small and large groups, learning stations (centers) for independent or small-group learning activities, cooperative peer groups, and individual independent learning activities.

- All classrooms will utilize appropriate "hands-on" learning materials and activities and will provide integrated learning activities that incorporate simultaneous learning experiences in several content areas.

- All classrooms will provide intrinsically satisfying experiences in which learning is an enjoyable activity designed to help each student develop a more positive self-concept and a feeling of self-worth.

- All classrooms will have programs based on the Leal Rights and Responsibilities to help students develop social responsibility.

- All classrooms will contain a representative mixture of the cultures and backgrounds of the total student population of the school.

Because all classrooms adhere to the same school philosophy, because all classrooms have the same basic beliefs in common, because there is a common base curriculum for each classroom at a given age level, and because all classrooms have many organizational and instructional strategies in common, there will be more similarities among the classrooms than differences between them.

However, at Leal, we believe that a quality education can be obtained through alternative methods, all of which adhere to the school philosophy and embrace the common basic beliefs. No one alternative is objectively better than another. Teachers as individuals may feel more comfortable working in one alternative than another and are, thus, likely to be more successful. The same may be true for the learners.

Example 1

Alternative 1: Self-Contained, Multiage Classroom

This is a mostly self-contained, multiage classroom. This alternative provides that one teacher will spend most of the school day with a classroom of students of two age levels rather equally distributed—either grades one and two or grades three and four or grades five and six.

Alternative 2: Team-Taught, Multiage Classroom

This is a two-classroom cluster of a multiage group of students. This alternative provides that two teachers will share the responsibility for two classrooms. Each classroom will consist of two age levels rather equally distributed—either grades one and two or grades three and four or grades five and six.

Alternative 3: Self-Contained, Single-Age Classroom

This is a mostly self-contained classroom of students of one age level. Two of these classrooms will be paired at grades one and two, two will be paired at grades three and four, and two will be paired at grades five and six. A single teacher will stay with the same class for 2 years. Thus, the teacher in each pair would teach one level the first year and the other level the following year.

Example 2

Option A

Serves children of all abilities who want and need the security of structure. Also serves the child who, while not needing the structure, will accept it and function within it. Because the classroom is individualized, it is not the "old, traditional" classroom.

The teacher has the primary responsibility for making decisions about subject matter and the use of time.

Generally, the majority of students work on language arts or math at the same time. Grouping is flexible, depending on the varying needs of children and teachers. Both large and small groups are used for instructional purposes. Other content areas tend to be total class experiences with follow-up assistance provided to students according to their individual needs.

Materials are primarily teacher chosen and of a great variety. Textbooks, supplementary materials, and teacher-made items are all used.

Teachers will have differing expectations and requirements, both academic and behavioral, for individual children. Each child is encouraged and challenged to better his or her own past performance.

Classrooms are essentially self-contained, with possibly some limited team teaching depending upon teacher preference. Each classroom contains children of two grade levels: first and second, third and fourth, or fifth and sixth.

Option B

Serves children of all abilities who want or need freedom, but within the security of an essentially self-contained classroom.

The teacher has the primary responsibility for determining the educational objectives of the classroom, but the children and the teacher share the planning of how to accomplish those objectives. Children are encouraged to assume increasing independence in the daily use of time, materials, and class assignments.

A "typical" day would include children meeting in small teacher-led skill groups and/or one-to-one with the teacher for instruction and evaluation, working on individual activities and assignments and participating in total class instruction. An informal atmosphere prevails.

Learning resources include teacher-made activities, paperback books, textbooks, educational games, and library materials. Community resources and facilities supply a major source of enrichment.

Realizing that each classroom contains children of varying strengths and weaknesses, the teacher will have different expectations and requirements for each child, both academic and behavioral. Each child is encouraged to better his or her own performance.

Classrooms are essentially self-contained, with possibly some limited team teaching. Each classroom contains children of two grade levels: first and second, third and fourth, or fifth and sixth.

Option C

Serves children of all abilities who want to take major responsibility for their own learning. Option C teachers believe that children need and thrive on a school experience of both structure and freedom.

Students are under the direct supervision of teachers, either in group meetings or one-to-one, for about two-thirds of the day. During the other third of the day, the student is responsible for deciding how to use the time to accomplish the assigned tasks and to pursue other activities of interest to the student. New students are given much guidance in organizing their work for this time. Learning to use this freedom responsibly is considered to be an important goal of Option C, and the teachers take every possible opportunity to help the students develop an attitude of responsibility and self-direction. Students entering Option C are not required to be mature and self-directed; rather, it is assumed that they and their parents desire that they work toward achieving that goal within the setting of the option.

Students do not have desks or assigned seats. They may move around during their independent work time but must learn to do this without bothering others as they work. Likewise, they should be tolerant of others moving in the room and able to concentrate despite a large variety of active learning activities and movement in the classroom. Conversation is also permitted during the independent work period, but measures are taken to keep this within reasonable limits.

A strong emphasis is put on one-to-one guidance and small group work, but some subjects are taught in larger groups. All subjects utilize flexible groupings based on children's needs. Math and language groups are formed according to the skill levels of the children. Grade level is a strong criterion for determining group placement, but other factors may necessitate exceptions to this. Social studies, science, and health are usually taught in large groups.

Option C is based on the following assumptions: Children learn best those things in which they are interested, but some things are necessary to learn regardless of one's interest. Children vary in the levels of skill and subject matter they need. Individuals vary in learning style, and thus varied approaches must be used in presentations. Since children learn best when they develop a caring relationship with their teachers and their peers, activities should be planned to promote this relationship.

Classrooms include children of two grade levels, either first and second, or third and fourth, or fifth and sixth. Each child has access to both rooms and both teachers of his/her level. Team teaching and the development of teacher specialties is an integral part of the program.

These descriptions show that programs of the various options will provide variety at each age level. It must also be noted that variations will occur within the same option from age level to age level. Much of that variation is due to the maturity level of the students. Also, some variations occur between classrooms of the same option at the same age level due to the style, preference, and personality of the individual teacher.

Secondary schools also can be organized to offer parents and students choices beyond the traditional option of the elective course. The core curriculum can be structured to offer program variety in much the same way as in an elementary school. A large school could be divided into "schools within a school," with each of the smaller schools specializing in a curriculum-unifying theme: for example, the practical arts school, the aesthetic arts school, the scientific process school, the independent study school, and so on. The creation of schools within a school should not be a form of tracking to sort out college-bound students from those who will seek technical training beyond high school and those for whom high school represents the end of study; rather, it should embody distinctly different ways to organize and facilitate learning.

FAMILY INVOLVEMENT IN THE LEARNER'S SCHOOL EXPERIENCE

The lead-manager principal of the school for quality learning realizes that some—perhaps many—parents or family members will not choose to be involved with the school because, for various reasons, they do not see the school as need fulfilling. The principal leads the school staff to recognize that these family members are doing the best they know how to do and that they are not sending the message that they do not care about their children or their children's education. The principal encourages the staff to develop strategies for involving such families meaningfully in their children's education.

Involvement in a child's school experience does not depend on direct, active involvement with the school. The school staff accepts the responsibility to help the student and the family communicate about the school experience. Often, a child, when asked, "What did you do (or what did you learn) in school today?" replies, "Nothing!" Perhaps the child simply does not know how to verbalize the experience. The teacher can help the student by summarizing and prompting: "This is what you did at school today, and this is what you learned." This support is important whether the student has learned to count by two in elementary school mathematics or dissected a fetal pig in high school biology.

The teacher in the school for quality learning communicates regularly with families through a brief classroom newsletter that tells what the class is learning and what is planned for the immediate future. Most important, the newsletter presents some questions for family members to ask the student. A one-page newsletter requires little of the teacher's valuable time, yet the potential payoff in family support is significant. The newsletter format can vary, but it should be simple so that information can be recorded quickly as the week progresses, and it should be consistent so that the readers will become familiar with it and understand the information readily. The newsletter should be sent home on the same day each week. Figure 9.1 shows a sample format for a classroom newsletter.

Figure 9.1   Sample Classroom Newsletter

OUR WEEKLY NEWS NOTE

Teacher _____ Week of _____

What we learned this week . . .	Questions to ask your child . . .	What is planned for next week . . .

Special notices:

The newsletter may be handwritten and photocopied, or it may be generated on a computer. Usually the teacher fills in the newsletter gradually by jotting down major concepts or ideas presented during the week, along with appropriate questions; often these questions come from the learners. The teacher also indicates major plans for the coming week. The special notices section can alert family members to field trips, special assemblies, or classroom speakers; request special materials; suggest an out-of-school activity for the student and family members; indicate a media event that is relevant to classroom activities; and so on. Compilation of the newsletter can actually be a student activity, especially the "what we learned" and "questions to ask" sections. It may be done by the entire class working together, by a newsletter committee, or by a single classroom reporter.

To help ensure that students and their families communicate about school, the teacher follows up by occasionally asking students about conversations at home. The class might devote a class meeting to the question, What did you and a family member discuss about school yesterday? If it seems evident that student-family dialogue is not taking place, the teacher may further assist the student by suggesting and practicing ways to initiate and sustain such dialogue. Follow-up with the family is also desirable.

Though the newsletter provides information about the class, families also need information specific to their children. Nearly all parents and family members welcome good news from a teacher. Telling them what their child is learning is imparting good news. When family members realize that the child is involved in a quality learning experience, they will be supportive of the school's efforts. They may still be unable to choose to be actively involved with the school, but they will convey a feeling of pride in their child and will encourage his or her continued involvement and success.

CHAPTER 10

Inclusive System of Support for Teachers and Learners

The school for quality learning is inclusive: Everyone belongs, is accepted, gives support, and is supported by others. "Everyone" includes both adults and learners. William Stainback and Susan Stainback (1990), in *Support Networks for Inclusive Schooling*, state that "inclusive schooling is the process of carrying out the operation of supportive schools" (p. 4). That process entails managing the classroom and the school as a supportive community where the needs of all members are met and where each member accepts responsibility for supporting and helping others to ensure that those needs are met. In the school for quality learning, everyone contributes to the effort to develop a total school community and individual classroom communities that nurture and support both teachers and learners in the mission of quality learning. An inclusive system requires support networks for both teachers and learners. This chapter discusses a system of support for teachers that includes collaborative service teams, team teaching, and administrative support services, all of which ultimately affect the learner and the quality of learning. (Chapter 15 will deal specifically with a system of support for learners.) Creation of an inclusive system of support involves rethinking the school's administrative structure, instructional support structure, and special education structure.

RATIVE STRUCTURE

element of the school includes people other than the and the classroom teachers. In chapter 4, we recommend redefining middle management positions such as assistant principal, dean, department head, and the like, which are conceived as operational or communication links between the classroom teacher and the principal. It is vital for principal and teacher to have a direct line of communication concerning decisions about curriculum, instruction, discipline, budgeting, evaluation, and staff development. The traditional middle management positions can be redefined as support positions with the purpose of helping the principal and the teachers find solutions to identified problems. Alternatively, the school can be reorganized into smaller aggregates—"schools within a school"—with each former middle management administrator assigned a particular group of teachers.

Administrative Support Service Strategy

When the school structure is changed to redefine middle management as administrative support positions, it is essential to ensure that such support services do not allow the principal and teacher to abrogate their decision-making and operational responsibilities, especially in the critical areas of curriculum, instruction, discipline, and evaluation, as well as in such related areas as budgeting and staff development. For example, the teacher must assume the major role in learner responsibility education and discipline. A dean or assistant principal in a support role might help by meeting with the teacher and learner as they address a problem behavior and by mediating as the two parties work to develop a plan for new behavior. Alternatively, the support person might help the learner develop a plan for new behavior after the teacher and learner have together identified the problem; this would free the teacher to resume other activities. The support person might simply provide a time-out or cooling-off alternative until the teacher and learner can meet to address the problem. In this capacity, the dean or assistant principal might formally serve as the in-school time-out teacher (to be discussed in chapter 16). In any event, the teacher cannot escape dealing with difficult behavior problems simply by referring them to the dean or assistant principal, nor can that individual override the teacher's decisions.

As is often the practice, the principal may not assign the responsibility for evaluating a portion of the teaching staff to an assistant principal. The assistant principal might support the principal's efforts in evaluation by doing classroom observations, providing instructional support, arranging for staff development activities already agreed upon by the principal and the teacher, and so on. Although the assistant can help in a variety of ways, he or she cannot replace the principal in the goal-setting effort and in the evaluation dialogue with the teacher.

The specific roles of administrative support service staff members vary, but all embrace the inclusive operational notion that their mission is to help the principal and the teacher determine what they want to do and then help them get it done. Administrative support staff are valuable human resources who assist the principal and teacher in finding alternatives, examining consequences, investigating resources, and so on. However, they do not have the authority to dictate policy or practice to either the principal or the teacher.

School-Within-a-School Strategy

When a school is organized into smaller aggregates, with the former middle managers assigned specific groups of teachers, each such group functions as an autonomous unit within the school and serves a unique group of students. The administrator assumes the responsibilities of a lead-manager principal for his or her "school within a school." One rationale for this type of organization lies in the decision-making process recommended earlier. Some decisions require total staff participation and must be achieved by consensus. Reaching consensus is challenging in a small group—extremely difficult in a large group. The practice of many large schools, which use some form of representative assembly to make such decisions, could be counterproductive in the school for quality learning. The real value of the consensus process is very often the protracted discussion that it entails. The discussion gives each participant the opportunity to hear and question various viewpoints. In the representative assembly model, the commitment to the consensus decision is only as strong as the weakest representative. Moreover, it is questionable whether each representative can fully articulate to the decision-making body the opinions and concerns of the people represented. Likewise, the representatives may have trouble communicating the spirit of the agreed-upon decision to all of the individuals they represent.

Another argument in favor of reorganizing the large school into smaller units of governance relates to evaluation. To effectively use the evaluation process described in chapter 6, the lead-manager principal should have no more than 20 to 25 teachers to evaluate. Further, such reorganization can make it easier to provide parent/learner choice, as suggested in chapter 9. It can certainly facilitate the development of an integrated curriculum (to be discussed in chapter 14), especially when the integrative nature of the curricular offering defines one or more of the choices offered to parents and learners.

INSTRUCTIONAL SUPPORT STRUCTURE

Nearly every school has some staff members who can appropriately be categorized as instructional support personnel—for example, librarians or media specialists. They assist classroom teachers in organizing or developing instructional resources, and they help learners carry out activities initiated in the classroom. Other instructional support comes from content specialists who, particularly at the elementary level, deliver their curriculum to the learners—commonly in areas such as music, art, physical education, and foreign languages, and perhaps in drama and computers. The lead-manager principal is aware of the increased importance of support personnel and the increased need for their collaboration with the classroom teachers, particularly to achieve an integrated curriculum and to expand the human resources available to learners. (The latter issue will be discussed in chapter 15.) Guidance counselors, especially in their nonadministrative functions, also represent a valuable resource to learners, as they can assist in the pursuit of both quality behavior and quality learning.

Principals also have responsibility for other nonteaching staff members, such as nurses, secretaries, clerks, custodians, cafeteria workers, and so on. The lead-manager principal makes clear to these individuals that they are important contributors to the school's overall effort. To relieve the classroom teacher of as many nonteaching responsibilities as possible, the principal will make sure that those responsibilities are assumed by the appropriate people. The lead-manager principal involves each staff member in clearly defining his or her responsibilities, gives each one the same degree of freedom in fulfilling those responsibilities as the classroom teacher has in promoting quality learning, and forms with each one an evaluation relationship similar to the principal-teacher relationship described previously.

In many schools, teachers are expected to perform a variety of nonteaching tasks, which detract from their primary function. In such schools it often appears that the classroom teacher exists in part to support the nonteaching positions in the school. Why else would teachers collect lunch money or take lunch counts? Why else are teachers burdened with completing administrative reports? Why else would teachers be expected to straighten up classrooms before they can be cleaned?

In the school for quality learning, every staff member— certified or noncertified, teaching or nonteaching—is a potential learning resource person for one or more students. This sharing of responsibility is central to the development of a community of learners, and it provides further opportunity for staff members to gain stature and to meet their own basic psychological needs. Too often, in attempting to link learners with appropriate resource people, teachers overlook the hobbies, talents, and special attributes of some staff members. Perhaps the office secretary is the most knowledgeable computer specialist in the school; the custodian may have the skill to assist a learner in constructing a model to demonstrate a learning outcome; the counselor may be able to help design a questionnaire or organize social data; and so on. In addition to talents and interests directly related to job responsibilities, staff members have lives beyond the school. Their personal interests and special abilities can, if tapped, contribute much to the total school learning environment.

SPECIAL EDUCATION STRUCTURE

Job titles, labels, and formal and informal role definitions determine the ways in which workers behave within the school. In the school for quality learning there should be no need to label learners with terms such as *learning disabled, gifted,* or *behaviorally-emotionally disordered.* Likewise, there should be no need to label teachers as "the L.D. teacher," "the gifted teacher," or "the B.D. teacher."

The title of a special education teacher often carries a set of expectations. For example, the "L.D. teacher" usually works in a separate room; learners must leave their regular classrooms to receive services from this teacher, and only the "learning disabled," identified by the special education staff through a rigorous process, may benefit from this teacher's expertise. These circumstances lead to exclusion. The special education teacher is excluded from the learner's classroom teacher, the learner's classroom, and the other learners. The learner is excluded from the classroom teacher, classroom activities, and peers. The real tragedy of exclusion is the effect on the individual learner; it is not unlike the acknowledged effect of school segregation on whole segments of our population. As Chief Justice Earl Warren noted in *Brown v. Board of Education* (1954),

> Separateness in education can generate a feeling of inferiority as to children's status in the community that may affect their hearts and minds in a way unlikely ever to be undone. This sense of inferiority . . . affects the motivation of a child to learn . . . and has a tendency to retard . . . educational and mental development. (p. 493)

Promoting collaboration between classroom teachers and special education teachers is a challenge for the lead-manager principal of the school for quality learning. Historically, there has been a monumental lack of cooperation between those two groups, with special educators working in isolation from the rest of the school, often in a separate facility, and their students separated from the mainstream school culture. The prevailing attitude of classroom teachers was that they had no responsibility for special education students once they had identified those students as having special needs; students with academic or behavioral needs that deviated from the average could be better served by a specialist who enjoyed a learner-to-teacher ratio far more favorable than that of the regular classroom. Special educators supported this same system with their prevailing attitude that learners with special needs could not survive in classrooms where they received inadequate teacher attention. These attitudes were most marked with regard to students with physical or sensory disabilities.

With the passage of Public Law 94–142 and the resultant attempts to mainstream the special needs student into school culture, these prevailing attitudes often solidified into distrust and belligerence. Many classroom teachers essentially told the special education teachers, "Take this kid and fix him, and don't ask me to take him back until he can function properly. I cannot spend the necessary time with this student when I have 25 other kids to teach. You work with him individually or in a small group. That is too different from what he experiences in the classroom." The special educator often took the position with the classroom teacher, "This kid could easily be successful in the classroom if you would adapt the materials to her level and adjust your expectations to support and challenge her appropriately." Too often, the supposed cooperation between the classroom teacher and the special educator was actually an unresolved conflict of opposing philosophies and a general distrust that clearly did little to support the learner. If the cooperative venture did help the learner, it was usually because either the special educator or the classroom teacher acquiesced to the other's judgment "for the good of the student." Though recent years have seen some attempts at collaboration between special education teachers and classroom teachers, these attempts typically have meant fitting learners into the existing coercive system instead of designing a support system that would enhance the learners' ability to get their needs met.

In the school for quality learning, the special education teachers' job titles and responsibilities are redefined. Deming's (1986) Point 9 (break down barriers between staff areas) provides the rationale for this important restructuring. These specialists become support workers who no longer confine their activities to a separate room but rather provide support to other teachers through modeling, consultation, coteaching, collaborative problem solving, and inservice training. They also continue to provide strong support to learners who need it, but not in isolation from the classroom and its learning activities.

Breaking down the barriers between the special education teacher and the classroom teacher creates a collaborative environment in which they may combine resources to help improve the quality of service and thus the quality of learning. This redefinition means that every learner is in a classroom that is sensitive, flexible, and adaptive to his or her unique needs. It means that all learners have the freedom of choice they need to get their individual needs met and that all receive the support and assistance they need for quality learning. It means that no learner is excluded from the expectation of quality learning.

COLLABORATIVE SERVICE TEAMS

School staff members whose responsibilities require special certification, such as counselors, social workers, psychologists, special education teachers, teacher aides, and the like, must be expected to work with classroom teachers according to a *colleague consultation model*. In this approach, characterized by consensus decision making, professionals involved with a single learner are a team whose services are focused on the learner and are coordinated toward a common purpose. Team members support one another so the learner can realize the maximum benefit of their collective efforts to support the learner's venture into quality learning activities.

In most schools, the learners served by such teams are those who frequently or consistently exhibit unacceptable behavior, difficulties with learning activities, or difficulties with both behavior and learning. The lead-manager principal knows that these learners pose the greatest challenge to the fulfillment of the mission of the school for quality learning. For this reason, the principal will become part of the teams that work with these learners. Too often, each of the specialized service providers works with a learner in virtual isolation from the other professionals involved with that learner. The true outcome, if not the goal, of such an approach appears to be to help the learner simply survive in the system, to achieve the minimal success needed to continue. This is not an acceptable outcome in the school for quality learning.

In the school for quality learning, team members collaborate to plan for each learner who is experiencing difficulties in the classroom or in school life. The team (which in Deming's terminology would be a QC circle) raises questions such as these to facilitate the planning process:

1. What is the learner's picture/dream/want for himself or herself? What does the learner want to do?

2. What is the team's picture/dream/want for the learner? What does the team want the learner to be able to do?

3. What is the learner doing?

4. What is the team doing?

5. Is what the learner is doing helping the learner achieve quality?

6. Is what the team is doing helping the learner?

7. What are the learner's strengths?

8. Which of the learner's needs are not currently being met?

9. How can the team support the learner in getting these needs met?

10. What must the team do to make this happen?

11. How will it be done?

12. Who will do what?

13. When and where will it be done?

All certified personnel in the school for quality learning collaborate with classroom teachers in planning, service delivery, and the continual effort to improve learning opportunities for all learners. The diversity of the learners requires educators to challenge their isolated working routines of the past. Professional collaboration breaks the cycle of exclusion, allowing staff members to utilize their expertise in a planned, coordinated way that yields quality results that individual efforts would not produce. Such collaboration may improve the adult-to-student ratio in any given classroom and result in an exchange of professional skills. Collaboration maximizes educators' potential to ensure quality learning for all learners. In addition, it creates a sense of belonging and empowerment. As staff members work together, they are listened to, affirmed, and respected; they have a sense of mutual caring and are supported in their efforts to achieve common goals.

CONCLUSION

The lead-manager principal, pursuing the mission of quality learning for each learner, recognizes that the classroom teacher plays the key role in the accomplishment of that mission. The principal realizes that the school's entire adult element must be organized to support the teacher's efforts to facilitate quality learning for each learner. The principal understands that the way in which this support is organized and delivered can significantly affect the school climate. Staff members who must constitute the support system for the classroom teacher all have needs to be met in the workplace. It is unlikely that they will obtain satisfaction if they see their roles as secondary. The lead-manager principal facilitates working relationships and maintains the focus on the learner. The inclusiveness and the attitude that "we are all in this together" have one purpose: to engage students in quality learning. Every staff member's role is critical to that purpose; if it is not, it should be redefined or eliminated.

CHAPTER 11

Understanding the System: District Responsibilities

According to Pat Dolan (1991), a prominent labor management consultant who spoke at a seminar sponsored by the American Association of School Administrators, a growing number of organizations are recognizing that much of the loss of the competitive edge is traceable to organizational principles and practices that have resulted in loss of quality and productivity. A top-down pyramid model has been applied universally for organizing people in work settings. The roots of this system are deep in our culture. It is the embodiment of the industrial worldview, and education has not escaped its influence. School districts exhibit a top-down pyramid organization; typically, each school in the district mirrors that same organization, and each classroom is similarly structured.

THE TRADITIONAL TOP-DOWN PYRAMID

The traditional organizational, or top-down, pyramid, illustrated in Figure 11.1, puts people in charge at the top and gives them the authority and responsibility to control the human and technical systems below. The structure is operationalized through layers of people down through the organization, with each layer having

Figure 11.1   The Top-Down Pyramid

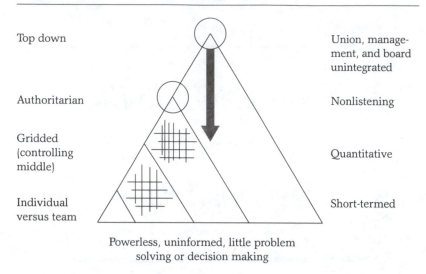

Top down — Union, management, and board unintegrated

Authoritarian — Nonlistening

Gridded (controlling middle) — Quantitative

Individual versus team — Short-termed

Powerless, uninformed, little problem solving or decision making

Note. From *The Pyramid Organization,* by W. P. Dolan and Associates, 1991, Overland Park, KS: Author. Copyright 1991 by W. P. Dolan and Associates. Reprinted by permission.

less authority than the one above. The result is a top-down, authoritarian hierarchy, controlled from above and responded to from below.

The system is further defined and refined by "gridding," the creation of functional departments in the middle of the system. The grids, or departments, represent specialties—business or finance, curriculum, staff personnel, pupil personnel, maintenance, special education, technology, special programs, and so on —that perform specific tasks within the system. The departments develop relatively well-defined boundaries, and each is encouraged to maintain tight control over its piece of the system.

The structure tends to be "nonlistening" because it is assumed that the intelligence and talent to achieve goals, to structure and guide work, and to solve problems increases as one moves up the pyramid. In addition, the system tends to be characterized by poor communication in all directions. Information from the top consists primarily of commands and demands. The amount of downward-flowing information decreases as one moves toward the bottom because of the need-to-know principle and the tendency to withhold critical data for fear that employees will misuse it. Information does not move up the system well because information from below tends not to be valued and the layers and grids have a filtering, protective effect. The same "filter" also inhibits the movement of information across the grids and across the lines at lower levels in the system.

Within this traditional structure, management tends to have a short-term, crisis-oriented time frame in which efforts are monitored and judged on the basis of immediate results. Daily, weekly, monthly, quarterly, even annual reports—regardless of medium to long-range direction—become the driving force. In this system, rewards and punishments are fairly narrowly defined. They include so-called positive motivators, in the form of money and benefits, and so-called negative motivators, in the form of lack of advancement or even loss of job. There are rarely any conventions for recognizing employee contributions that relate directly to job responsibility.

Very often, superimposed on this pyramid is a labor/management model of confrontation, distrust, and poor communication. To a slightly lesser degree, these same behaviors or attitudes of confrontation, distrust, and poor communication are exhibited toward everyone outside of the pyramid, especially the community and the parental clientele.

The pyramid structure has proven to have several debilitating characteristics. First, in the classic top-down hierarchy, people at the top have great difficulty hearing and learning from the people below. Second, because of the control and punishment mechanisms and the heavy reliance on quantitative information as the only basis for success, top managers are not able to get good quality and broad data from below. Often this structure and its value system not only fail to encourage but actually discourage team integration across the grids. This lack of integration, combined with the power/control focus at the top, means that those in the middle of the system share little information and invest considerable energy in protecting turf. The middle monitors and hoards information moving down the system, thus creating an information deficit at the lower levels. The middle also filters the information moving up the system and transmits upward only that information which conforms to the principles of obedience and success. The structure is unwelcoming and often adversarial to those outside it. It shares information selectively with outside audiences. Thus, a school does not typically fully inform parents or community about its processes, procedures, or goals.

Workers in such a system, be they teachers in the school or learners in the classroom, expend only enough energy to perform their specific functions and, at first sight, do not appear to care deeply about either productivity or the quality of the product. However, according to Dolan (1991), it is important to distinguish between not caring and not appearing to care. He maintains that the traditional structure gives workers little opportunity to demonstrate their skill, experience, or concern; as a result, they appear not to care. However, most organizations that have altered the pyramid to involve the workers more deeply in the determination of the work and the work setting have found that the workers do, in fact, care a great deal.

The school system, the school, or the classroom will not take kindly to being characterized as a pyramid. Every system, school, and classroom would prefer to believe that its structure is more responsive to and more accepting of its workers. But boss management is the pyramid organization operationalized, and change is difficult. However ineffective the pyramid organization may be, it has vast powers to preserve itself. The lead-manager principal understands this fact and uses it in facilitating the changes required for the school to become a school for quality learning. The school, however, is not an island. Nearly all schools are part of a larger organization—the school district. What happens (or does not happen) in the district affects the school. The lead-manager principal of the school for quality learning, understanding this, seeks and accepts district responsibilities with two basic purposes in mind:

1. To use every opportunity to persuade others in the district to accept the mission of quality learning for each learner

2. To help prevent the district from developing policies and procedures or issuing demands that, when implemented as required, would hamper the development of the school for quality learning

The lead-manager principal becomes involved in district activities at every possible opportunity because nearly every school district is organized on the top-down pyramid model, with district level administrators of the boss-manager type. The principal understands that the classic boss-manager behavior is to withhold or manipulate information in order to maintain control. The principal needs a thorough understanding of the district to advocate effectively for the staff and program of the school for quality learning.

The lead-manager principal seeks out information—even hidden information—and shares it with the school staff. Principal and staff cooperate to ensure adequate representation of their school in any district endeavor—be it a textbook adoption committee, a curriculum committee, a committee to develop districtwide discipline standards, a committee to specify learning outcomes, an ad hoc committee of the governing board to study long-range plans for the district, and so on. Representation is crucial if the school is to accomplish the two purposes for district involvement. Early involvement is especially crucial to the second purpose identified—to have significant input into policies and procedures. The principal and staff should view each interaction with the district as an opportunity to build relationships with others in the district while negotiating to achieve the goals of the school for quality learning.

Roger Fisher and Scott Brown (1988), in *Getting Together: Building Relationships as We Negotiate*, say that successful negotiation depends on building a relationship that can deal well with differences. In developing the school for quality learning, the lead-manager principal must foster relationships that deal well with differences. Fisher and Brown outline the elements that contribute to this.

Balancing reason and emotion helps. "We need both reason informed by emotion and emotion guided and tempered by reason. This balance between logic and emotion is a practical definition of working rationality" (p. 9).

Understanding helps. "If we are going to achieve an outcome that will satisfy the interests of both . . . and leave each of us feeling fairly treated, we will need to understand each other's interests, perceptions, and notions of fairness . . . the better we understand each other, the better our chance of creating a solution we can both accept" (p. 10).

Good communication helps. "The more effectively we communicate about our differences, the better we will understand each other's concerns and the better our chances for reaching a mutually acceptable agreement. . . . And the more we believe the other side has heard and understood our views, and we theirs, the more likely we will feel that an agreement is fair and balanced" (p. 10).

Being reliable helps. "Well-founded trust, based on honest and reliable conduct over a period of time, can greatly enhance our ability to cope with conflict. The more honest and reliable we are with respect to each other, the better our chance of producing good outcomes" (p. 11).

Persuasion is more helpful than coercion. "At one extreme, I can try to inspire your voluntary cooperation through education, logical argument, moral persuasion, and my own example. At the other extreme, I can try to coerce you by worsening your alternatives and by warnings, threats, extortion, and physical force. The more coercive the means of influence, the less likely it is that the outcome will reflect both of our concerns, and the less legitimate it is likely to be in the eyes of at least one of us. The less coercive the modes of influence, the better our ability to work with each other" (p. 11).

Mutual acceptance helps. "Feeling accepted, worthy, and valued is a basic human psychological need. Unless you listen to my view, accept my right to have views that differ from yours, and take my interests into account, I am unlikely to want to deal with you. And if we do not deal with each other, we will not even begin to resolve our differences" (p. 12).

The lead-manager principal avoids taking a confrontational approach, choosing rather to educate others to develop an understanding of what constitutes quality learning. Consistently advocating for teachers and learners, the principal influences district policy and practice by frequently asking, "Will what is being proposed improve teachers' abilities and opportunities to provide quality learning experiences for all learners?" and "Is what is being proposed good for all learners?"

On the other hand, especially early in the development of the school for quality learning, it is important not to alienate the district level administration or the other district schools by being too zealous in pursuit of the first purpose—to win others to the cause of quality learning. The lead-manager principal recognizes that change in any part of the pyramid threatens stability in every other part. Change can be threatening, even to those who see a need for change: They may fear that they will have a certain change imposed on them rather than having the opportunity to design their own destiny. If one understands the pyramid structure, one knows that this fear is not unfounded. The lead-manager principal fully understands the need for effective working relationships, has the skills to disentangle relationship issues from the substantive issues of the school for quality learning, and is consistently and unconditionally constructive in thoughts and actions.

needs, in the coordination of pr
evaluation of staff.

Goal and task orientation.
task oriented—in other words, a
approaches to program developm

Good organization. Effecti
organized, create workable yet
in the school, and demonstrate s
others. These principals achieve
leadership and maximum autono

High expectations for staff
pals set and communicate high
and themselves. The principals n
their schools' mission and emph
They seek and promote greater i
bers of the school community.

Well-defined policies and
have effective in-house commun
fined and written down. Each el
knows what is to be achieved a
ties are.

Classroom involvement. Ef
and observe classrooms. These
variety and with a preconceived
or instructional assessment, allo
needs and understand what assi
ers. The principals use classroom
act with learners, especially in th

High visibility and availa
Effective principals interact ofter
schools and assume leadership i
and in helping individual learners
responsive to learner and staff in

Strong support for the tea
support teachers' classroom effort
tions to the learning process. The
porting teachers and in providing

principals also promote staff devel-
of their schools' mission.

...unity relations.** Effective princi-
ons skills in communicating with
ers. They possess high verbal flu-
munication style and substance to
n the audience, and avoid educa-
s tend to be informal in personal
riety of communication vehicles,
tings, open houses, phone discus-
policy prevails in their schools.

for quality learning must exhibit
management to an extraordinary
chool's mission depends in great
lities in these dimensions. For the
also an added set of expectations.
es of the lead-manager principal
ose of any effective principal, the
nisms, and interactions for meet-
y different. These differences re-
ement of specific attitudes and
s and behaviors are very different
a principal; some differ only in
ree is crucial. The following are
to the lead-manager principal.

The lead-manager principal must
derstanding of the psychological
knows and uses reality therapy
it applies to education.

...anager principal, like everyone,
al's position is one of recognized
al perceives power as the free-
hat to do rather than perceiving
tell others what to do. The prin-
n and challenge in urging others

principal listens equally care-
analyzes the messages received,
senders and the messages, and

communicates in a manner that conveys an understanding of each message. If the message is a call for action, the principal either acts and makes certain that the sender knows of the action or lets the message sender know why no action was taken. Such communication must be timely. This behavior contrasts with that of the typical boss manager, who tends not to listen and not to acknowledge communication from lower echelons of the organization.

Questioning. The lead-manager principal has highly developed and diverse questioning skills. Questioning is essential in assisting others in the self-evaluation/planning process discussed in the context of reality therapy. Highly developed questioning skills allow the principal to influence behavior without dictating behavior.

Consistency. The lead-manager principal's observable personal behavior is the primary mode for communicating high expectations and demonstrating desirable behavior to others in the school community. The principal is constantly aware of and concerned with the congruency and compatibility of his or her verbal messages and overt actions.

Mediation. The lead-manager principal knows that, in a people-dominated organization like a school, conflict is inevitable. Because the principal is called upon to mediate disputes between staff members, between learners, between staff and learners, and between parents and staff, he or she must understand conflict and be well-versed in conflict resolution strategies. The lead-manager principal views conflict as a positive opportunity for the conflicting parties to grow.

Avoidance of adversarial confrontation. The lead-manager principal avoids confrontation because the adversarial stance diminishes cooperation and has a detrimental effect on the achievement of the school's mission. Glasser (1990) maintains that lead managers try to keep rules to a minimum because they know that, whenever they are put in the position of enforcing rules, they become the adversaries of the rule breakers. The lead-manager principal will be a rule reducer rather than a rule generator.

People orientation. The lead-manager principal is goal and task oriented, and focused on the fulfillment of the school's mission. At the same time, the principal strives not to allow this strong focus to diminish his or her accessibility to any member of the school community. The lead-manager principal understands that the development of a personal, caring relationship with each individual is necessary to the development of a school for quality learning. There is no professional role higher than that of friend.

Support. The lead-manager principal, in the knowledge that each member of the school community is doing the best that he or she knows how to do, accepts the performance and supports the performer. The principal uses nonconfrontational questioning to challenge the individual to choose and develop behaviors that are of higher quality. When a behavior is clearly unacceptable, the principal skillfully distinguishes the behavior from the person by demonstrating acceptance of the person while asking him or her to reject the unacceptable behavior.

Involvement as resource person and linkage agent. The lead-manager principal knows individual staff members' problems and concerns as well as the distribution of strengths among the staff. The principal is also knowledgeable about potential staff development resources, both within and outside the school district. In providing and promoting staff development activities, the principal can serve as a resource person in the growth endeavors of a staff member if he or she has the appropriate knowledge and skills and if the staff member has a comfortable trust relationship with the principal. In other instances, the principal can best facilitate staff development by linking staff members with other resource people or places. The principal understands that even when he or she possesses the knowledge to be an effective resource, it is important to consider the comfort level that exists in the relationship. For example, a teacher may genuinely desire to improve the classroom mathematics program, and the principal may be a mathematics expert. However, the teacher may not be willing to reveal what he or she perceives as a professional weakness to a supervisor. Another teacher might be a more effective resource person because that teacher is perceived as less of a threat. In brief, the fit of personalities between the helper and the person to be helped is an important consideration in staff development.

Risk taking. The lead-manager principal, in collaboration with the staff, will continually evaluate and strive to improve the school program. Change is an expected feature of the effort to make the school a place of quality learning for each learner. The principal encourages innovation and experimentation in keeping with the school philosophy, as well as with district policy and the laws of school governance. When a seemingly reasonable solution to a problem or a promising idea for addressing a concern surfaces, the lead-manager principal does not seek permission for the school to develop and implement an action plan; rather, he or she sanctions the plan and promotes its development and implementation. The principal realizes that the district power structure will likely be resistant to change and discourage the development of a new idea if its permission is sought. If the idea or plan is clearly contrary to current policy or law but the school community sees it as desirable, the principal will lead an effort to change the policy or law. Deming (1986) charges management with the responsibility to change the system.

Vision. The lead-manager principal maintains an unobstructed view of the school's mission, is thoroughly knowledgeable about changes currently under way, and is aware of further changes required to realize the mission. The principal is a problem finder and a problem solver with a thorough understanding of the school as a social system. A keen sense of timing tells him or her when to urge forward movement and when to allow current efforts to come to fruition.

As we noted earlier, it is not impossible for a boss-manager principal to succeed in developing many of the essential characteristics of an effective school. That school will then likely be judged effective because it has improved on its own previous record or because it surpasses other schools. Still, it is possible that a high percentage of that school's learners are not engaged in quality learning. Quality work and quality learning are different notions; one can produce a quality product (work) by repeatedly doing the same activity well, whereas quality learning requires one to engage in growth activities and to aspire to do all things well—new and old alike. Moreover, the expectation for the school for quality learning is not merely that the student body as a whole will perform at a higher level but rather that each learner will participate in quality learning.

Only a lead-manager principal can lead a school to become a school for quality learning for each student. The structures and measures outlined here in Part 2 represent an extraordinary departure from traditional school organization and an extraordinary change in the principal's responsibilities and performance modes. If the school is to become a school for quality learning, all remnants of hierarchical structure and authoritarianism must be removed. Trust must underlie the operations. The employee time cards or sign-in, sign-out sheets must disappear, to be superseded by the concept of the professional day. Each employee's responsibilities are crucial to the organization's effort to provide quality learning for each learner. All employees are expected—and trusted —to meet the highest standards of which they are capable. They are not merely doing "the best they can do"; they are making what they understand to be their specific contributions to the entire mission. Facilitating and orchestrating this endeavor is an awesome task for the lead-manager principal; it would be an impossible task for a boss manager.

PART THREE

Managing the Classroom for Quality Learning

CHAPTER 13

Overview: The Classroom for Quality Learning

In Part 2, the emphasis was on managing the school for quality learning, and the focus was on the school principal as the non-coercive lead manager; in that context, the teacher was the worker. In Part 3 we will emphasize the classroom and focus on the teacher as the noncoercive lead manager of the learning environment; in that environment, the student learner is the worker.

The management of the classroom for quality learning is the primary dimension of the school for quality learning. A school will not be a school for quality learning until each learner participates fully in the goal of quality learning; that goal cannot be achieved until each classroom is a classroom for quality learning. The expectation of full participation by each learner radically changes the mission of the school and, consequently, the responsibilities of the teacher as manager of the learning environment.

Western culture either is in the midst of or has already made a paradigm shift away from an industrial worldview toward an information- and knowledge-based worldview. The industrial worldview stresses repetitive thinking and labor: Individual needs are subordinate to production requirements, and personal contribution is subordinate to structured order. Under this view, the self is relatively simple and is largely shaped by social influences; education emphasizes the collective and the willingness to follow the guidelines of peers and traditional authorities. This is the view according to which nearly every school is organized. Mission statements or school district goals might suggest otherwise, but an examination of the actual operation of schools and classrooms will reveal that they reflect the industrial worldview. Most of the tactics and strategies of the education profession are based on a view of the learner as ward—the (it is hoped) properly grateful recipient of curricular downloads. The education of each learner is controlled by parents and community. Community is represented by the school board that establishes policy, along with state and federal mandates, to be implemented by the professional staff. Parents exercise their choices by deciding where to reside and by selecting options provided within a school.

In contrast, a knowledge-based worldview stresses rapid change and innovative thinking and work. Satisfaction of individual needs is meshed with socially desirable results, and personal contribution is meshed with societal welfare. In this view, the self is relatively complex and is formed independently from within; education emphasizes the individual and the willingness to collaborate with peers and traditional authorities. The mission of education is no longer to produce the like-minded learners required under the industrial worldview. It becomes, rather, to encourage and support functionally unique individuals. Education is controlled by the learner—the customer of the school. The age of knowledge requires new, appropriate, and timely educational services and customer-oriented school cultures. The system must respond to the needs of its customers.

Many current school reform efforts are still focused on learners in the aggregate. Policymakers consistently urge greater rigor in current practices and greater accountability (through testing) for outcomes. This approach was lent credibility by the National Commission on Excellence in Education (1983) in its report *A Nation at Risk*. However, the important questions about learning and about quality cannot be answered in the aggregate; they can only be addressed by and for the individual. Quality in learning is not about requiring learners to work longer and harder at what they have been asked to do in the past.

The lead-manager teacher in the school for quality learning creates a learning environment that corresponds to the knowledge-based worldview. Following are the features of that environment:

1. It affords diversity, novelty, and openness to stimulate curiosity and exploration.

2. It provides options both within and beyond the classroom and the school, and it most certainly involves new players in the education of the learner as the truth that learning occurs everywhere, not just "in school," is recognized.

3. It is learner-centered, featuring personalized experimental and experiential learning opportunities.

4. It stimulates teamwork, flexibility, and problem solving.

5. It frees and/or teaches learners to think creatively, critically, and evaluatively.

6. It increases accountability for everyone and engages all in decision making.

7. It promotes cooperation, social conscience, and group interaction.

8. It encourages risk taking and stresses the use of skills necessary to adapt to and to bring about change.

In this environment, the focus is more on outcomes than on inputs. Outcomes are significant and relevant both to the learner and to society. Outcomes are viewed in terms of skills and abilities in which learners are required to demonstrate quality achievement. Following are some examples:

1. Ability to communicate effectively with all members of a multicultural, diverse society

2. Facility in social interaction

3. Self-esteem

4. Analytical capabilities

5. Problem-solving skills

6. Intellectual open-mindedness

7. Skill in making value judgments and decisions

8. Skill in creative expression and in responding to the creative work of others

9. Civic responsibility

10. Acceptance of, appreciation of, and respect for others in a multicultural world

11. Responsible participation in a global environment

12. Skill in developing and maintaining wellness

13. Skill in using technology as a tool for learning

14. Skill in life and career planning

15. Ability to function effectively in ambiguous and uncertain conditions

16. Ability to resolve conflicts through negotiation and mediation

These or similar outcomes ensure that learners (a) become self-directed in the pursuit of learning; (b) apply problem-finding, problem-solving, and decision-making skills; (c) master communication and group interaction skills; (d) express themselves creatively, proactively, and responsibly; (e) use the skills necessary to adapt to and/or to bring about change; (f) enhance and sustain their self-esteem; and (g) demonstrate concern, tolerance, and respect for others.

The outcomes of quality learning are significant and broad. It follows that one would be foolish to assume that any single curriculum, program, or strategy should be required. That would run counter to the view of the learner as the customer of the school. Variety and learner involvement are hallmarks of the school for quality learning. The lead-manager teacher will create an individualized learning environment that empowers each learner and provides each the opportunity to develop the following talents:

1. Responsibility: The facility to exercise personal freedoms without infringing upon the freedoms of others

2. Self-direction: The ability to choose personal goals and to design strategies for attaining those goals

3. Decision making: The skills and thinking abilities to choose among alternatives by examining the probable consequences and implications of various choices

4. Self-awareness: The acceptance of one's own humanity and the development of an appreciation for the humanity of others

5. Critical thinking: The use of convergent, divergent, and evaluative thinking skills to define and solve problems

6. Knowledge utilization: The ability to collect, process, and utilize data to make sound generalizations

7. Learning style: The ability to find one's most effective learning mode and to develop the skills to enhance that mode

8. Self-evaluative skill: The ability to learn to use information
about one's own behavior and the behavior of others
in order to design new behaviors

This notion of talent development is fundamental to the
school for quality learning. Each learner is capable of developing
all of the talents just listed. Moreover, each one has unique talents
and is capable of further developing that uniqueness.

The lead-manager teacher has two major responsibilities,
which are sometimes distinct but are more often closely intertwined. The teacher both creates the environment and facilitates
learning within that environment. Thus, the teacher operates
both on the environment and within the environment. He or she
must understand the nature of learning and the impact of the
environment on learning.

Rogers (1969) characterizes the learning process in a way that
is highly relevant to the school for quality learning:

1. Human beings have a natural potentiality for
learning. . . .

2. Significant learning takes place when the subject
matter is perceived by the learner as having relevance
for the learner's own purposes. . . .

3. Learning which involves a change in self-organization —
in the perception of oneself — is threatening and tends to
be resisted. . . .

4. Those learnings which are threatening to the self are
more easily perceived and assimilated when external
threats are at a minimum. . . .

5. When threat to the self is low, experience can be
perceived in differentiated fashion and learning can
proceed. . . .

6. Much significant learning is acquired through doing. . . .

7. Learning is facilitated when the learner participates
responsibly in the learning process. . . .

8. Self-initiated learning which involves the whole person
of the learner—feelings as well as intellect—is the most
lasting and pervasive. . . .

9. Independence, creativity, and self-reliance are all facilitated when self-criticism and self-evaluation are basic and evaluation by others is of secondary importance. . . .

10. The most socially useful learning in the modern world is the learning of the process of learning, a continuing openness to experience and incorporation into oneself of the process of change. . . . (pp. 157–163)

These notions about learning will guide the lead-manager teacher in developing the learning environment. Following is a description of that environment:

1. The learning environment is designed to provide all individuals with opportunities to meet their needs. The lead-manager teacher proactively constructs, modifies, redesigns, and redefines the environment toward this end.

2. The learning environment is fluid and flexible in design so that the learner and/or the teacher may adjust it to fit the learner, rather than expecting that the learner's behavior and needs must be modified to fit the environment and/or the teacher.

3. The learning environment provides activities that allow both the learner and the teacher to learn about themselves —to assess their strengths and weaknesses, their goals and aspirations, their beliefs and values, their successes and failures, and their thoughts and feelings. Further, it gives them opportunities to share what they know about themselves. Learning about oneself and others is valued highly.

4. The learning environment is designed to foster, encourage, demand, and utilize cooperation.

5. The learning environment is psychologically safe for the learner and the teacher. Both must feel free to take risks, explore, inquire, create, discover, think, value, share, receive, give, succeed, and fail.

6. The learning environment is open-ended. Questioning is valued perhaps more than answering. Each learner is seen as capable of uncovering his or her own answers. Knowledge is viewed as dynamic, not static.

7. Though the physical and material resources may be modest, the learning environment is rich in human resources. The learning environment is the sum of the human interactions within—no more, no less. Activities are designed to make maximum use of all those human resources.

The environmental design of the classroom is of utmost importance because the environment either will afford the teacher the freedom, flexibility, and tools to facilitate each learner's efforts toward quality or will stifle and frustrate the efforts to individualize learning opportunities. Still, even a dynamic and near-ideal environment will not result in quality learning if the teacher does not understand the psychological framework of learning and assume proactively the responsibility to facilitate learning.

In the school for quality learning, the relationship between the teacher and the learner is crucial. In making operational the notion of learner as customer, the challenge is to ensure that all learners become fully engaged in learning activities that are relevant and challenging to them. To facilitate learning skillfully, the lead-manager teacher must know each learner intimately, and each learner must know and trust the teacher. Such knowledge and trust develop only with time. A school for quality learning will seek ways to optimize the development of the knowledge and trust relationship between learners and teachers. To do so, the school must address at least two issues in its organizational design:

1. The initial matching of learners and teachers should ensure an acceptable match. Personality types and learning or teaching styles should be considered in the assignment of learners to teachers. Allowing learners and/or parents to exercise choice, as suggested in chapter 9, is one way to increase the likelihood of good initial matches.

2. Once a favorable match is achieved, it should be nurtured over time. The knowledge/trust relationship, even in initially good matches, takes time to materialize. For the relationship to yield the best results in terms of quality learning, it should last as long as feasible. At present, however, the organization of most schools imposes considerable time constraints: Either (a) the learner spends short periods each day with different teachers (secondary school organizational scheme) or (b) the learner is in a self-contained classroom and has a new teacher each year (elementary school organizational scheme).

Different organizational strategies create better conditions for the teacher-learner relationship to flourish. Interdisciplinary teams of learners and teachers who work together for long periods each school day extend their opportunity to become well acquainted and attuned to one another's needs. Multiage groupings that let teachers and learners stay together for more than a single year likewise strengthen their relationships.

The mission of the teacher in the school for quality learning is to facilitate the full participation of each learner in quality learning. There is no more important role in the school. The lead-manager teacher demonstrates that he or she has the ultimate responsibility for quality learning but has no authority to dictate to the learner either what to learn or how to learn. The teacher develops with each learner a relationship of mutual trust that is open, warm, caring, pleasant, and accepting. A crucial responsibility of the lead-manager teacher is to communicate high expectations to each learner and to support and challenge each one in a way that engages him or her in quality learning.

In the school for quality learning, many of the teacher's responsibilities in the classroom parallel the responsibilities of the lead-manager principal. Just as the principal involves the teacher in decision making (as recommended in chapter 5), so must the teacher involve the learner in decision making. Just as the principal involves the teacher in self-evaluation (as recommended in chapter 6), so must the teacher involve the learner in self-evaluation. The remainder of Part 3 examines the required transformations in which the lead-manager teacher plays the key role.

CHAPTER 14

Quality Curriculum

Glasser (1990) observes that curriculum is largely standard and compulsory during the first 10 years of education. Educators appear to know what students must learn but also seem dissatisfied with students' mastery of that curriculum. Glasser asserts that there is actually little wrong with the curriculum:

> What is wrong is our inability to persuade more than
> a small percentage of students to learn it well. . . .
> If we pressure students to learn what they do not
> want to learn, and then punish them with low grades
> when they do not learn it, they counter by taking school-
> work out of their quality worlds, and we lose them as
> learners. (pp. 118, 119)

Curriculum—meaning what is to be learned and how it will be learned—must receive serious scrutiny in the development of the school for quality learning. It is, of course, central to the schooling process, and many including Glasser maintain that the present schooling process is not producing the quality we should expect. Actually, there is something wrong with the curriculum— namely, that the decisions about what should be learned have been made by people far removed from the learner.

School restructuring during the past few decades has centered almost entirely on climate and institutional features. As is apparent from Part 2 (especially chapter 11), we do not dispute the need to address these very important matters. Still, it seems that however radical restructuring may be, it rarely touches on the curriculum itself. In that sense, much of what passes for restructuring amounts merely to new bottles for old wine that clearly has not improved with age. Efforts to "fix" the schools have largely focused on issues such as increased teacher accountability, more high-stakes standardized tests, higher academic standards (usually meaning more and stricter graduation requirements), more rigorous expectations for existing curricula, and more and better teacher training. Most recently, the emphasis in "fixing" has shifted somewhat to school restructuring, site-based management, and parental choice of schools. There has been little discussion about how students learn; instead, the restructuring discussion has assumed a failure of student effort and sustained the view that schools will succeed if only learners will work harder, or longer, or both to learn what is expected. Can we truly claim to speak of school reform without addressing the centerpiece of the school, the curriculum?

For more than a century, schools in this country have operated on the principle that students learn by mastering the component parts of complex material before grasping the whole. In the traditional system, a carefully sequenced curriculum spanning the years from kindergarten to graduation is determined largely by experts outside of the schools (perhaps self-proclaimed experts, perhaps experts designated by the community of educators). From that curriculum, teachers and textbooks transmit information to students, who spend most of their time as docile recipients. Students study structured textbooks containing drills and exercises that reinforce skills and knowledge that they often see as irrelevant to the world outside the classroom. Emphasis is on memorization of facts rather than on problem solving and creative thinking. Students are tested, drilled, and retested regularly to ensure that they have learned the facts and absorbed the information.

The prevailing theory is that learning is hard work and that students must be persuaded to undertake it and stick with it. A system of external rewards and punishments, largely in the form of grades and credits, provides the incentive to achieve. Learning is considered primarily an individual activity, and students are discouraged from collaborating with one another; indeed, working together is frequently viewed as cheating. According to this view (which corresponds to McGregor's, 1961, theory X view of human nature), students naturally dislike hard work and would rather be playing than learning. Thus, the teacher's main challenge is to maintain order and control the students so that teaching and learning can take place.

Postman and Weingartner (1969) argue that the only learning that actually occurs in classrooms is that which is directly communicated by the classroom structure and the operating practices within it. They observe that the following list, although not the stated intended outcomes, partially characterizes what can be learned in our schools:

> Passive acceptance is a more desirable response to ideas than active criticism.
>
> Discovering knowledge is beyond the power of students, and is in any case none of their business.
>
> Recall is the highest form of intellectual achievement, and the collection of unrelated "facts" is the goal of education.
>
> The voice of authority is to be trusted and valued more than independent judgment.
>
> One's own ideas and those of one's classmates are inconsequential.
>
> Feelings are irrelevant in education.
>
> There is always a single, unambiguous Right Answer to a question.
>
> English is not History and History is not Science and Science is not Art and Art is not Music, and Art and Music are minor subjects and English, History and Science are major subjects, and a subject is something you "take" and, when you have taken it, you have "had" it, and if you have "had" it, you are immune and need not take it again (The Vaccination Theory of Education?). (pp. 20–21)

In its 1988 report entitled *Rethinking Curriculum: A Call for Fundamental Reform,* the Curriculum Study Group of the National Association of State Boards of Education (NASBE) concluded that

> there is a fatal flaw in the American education system: our use of outmoded curriculum and instruction that not only fail to prepare students for success in our rapidly changing society, but also alienate large numbers of students, contributing to unacceptably high dropout rates that threaten our national unity. . . . The NASBE Curriculum Study Group concludes that fundamental changes are required if we are to have schools that actively engage students in learning and that provide them with a solid foundation for further education and employment. (p. 3)

The fact is that the segregated and segmented subject matter curriculum has been prevalent for a long time and is deeply entrenched in our school systems. It has virtually paralyzed the educational establishment's capacity to imagine something different. An almost intransigent force comprising a network of educational elites—scholars, federal and state departments of education, certification bureaus, and text and test publishers—makes serious curriculum reform seem almost impossible. According to Beane (1991), there is barely a language left to describe other possibilities for the curriculum.

Curriculum reform is not a call to eliminate the basic school subjects; they represent modes of understanding that have proven enormously useful. However, many of the most urgent and interesting curriculum topics, and many of the outcomes we most value, do not fit into a single subject area. Integration of curriculum appears to be a logical and promising direction that could result in school learning more in tune with desired outcomes (such as those detailed in chapter 13) and more relevant to learners' needs. Such reform in turn would facilitate the development of the school for quality learning. The whole-language approach, which has made strong inroads at the elementary level and has in a few instances been used successfully at the secondary level, holds real promise for an integrative curriculum.

Whole language is an entire philosophy about teaching, learning, and the role of language in the classroom. Its adherents stress that language should be kept whole and uncontrived and that children should use language in ways that relate to their own lives and cultures. In a whole-language classroom, the final product—the "answer"—is not as important as the process of learning to define and solve problems. The whole-language classroom is child centered: Students enjoy learning because they find the material meaningful and relevant to their lives. The teacher is not an authoritarian figure but a resource, coach, and colearner who shares power with the students and allows them to make choices. Learning in such a classroom is a social act, and children learn from and help one another. The challenge to the teacher is to adapt the curriculum and activities to the interests and talents of the learners, to provide a material- and resource-rich environment, and to ensure that all students are continually engaged in learning.

Middle-level and middle-school educators have for the past several years been trumpeting a reform that features interdisciplinary teams, advisory programs, block scheduling, and core curriculum. However, a close examination of the practices at many middle-level schools will reveal that even these recent promising changes are based on, or at least designed to accommodate, the old curriculum. Recent calls by national subject-area associations for integration may eventually lead to the demise of the hard subject boundaries that characterize the middle and high school curriculum and organization. The curriculum at all educational levels must be truly integrated if the rhetoric of our concern for the young, the rhetoric about our knowledge of the learning process, and the rhetoric about the desired outcomes of our schooling are to become a reality. This integration will be a long and arduous task, which, however, is essential to the mission of the school for quality learning: to have all learners fully engaged in quality learning.

Professional journals of the late 1980s and early 1990s are replete with examples of whole-language programs and other integrative curriculum efforts. The educator should consult *Teacher Magazine, Instructor Magazine,* the *Phi Delta Kappan,* publications of various subject area associations, publications of various professional organizations, and so on. *Educational Leadership,* the journal of the Association for Supervision and Curriculum Development, features integrated curriculum in its October 1991 issue.

Integration requires that curriculum design focus on the way students learn rather than on the information to be transmitted. Our present educational structure creates barriers to integration that are, for many, nearly insurmountable. One very significant barrier is personal: Teachers, especially at the secondary level, have become so identified with their subject areas by virtue of their training, the culture of the departmentalized school, and their personal learning preferences that they may have difficulty relating their subjects to other subjects, though they may see the advantage of doing so. Elementary teachers often face a different barrier: Their training may not give them sufficient background in the various disciplines to know how to integrate them effectively. Teachers need to surmount these barriers so they can answer the learner's call for relevancy: Why should I learn this? How does this fit with my life? This makes no sense—how does it relate to anything else? Teachers cannot help learners see the connections between school subjects unless those connections naturally exist in the school environment. If we persist in favoring subject isolation, then we accept the argument that it actually helps the learner to have no deliberate connections between the disciplines. This notion sounds absurd, but current practice seems to endorse it.

Integration has a further important potential. Although knowledge continues to expand, the school day, term, and total experience remain rather constant in length, a condition that is not likely to change substantially. The time available in the school day is already overloaded with information now required to be taught, allowing no room for new knowledge. Further, much of the newest and most current knowledge falls between the cracks of the conventional subject areas and thus does not find a place in the school curriculum. Integration can address this issue in two ways: by increasing efficiency in the use of time and by providing a vehicle to introduce truly interdisciplinary concepts and ideas.

The development of an integrated curriculum requires that conventional curriculum design be discarded. With an integrated curriculum, the organizing principle is most often a theme, which could be a concept, an outcome, a skill, a learner behavior, and so on. The curriculum focus might be literacy, numeracy, collaborative learning, or storytelling; it might be a research skill or a thinking skill. The possibilities are many and varied.

Development of an integrated curriculum is likely to proceed through at least three stages.

Multidisciplinary (more than one) approach. Two or more subject areas incorporate a theme as the focus of their separate efforts with learners. The actual interactions between the content areas are indirect; the learner links them by studying the theme simultaneously in the various subject areas.

Interdisciplinary (mutually or together) approach. Teaching in two or more subject areas focuses on the theme by highlighting the overlapping content of the subjects through shared strategies. Distinctions between subject areas are downplayed; the learner is not concerned with classifying the learning into the subject areas involved.

Transdisciplinary (beyond or above) approach. The content and the theme are identical, and any attempt to introduce a division into subject areas is seen as artificial and counterproductive. This approach requires a true cooperative effort among the teachers in the individual disciplines.

According to Fogarty (1991b), there are 10 views of curriculum integration. Six of those views seem to depart significantly from the norm and seem applicable to the school for quality learning.

The nested view. Within each subject area, the teacher targets multiple skills—a social skill, a thinking skill, and a content-specific skill. For example, the teacher designs the unit on photosynthesis to simultaneously target consensus seeking (social skill), sequencing (thinking skill), and plant life cycle (science content).

The sequenced view. Topics or units of study are re-arranged and sequenced to coincide. Similar ideas are taught in concert while the subjects remain separate. For example, an English teacher presents a historical novel set in a particular period while the history teacher teaches about that same period. A study of the stock market in math could be linked with the study of the Great Depression in history.

The shared view. Shared planning and teaching take place in two disciplines in which overlapping concepts or ideas emerge as organizing elements. For example, a science and a math teacher use data collection, charting, and graphing as shared concepts that can be team taught.

The webbed view. A fertile theme is webbed to multiple curriculum contents and disciplines; in subject areas the theme becomes a way to sift out appropriate concepts, topics, and ideas. For example, a teacher presents a single topical theme such as the circus and webs it to the various subject areas. A conceptual theme, such as conflict, can be webbed for more depth in the approach. Using local architecture as the theme, an elementary teacher can teach all subject areas in an arena of interest to all learners. Some other themes that support webbing are inventions, patterns, and fairy tales or other literary genres.

The threaded view. The metacurricular approach threads thinking skills, social skills, multiple intelligences, technology, and study skills through the various disciplines. For example, teachers in reading, math, and science lab target prediction, while the social studies teacher targets forecasting current events; the skill of prediction is thus threaded across the disciplines. Any thinking skill or problem-solving strategy can provide the basis for threaded units.

The integrated view. The interdisciplinary approach matches subjects for overlap in topics and concepts and uses some team teaching in an authentic integrated model. For example, in math, science, social studies, fine arts, language arts, and practical arts, teachers look for patterning models and approach content through those patterns. The concepts of argument and evidence can integrate math, science, language arts, and social studies. The whole-language strategy, in which reading, writing, listening, and speaking skills spring from a holistic, literature-based program, is an example of the integrated view in action.

Any of the foregoing views will likely yield learning opportunities that are less fragmented for the learner than those now offered by the rigid, disassociated curriculum. The nested, sequenced, and shared views represent starting points for the interested and committed novice; the webbed, threaded, and integrated views make possible significant movement toward interdisciplinary learning. If most learning activities were organized according to the latter views, learners would much more easily see the relevance and value of learning, and a first important milestone on the path to quality would be reached. However, it would be only one milestone. At least as important as curriculum integration is the issue of who will decide what is to be learned. The central question in curriculum reform is whether educators—at least those in the individual school—are willing to make a leap of faith on behalf of the school's intended customers. Are the educators willing to turn themselves over to the learners rather than maintain allegiance to the abstract subject categories and artificial purposes that plague our present efforts? Will teachers be willing and able to gear curriculum decisions and pedagogical choices to individual learners? And, more precisely, will they be willing and able to make those decisions and choices in concert with each learner? The school for quality learning requires affirmative responses.

In chapter 5, we advocated that the individual teacher have broad discretion in curriculum-related decisions. At the least, the teacher should be free to choose the teaching strategies and the materials to be used. Further, to the extent possible, the teacher should be able to choose the curriculum content. These decisions are essential for designing quality learning experiences for individual learners. To make relevant curriculum decisions, one must know the learners and the learners' needs and wants.

In the school for quality learning, the lead-manager teacher will be responsible for deciding what to teach and how to teach it. However, the teacher will share that responsibility with the learners, both with each individual and with the class as a whole. In the absence of a partnership of shared responsibility for these two basic decisions about the nature and structure of the learning environment, the philosophy and the desired outcomes discussed in chapter 13 cannot be realized.

Glasser (1990), in further discussion of curriculum, suggests the following:

> Instead of telling students what they need to learn and
> then losing so many of them in the process, we should
> separate from the bulk of the curriculum the most
> obviously important parts and ask students if they will

accept learning these components well . . . we should explain much more than we do now . . . about why we teach the things we do. Then we should break down what we teach into recognizable parts . . . we should ask students if they agree that these definite and understandable components are worth learning. . . . If we cannot figure out how to present what we teach in a way that students will easily see that it is worth making the effort to learn, we should not teach it. More often than not, to try to force learning on the unwilling is to promote ignorance. (pp. 119–121)

When designing the learning environment and seeking answers to the questions, What should be taught? and How should it be taught? the teacher should remember that a learning activity has the following four basic dimensions:

1. Problem dimension

   What will the learner do?

   What will the learner learn?

2. Process dimension

   How will the learner do it?

   How will the learner learn it?

3. Product dimension

   What will the learner have when finished with the activity?

   What will the learner be able to do when finished with the activity?

   What will the learner be when finished with the activity?

4. Evaluation dimension

   What does the learner want or need feedback on relative to the activity?

   Who can give the learner this feedback?

   What will the learner do with this feedback?

The lead-manager teacher of the school for quality learning knows that the learner must be involved in the basic decisions within each dimension. By having the learner rephrase each question to pertain to himself or herself and carefully considering the learner's answer to each question, the teacher can facilitate quality individual learning experiences. The answers will not necessarily mean different learning activities for each learner, but they will mean appropriate learning activities for each learner. Excluding the learner from these basic decisions will serve only to perpetuate the status quo. Even if curriculum is reworked—perhaps even to the point of true integration—simply doing harder or longer what others tell one to do has not, does not, and will not fit into the learner's quality world.

Even a cursory examination of present practice leads to the conclusion that integration of curriculum represents a monumental change; the same is true for the creation of a classroom environment where the learner is a primary decision maker in all dimensions of learning activity. In present practice, learners are rarely involved in the decision process and become less involved as they progress through the system. In present practice, the more experienced learners become, the less they are allowed to decide: As they advance from elementary to middle to high school, curriculum demands become more and more rigid and less and less responsive to learners' needs. Secondary school curricula are largely textbook driven. To argue that textbook authors and publishers understand individual learners and their varying needs is to argue that the learners or the teachers are to blame for the alarming dropout rates and the disenfranchisement of students everywhere. The suggestion that the fault lies with ineffective teachers comes from that same intransigent group of educational elites—scholars, federal and state education departments, certification bureaus, and text and test publishers—who make serious curriculum reform nearly impossible. The suggestion that the fault lies with the learners either supports the "longer and harder" notion (advanced by this same elitist group) as the answer to the failings of our educational system or implies that the learners are innately defective and not capable of success in school.

For quality learning to occur, decisions about learning activities must involve each learner, not just consider the perceived needs of learners as a collective. Involving the learner in decision making removes barriers to pride of workmanship (Deming's, 1986, Point 12). The responsibility for involving the learner in decisions about learning activities lies with the classroom teacher. To enable the teacher to meet this responsibility, the school for quality learning guarantees teachers the conditions, outlined in Part 2, that will create the comfort level they need if they are to change their own practices. Change will proceed slowly, and the change process will likely be ragged, characterized by false starts, bold ventures and retrenchments, successes and disappointments, changes of direction, uncertainties and ambiguities, and so on.

The lead-manager teacher must begin somewhere, at a point of relative comfort, in starting to rethink what should be taught. Following are three decisions that will help teachers move toward an integrated curriculum and free themselves to deal with individual learners.

DECISION 1. The teacher should stop asking what should be taught and instead ask what is worth learning. This changes the focus of concern from teaching to learning. The teacher should ask, What am I going to ask my students to learn? Why is it worth learning? and How do I know that?

DECISION 2. The teacher should examine the content now being taught in his or her subject area(s) and determine what he or she deems essential—what is worth learning for *every* learner. This scrutiny should reduce the original content by at least half and probably will result in an even greater reduction. The questions should be about learning rather than about teaching.

DECISION 3. The teacher should determine what other learning, beyond that identified as essential content, he or she considers acceptable for individual learners to pursue. Content that may not be essential for all learners is very likely to be of interest and value to some learners.

The process involving these three decisions results in a curriculum structure—what is to be learned. The teacher is focused on learning rather than teaching, has identified what all learners will be persuaded to learn, and has identified other acceptable learning activities. As the lead-manager teacher grows in the ability to facilitate quality learning, he or she will involve the learner more and more in the process of deciding what is essential and what is acceptable. Once the curriculum structure for the classroom is determined, the teacher can begin deciding how to teach that curriculum or, better, how to facilitate learning.

CHAPTER 15

Facilitating Learning: Organization and Strategies

According to Glasser (1990), "being an effective teacher may be the most difficult job of all in our society. . . . An effective teacher is one who is able to convince . . . essentially all of his or her learners to do quality work in school. This means to work up to their capacity" (pp. 14–15). Glasser holds that

> all work falls into one of two major categories: managing things and managing people. When we manage things, the essence of the job is to perform an operation on a thing or even on a person (who may be acting as passively as a thing) that improves its value. What is characteristic of a thing (or a person behaving like a thing) is that, hard as the operation may be, the thing never actively resists the person managing it. . . . Jobs in which things are managed . . . are in some sense much easier than jobs managing people. . . . Regardless of the skill and creativity of the manager, managing people depends for its ultimate success on the cooperation of the people being managed. (pp. 15–16)

When the stakes are raised from expecting quality work of essentially all learners to expecting quality work of all learners, we can entertain no doubt that effective teaching is the most difficult job in our society.

As we stated in chapter 13, the lead-manager teacher has two major responsibilities, sometimes distinct but more often closely intertwined. The teacher both creates the environment and facilitates the learning within that environment. Creating the environment is largely, though not entirely, a job of managing things, whereas facilitating learning is largely a job of managing people. The teacher wishing to develop the classroom for quality learning will invest a great deal of energy in the latter job, the more difficult one.

In facilitating learning, the lead-manager teacher has two major responsibilities, rarely distinct and usually closely intertwined. The teacher is responsible for determining both what is to be learned (even when the teacher involves the learner in the decision, it is still the teacher's responsibility) and how that learning can be facilitated. Chapter 14 dealt with the first process, which is primarily a job of managing things. The teacher wishing to develop the classroom for quality learning will also invest considerable physical and mental energy allowing or causing learners to be engaged in quality learning.

What is a quality learner? What does a quality learner believe? How does a quality learner behave? In designing activities and strategies that will lead to quality learning, the teacher can find clarity of purpose and direction by considering those characteristics. Following are some traits of quality learners (adapted from Postman & Weingartner, 1969). Learners who possess these traits will be effective in realizing the outcomes detailed in chapter 13.

Quality learners are curious. Most preschool children are curious. Most preschool children are quality learners. Recognize what most children accomplish before school age: They develop incredible fine and gross motor abilities; they master a very complicated language (the average first grader has a 10,000-word vocabulary and facility with grammatical structure); they learn to observe, listen, and question. Quality learners of all ages exhibit the desire to know—they maintain that initial curiosity.

Quality learners have confidence in their ability to learn. Although they may sometimes be frustrated and discouraged, they show a profound faith that they are capable of solving problems. If they fail at one problem, they are not incapacitated in confronting another.

Quality learners enjoy solving problems. They are intrigued by the process, and they may actually resent others who want to "help" by giving them the answers.

Quality learners are tenacious. They are willing to stay with a project or a problem they perceive as relevant and significant until they achieve a satisfactory resolution. They may be very impatient with those who try to impose time constraints upon them.

Quality learners seek challenging learning opportunities. They may, however, quickly tire of activities or tasks that they perceive as too easy. In contrast to their tendency to be tenacious, they may abandon those too-easy activities well before they have produced a product. (This behavior may result in the learner's being labeled as lazy or underachieving.)

Quality learners appear to know what is relevant to their survival or success and what is not. They are apt to resent being told what is "good for them to know." Even if they concur, they resent being told. They prefer to rely on their own judgment. As they mature, quality learners become increasingly suspicious of authorities, especially of any authority who discourages them from relying on their own judgment.

Quality learners rarely fear being wrong. They recognize their limitations and do not suffer trauma in concluding that what they once believed was apparently incorrect. They change their minds; in fact, restructuring and reformulating their system of knowledge and belief is their avocation. This trait enables these learners to formulate hypotheses.

Quality learners are flexible. Although they almost always have a point of view about a situation, they are capable of shifting perspectives to see what they can find out. Quality learners seem to understand that answers are relative, that everything depends on the system within which one is working. Their answers are frequently qualified by "it depends."

Quality learners have a high degree of respect for facts, which they view as tentative and system bound. They are also skilled at distinguishing statements of fact from other kinds of statements and at discerning what is and what is not relevant to their particular learning pursuit.

Quality learners know how to ask meaningful questions.
They are persistent in examining assumptions; their own included. They are apt to be cautious in making generalizations.
They continually verify what they believe and test their own
knowledge and beliefs.

Quality learners are emphatically not fast answerers.
They tend to delay their judgments until they have access to as
much information as they imagine will be available. (This trait
does not serve them well in most classrooms today.)

**Quality learners do not need an absolute, final, irrevoca-
ble resolution to every problem or question.** They can operate comfortably with uncertainty and ambiguity; they can accept
"I don't know." They seem to sense that some problems as yet
have no solutions, some questions as yet have no answers, and
some questions may never have answers.

Quality learners are self-evaluators. They do not rely on
the judgments of others to determine the value and quality of
what they have done or learned. They have their own sophis-
ticated criteria and their own high standards for judging their own
behavior and the products of that behavior.

Quality learners are individuals in search of knowledge—they
have inquiring minds. Simply stated, the ultimate goal of education is to produce learners with inquiring minds who can think
rationally and solve real-world problems. How does one search
for knowledge? Knowledge is produced in response to questions.
The lead-manager teacher, in the role of learning facilitator, understands that once learners have learned how to ask relevant,
appropriate, and substantial questions they will have learned how
to learn and cannot be prevented from learning whatever they
want or need to know. The most important intellectual ability that
can be developed is the art and science of asking questions, a
multidimensional talent that has the potential for continual development and refinement.

A quality learner learns by actively constructing knowledge;
weighing new information against previous understanding; thinking about and working through discrepancies, either independently or with others; and coming to a new understanding. In the
classroom for quality learning, the lead-manager teacher offers
learners numerous opportunities to explore phenomena or ideas,
conjecture, share hypotheses with others, and revise their original

understandings. The activities of the classroom are designed to foster development of the ability to ask questions. To nurture that ability, the lead-manager teacher takes the following measures (adapted from Postman & Weingartner, 1969):

1. Exhibits personal curiosity by raising genuine questions for the teacher and/or the learner to consider.

2. Takes on real problems and exhibits tenacity in pursuing solutions. The teacher participating actively in the environment as a learner in full view of the student learners provides a powerful model for quality learning—both of the expectations for and of the practice of quality learning.

3. Uses questioning as the primary mode of discourse with the learner in the pursuit of the learning activity, viewing the question as the instrument to open engaged minds to unsuspected possibilities or undiscovered factors.

4. Refrains from telling the learner what he or she thinks the learner should know because the teacher knows that the excitement of discovering something independently increases the learner's power.

5. Rarely accepts a single statement as an answer to a question. The teacher seeks the reasons, rather than a reason; the causes, rather than a cause; the meanings, rather than a meaning. The teacher promotes contingent thinking by helping learners understand the framework upon which a response depends. "It depends" is accepted as a valuable phrase modifying a statement of conclusion.

6. Encourages learner interaction by not acting as a mediator or judge of the quality of ideas expressed. Learners need to develop their own criteria for judging the quality, precision, and relevance of ideas. If the teacher is the primary arbiter of what is acceptable, learners fail to develop evaluative thinking skills and become dependent upon authority.

7. Interacts with learners in activities that pose real problems and that require learners to clarify the problem, make observations about the solution, and make generalizations based on those observations. Learners are encouraged to be engaged in activities that produce knowledge (if it is new to the learner, it is producing knowledge): defining, questioning, observing, classifying, generalizing, verifying, applying. Proficiency in these activities is the hallmark of a quality learner.

8. Insists that the learners ask questions and equips them with strategic questions that will guide them in problem solving. The strategic questions allow learners to better define problems and to analyze and evaluate the process used in pursuit of solutions. (The evaluation process presented in chapter 17 specifically addresses this teacher responsibility.)

A learner cannot possibly learn everything of value during the period of formal schooling, but the schooling experience can instill in the learner the lifelong desire to keep questioning. Individualized learning activities are those that develop self-directing, responsible, intrinsically motivated individuals by giving each learner maximum appropriate opportunities to manipulate and explore the environment. Individual learning activities based on self-assumed work and incorporation of self-evaluation provide individual freedom in learning within the instructional setting. The learner with the developing, inquiring mind is the increasingly independent learner.

Historically, individual programs, appropriately called *individualized instruction,* fall into three categories.

Continuous progress. A program in which different learners proceed through a commonly prescribed set of materials and/or activities arranged in a commonly prescribed sequence of learning tasks. This approach recognizes that learners do learn at different rates. Learners are encouraged to proceed through the activities as rapidly as possible, but each determines his or her own pace.

Performance criterion. A program in which different learners are presented a common set of materials and/or activities organized into convenient clusters (units), each with an explicitly stated performance standard (a product or a behavior). Each learner is responsible for demonstrating proficiency according to the standard, but the learner has latitude in determining when to do so and how to prepare to meet the standard.

Independent study. A program in which the learner exercises major responsibility for selecting a learning problem, designing a process for addressing the problem, and determining a product. The learner pursues the activity relatively independently and is evaluated individually on the basis of the problem selected and the product developed. The teacher usually structures parameters within which the learner may operate but does not organize materials or provide direct instruction concerning the learner's selected project. The teacher may or may not serve as a resource for the learner.

These various approaches all contain some provision for individual differences among learners that permits the teacher to individualize instruction. Each also emphasizes independent work. Typically, the teacher controls the content—what is to be learned—to ensure some degree of commonality for all learners. As one progresses through program types, from continuous progress to performance criterion to independent study, the learner has increasing responsibility for determining how to learn.

Another common approach to accommodating learner differences is instructional grouping within a single classroom. Groups are usually formed according to performance (ability) levels, and the teacher adapts the instruction according to what each group is ready to learn and how well its members can benefit from a particular instructional strategy.

Individualized instruction programs in their many variations and combinations may all be useful to the teacher seeking to facilitate quality learning. However, they will not in and of themselves guarantee quality learning any more so than will the almost exclusive use of instructional time to actively deliver information to a learner who listens passively. A program for individual learning comprises much more than individualized instruction. In individualized learning, the learner participates significantly in determining the learning activities or, at least, in determining the various dimensions of some of the learning activities. This is not the case in typical individualized instruction programs, which are basically dominated by teacher decisions.

In chapter 14, we stated that individualized learning does not necessarily mean different learning activities for each learner; rather, it means appropriate learning activities for each learner. Also, individualized learning most certainly does not mean that learners should pursue all learning activities independently of one another. Such an approach would not be an efficient use of learning resources, nor would it be an effective strategy for realizing the desired outcomes of the school for quality learning. Learning outcomes such as communication skills and facility in social interaction obviously require interaction among learners. It is difficult to imagine that most other desired outcomes could be fully realized if students did not interact through purposeful learning activities.

Glasser (1986) states that

> if we continue to use what is best described as the
> traditional classroom approach (that is, learners learning
> and competing as individuals with the teacher in charge
> of deciding both what is to be taught and how to teach it,
> usually through lectures), I believe our . . . schools will
> continue their downhill course. . . . What we need is to
> move to classrooms in which learners work in small
> learning teams. (pp. 74–75)

Glasser argues that such an approach offers learners need-fulfilling
opportunities because:

> 1. Learners can gain a sense of belonging by working
> together in a learning team. Teams should be as hetero-
> geneous as possible.
>
> 2. Belonging provides the initial motivation for the
> learners to work, and as they achieve academic success,
> those who had not worked previously begin to sense that
> knowledge is power and consequently work harder.
>
> 3. Stronger learners find it need fulfilling to help weaker
> ones because they want the power and friendship that go
> with a high-performing team.
>
> 4. Weaker learners find it need fulfilling to contribute as
> much as they can to the team effort because in this
> structure, whatever they can contribute helps the team.
> When they worked alone, their effort got them little
> reward because of the competitive, comparative nature
> of the evaluation and reward system.
>
> 5. Learners need not depend only on the teacher, but can
> depend a great deal on themselves, their own creativity
> and on other members of the team. This frees the learner
> from dependence on the teacher and provides the learner
> power and freedom.
>
> 6. Learning teams can allow learners to escape the
> superficiality that plagues schools and provides a vehicle
> to allow learners to learn enough in-depth to make the
> vital knowledge-is-power connection.
>
> 7. Teams are free to determine how to convince the
> teacher and other learners that they have learned some-

thing and are encouraged to use evidence to demonstrate learning that is other than tests.

8. Teams are changed on a regular basis to extend the opportunities for communication and social skill development and to broaden each learner's peer group, thus extending the learner's sense of belonging. (pp. 75–76)

A learning-team approach is essential to the promotion of quality learning. Learners can be organized into teams and directed to pursue activities in many different ways and in any of the typical content areas. Certainly, integrated learning lends itself to the team approach. Teamwork yields individualized learning experiences because each participant makes a unique contribution to the team effort, and, because all participants have different proficiencies at the outset, each learns something different in the process—even if their final products are identical.

Although the number of ways to organize and utilize learning teams is probably unlimited, the most prevalent current approaches are cooperative learning strategies. In cooperative learning, teams usually consist of four members, though the number can vary with the activity. Teams are heterogeneous relative to sex, ethnic group, and learner ability; they may also represent different age groups. A team works together toward a common learning goal. Each team member is expected to be able to demonstrate proficiency in the desired learning outcome, and each is responsible for helping the others develop that proficiency as well. The quality of the achievement of the learning goal may be assessed through a team evaluation process, through an individual self-evaluation process, or through some combination of team and individual evaluation.

Typically, cooperative learning activities have these common components:

1. Heterogeneous teams that represent a true cross-section of the class

2. Interdependence among teammates, whereby each team member's success depends on the success of all members

3. Team interdependence, whereby all members help the team reach a specific goal rather than simply competing against other teams

4. Accountability both for the team's attainment of its goal and for individual learning by each team member

5. Appropriateness of the group activity

Central to cooperative learning activities is the group goal or shared outcome. Group members interact with one another to problem solve. Sometimes the individual members are preassigned specific roles such as recorder, encourager, reporter, and the like, but all share in the thinking and problem solving that result in the group's solution. Cooperative learning assumes that no group member already has a solution to the common problem. A true cooperative learning activity requires the resources of each member to arrive at a solution. Following are some examples of cooperative learning activities:

1. The group agrees on answers to inferential comprehension questions based on a story or other common reading.

2. The group conducts a science experiment and agrees on an observed outcome.

3. The group organizes a panel discussion to exhibit understanding of a current events topic or a social studies concept.

4. The group writes, produces, and performs a short play to illustrate what they have learned.

5. Group members interact to solve a math word problem and present the group's solution to the class.

The most prevalent cooperative learning strategies are the Learning Together strategies developed by David Johnson and Roger Johnson (1975) and colleagues at the University of Minnesota; the Student Team Learning techniques developed by Robert Slavin (1987) and colleagues at John Hopkins University; and the Group Investigation method developed by Yael Sharan and Shlomo Sharan (1990) of Tel Aviv University. Cooperative learning is most consistent with the goals of the school for quality learning when the selected learning activity offers intrinsically interesting and challenging learning tasks, allows learners to make key decisions about how to perform these tasks, and emphasizes the value and skills of cooperation.

Some other learning activities, though not cooperative learning in the strictest sense, offer opportunities for cooperation that foster quality learning. The tutorial program in which one learner who has mastered a particular skill or concept helps another learner to gain the same proficiency is an example. This approach promotes quality learning for both parties: The one receiving the assistance or instruction improves in the ability to perform; the one providing the assistance has additional opportunity to practice what has been learned and is challenged to analyze it in-depth so it can be explained or demonstrated to the other learner. Further, the coach or tutor gains verbal fluency, becomes more adept at explaining and showing, or does both in demonstrating the skill or concept to the other learner.

Peer teaching and peer coaching programs provide active engagement in learning activities that build social skills and help students formulate relationships. Jigsaw, a strategy developed by Eliot Aronson (1978) and colleagues at the University of California, combines elements of cooperative learning and peer teaching or coaching. Cooperative learning and peer teaching facilitate the development of caring, cooperative relationships among learners. Other valuable individualized learning activities that lead to the social outcomes desired in the school for quality learning are simulation activities and educational games.

Group learning experiences that yield both individual learning and social learning outcomes are a necessary element in the classroom for quality learning. The lead-manager teacher must be adept at providing both individual learning activities and activities that engage each learner with others.

In chapter 14, we advised the lead-manager teacher to determine a curriculum structure by making three major decisions that shift the focus from teaching to learning, to identify the essentials that all learners should be persuaded to learn, and to identify other acceptable learning activities. These three decisions concern what is to be learned. The lead-manager teacher's next responsibility is to determine how to facilitate learning. The teacher must begin somewhere, at a point of relative comfort, in starting to rethink that responsibility. The following decisions, logical extensions of these first three, will help the teacher determine learning facilitator behaviors.

DECISION 4. The teacher should examine what was identified as essential for possible integration across subject areas. If the teacher has responsibility for more than one content area (as does the elementary teacher with a self-contained classroom), he or she should seek natural associations to economize on the time required to provide learning activities around the essential information and to make that information more relevant for the learners. (Remember, what the teacher decides is valuable to learn may not hold much attraction for many learners.) If the teacher, like most secondary teachers, is responsible for only one content area, he or she should seek out colleagues whose subject matter offers the potential for developing interdisciplinary learning activities around the essential concepts.

DECISION 5. The teacher should organize the essential material into learning activities or units and determine what learners must have or how they must behave (the learning outcome) to demonstrate satisfactory learning of the material. The teacher also needs to determine the order in which the learning activities or units will be introduced.

DECISION 6. The teacher should determine a strategy, or a variety of strategies, to engage the learners in the chosen learning activities or units. The teacher may decide that an activity or a unit lends itself to multiple approaches and may allow the learner to select the most enjoyable approach. For other activities or units, the teacher may decide that a common approach is preferable. Variety from unit to unit is advisable. The teacher should ask which activities or units lend themselves to a cooperative learning approach, a continuous progress approach, a performance criterion approach featuring peer coaching, and so on.

DECISION 7. The teacher should determine a time allocation plan, providing as much time as possible for the learners to satisfy the requirements of the activities or units but ensuring that all essential matter will be addressed in the time available—the reporting period, the semester, or the year.

DECISION 8. The teacher should organize the elective learning activities (those determined in Decision 3) into a learner choice menu. Learners should be oriented to understand that when the learning outcome (determined in Decision 5) for each essential activity or unit is demonstrated, they may use the remaining time (see Decision 7) to pursue learning activities of their choice.

This series of decisions is designed to help the teacher organize the curriculum deemed essential into pieces that may be more interesting and relevant to the learners and to engage the learners in learning activities that are potentially need fulfilling. This organization also gives learners an incentive to do quality work efficiently in order to demonstrate competence and then to gain the opportunity to select other activities. This element of choice allows learners to experience power, freedom, and fun because they are likely to choose activities that are personally satisfying. The greater the latitude for such learner choices, the greater the likelihood that all learners will be engaged in quality learning activities. As the lead-manager teacher grows in the ability to facilitate quality learning, he or she will involve the learners in the process of determining what is essential, what is acceptable, what the learning process will be, and what will be accepted as evidence of quality learning.

In the school and the classroom for quality learning, the use of technology is a further important consideration. Technology has enormous potential for assisting the lead-manager teacher in designing the learning environment and providing quality individualized experiences. Computers and other forms of assistive technology do not constitute a separate curriculum or program; rather, they are tools that can help teachers better meet learners' varying needs. Technology alone will not solve the problems of the educational system. It takes good teaching practices and a great deal of hard work to determine how best to improve learning activities. It is probably easier to develop a new technology than to apply it effectively to promote quality learning. In any case, technology is an important part of our world and as such is a vital component of the school for quality learning. The learning environment should mirror society and prepare learners for their future in the society; this is the acid test for relevance.

In an industrial society, those with capital have power. In an information- or knowledge-based society, those with information have power. Educational technology gives the have-nots the opportunity to access and manipulate information and to make decisions based on that information. When that occurs, the have-nots become the haves. More than any tool yet developed, educational technology has the potential to provide even learners who are currently disenfranchised the opportunity to gain power by acquiring information. Technology itself is not the solution, but the solution demands access to high technology. Although technology is not required for individualized learning activities, the use of technology significantly expands the available learning options. Quality learning for each learner demands access to as much technology as possible.

CHAPTER 16

Discipline in the Classroom

In Part 2 we discussed the importance of a healthy, positive school climate. As noted in chapter 8, the most important determinant of school climate is the behavioral expectations held for the learners. It is essential to have a responsibility education program grounded in total staff consensus and based on behavioral expectations and management procedures that ensure each learner the opportunity and support necessary to internalize acceptable behaviors. The classroom teacher is ultimately responsible for promoting acceptable and successful behaviors on the part of every learner. In the school for quality learning, each learner is expected to be fully engaged in quality learning activities. Because no student who feels threatened or coerced can engage in quality learning, the lead-manager teacher is unconditionally committed to managing the classroom without coercion.

To coerce is to compel or force another to act or think in a given manner—to dominate, restrain, or control another through the use of actual or implied force. The lead-manager teacher, who understands control theory and applies the questioning strategies of reality therapy, abandons as counterproductive the inclination to exercise forceful authority over the learners. The lead-manager teacher transfers the responsibility for acceptable behavior to the behavers—not through force or domination but through reason and support.

In chapters 14 and 15, we outlined eight decisions the teacher should make to begin developing the classroom for quality learning. Those decisions concern what is to be learned and how the teacher can facilitate the learning. The next decision deals with the learners' work and behavior.

DECISION 9. The teacher should establish guidelines defining the rules of work and of behavior for the learning environment. These guidelines, as simple and few as possible, are designed to guarantee that all learners will be engaged in quality learning and that they will not disrupt one another's learning opportunities through their behavior.

A work guideline, for example, may state that learners must choose activities to pursue; they may not elect to do nothing. A behavioral guideline might be that when a fellow learner asks for help, you should provide whatever assistance you can.

Is the idea of a discipline program and the notion of behavior management without coercion self-contradictory? The answer is a resounding no, but it is understandable that the question would be raised. Many existing discipline programs are misnamed. It would be more accurate to call them punishment programs. Punishment is coercive; discipline is educational. Table 16.1 contrasts punishment and discipline.

Punishment is a poor deterrent to undesirable behavior. It often results in an angry recipient who focuses on revenge behaviors or a compliant one who attempts to follow the rules out of fear. Because punishment does not teach appropriate behaviors, it frequently leads to repetition of the undesired (punished) behavior or the exhibition of an equally undesirable behavior.

Compliance is a recourse of the behaver who wishes to avoid punishment. The behaver acquiesces to an authority. A tendency to yield to others runs counter to the philosophy and the desired outcomes of the school for quality learning. Compliance negates thinking: The behaver accepts, at least temporarily, the logic of the authority. The compliant behaver does not examine alternative behaviors to find the one that would be most need fulfilling in the given situation. Because compliance rarely fulfills the behaver's needs, the compliant behavior tends to be inconsistently displayed in the presence of the authority and to disappear in the absence of the authority. In a school setting, it is true that a group of compliant learners is easily managed by a teacher. Boss managers strive to elicit compliance. However, the lead-manager teacher knows that quality learning and quality behavior bear little relationship to being compliant.

Table 16.1   Punishment Versus Discipline

Punishment	Discipline
1. Expresses power of an authority; usually causes pain to the recipient; is based upon retribution or revenge; is concerned with what has happened (the past)	1. Is based on logical or natural consequences that embody the reality of a social order (rules that one must learn and accept to function adequately and productively in society); concerned with what is happening now (the present)
2. Is arbitrary—probably applied inconsistently and unconditionally; does not accept or acknowledge exceptions or mitigating circumstances	2. Is consistent—accepts that the behaving individual is doing the best he or she can do for now
3. Is imposed by an authority (done to someone), with responsibility assumed by the one administering the punishment and the behaving individual avoiding responsibility	3. Comes from within, with responsibility assumed by the behaving individual and the behaving individual desiring responsibility; presumes that conscience is internal
4. Closes options for the individual, who must pay for a behavior that has already occurred	4. Opens options for the individual, who can choose a new behavior
5. As a teaching process, usually reinforces a failure identity; essentially negative and short term, without sustained personal involvement of either teacher or learner	5. As a teaching process, is active and involves close, sustained, personal involvement of teacher and learner; emphasizes ways to act that will result in more successful behavior
6. Is characterized by open or concealed anger; is a poor model of the expectations of quality	6. Is friendly and supportive; provides a model of quality behavior
7. Is easy and expedient	7. Is difficult and time-consuming
8. Focuses on strategies intended to control behavior of the learner	8. Focuses on the learner's behavior and the consequences of that behavior
9. Rarely results in positive changes in behavior; may increase subversiveness or result in temporary suppression of behavior; at best, produces compliance	9. Usually results in a change in behavior that is more successful, acceptable, and responsible; develops the capacity for self-evaluation of behavior

Punishment frustrates all of the recipient's basic psychological needs (belonging, power, freedom, and fun). The relationship between the recipient and the person administering the punishment is diminished, stymieing the recipient's ability to meet the need for belonging. Because of the negative focus of punishment, the recipient is likely to be ostracized by appropriately behaving peers and will seek out inappropriately behaving peers in an effort to belong. Punishment obviously restricts freedom and is not pleasurable—it causes emotional and sometimes physical pain. Punishment diminishes the power of the recipient, who typically blames the punisher for causing the problem and does not view himself or herself as the one in a position to solve it. The punisher is viewed as the one with the power to control behavior, and the recipient of punishment sees no reason to engage in self-evaluation of behavior.

Discipline, on the other hand, helps the individual learn acceptable behaviors. Discipline promotes self-evaluation of behavior. By learning to behave consistently in an acceptable manner, one earns freedom because those with the authority to manage choices trust that acceptable choices will be made and appropriate actions will follow. The more learners are in effective control of their behavior, the more powerful they feel. The more successful they are in choosing acceptable behaviors, the more likely they are to be engaged by others who behave appropriately. Thus, life in school becomes more need fulfilling and pleasurable, and school becomes a part of the learners' quality world.

Glasser (1965) holds that school discipline is problematic because administrators and teachers not only deal with a large variety of excuses for inappropriate behavior—some individual and some group excuses—but also ask for those excuses. Discipline is poorly understood. It has nothing to do with harming learners. Rather, it means helping learners first to realize that their current behaviors are not enabling them to meet their needs and then helping them choose more successful, need-fulfilling behaviors. It takes learners a long time to fulfill their commitments—especially the commitment to quality.

Learners, especially those with school experience, will scrutinize each teacher and try to determine if he or she will accept excuses. The real danger in accepting excuses for inappropriate behavior is in the message such acceptance sends to the learner. The message may be "You are worthless." The learner's translation is "You don't care." The teacher who refuses to accept excuses is saying, "You are a worthwhile person, and I am waiting for you to complete your commitment." For example, if a student fails to complete an assignment, rather than say, "Why didn't you do it?" the teacher should say, "When will you do it?" "Can you do it?" "Can you do it in school today?" "After school?"

The lead-manager teacher in the classroom for quality learning understands the necessity to communicate to learners high expectations regarding both learning and behavior. The teacher also realizes that it is impossible to elicit learning and behavior simply by declaring that they are desired and expected. The lead-manager teacher approaches the development and use of quality behavior as proactively as he or she approaches the development of quality learning. The teacher knows that discipline is a positive learning experience based on the learner's self-evaluation and choice.

Every lead-manager teacher develops a plan to engage learners in activities that promote responsibility education and quality behavior. The first step is to make sure that each learner fully understands the behavioral expectations of the school (the school constitution) and the process for resolving inevitable problems and conflicts. The Leal Rights and Responsibilities and the conflict resolution program discussed in chapter 8 are examples of a school constitution for behavior and a school process for resolving conflict. The next step is to engage learners in activities to help them understand the specific rules that govern behavior in their classroom. Obviously, classroom expectations must be congruent with those of the school, and discussions and other learning activities should be designed to help learners see the relationship between the two sets of expectations.

COMPONENTS OF A CLASSROOM DISCIPLINE PROGRAM

The remainder of this chapter describes the components of a classroom discipline program in the school for quality learning. It includes educational strategies for promoting responsible behavior (creating a vision of quality behavior) and intervention strategies for helping individual learners achieve quality behavior. The discipline program has five components: class meetings, life rules, C.A.R.E. (communication about responsibility education) time, time-out, and mediation. These components promote understanding of guidelines for behavior in the learning environment, and they provide the teacher and the learner with processes for solving problems. This program is designed to ensure that all learners will be engaged in quality learning and that they will not disrupt the learning opportunities of others.

Class Meetings

The social-problem-solving class meeting (Glasser, 1969) is an excellent vehicle for responsibility education. Although meetings appear to be time-consuming, they are critical to the success of the classroom. As a rule, such meetings require considerable time during the first week or so of the term, as this is the time for orientation, teaching, and reteaching. However, the real payoff comes when meetings are scheduled regularly throughout the term. Meeting activities are consistent with the desired outcomes of the school for quality learning. The activities provide a systematic way for learners to gain understanding and respect of self and others, to develop an understanding of conflict, and to develop the social-problem-solving skills they will need in life. These are all desired outcomes in the school for quality learning, outcomes that learners will not realize unless they have opportunities to explore behavioral alternatives and practice problem solving. Learners of every age experience difficulties in getting along with one another and find interpersonal problems most difficult to solve. Without help in resolving these difficulties, "learners tend to evade the problems, to lie their way out of situations, to depend on others to solve their problems, or just to give up. None of these courses of action [is] good preparation for life" (Glasser, 1969, p. 124).

Class meetings have the following functions:

1. They introduce behavioral expectations and help learners understand the reasons for rules in the social setting.

2. They help learners understand their basic psychological needs and wants, as well as the choices they can make to get their needs met.

3. They help learners understand diversity, conflicts, and problems.

4. They provide a forum for addressing individual and group educational and behavioral problems at both classroom and school levels.

5. They help learners discover that each one has both individual and group responsibilities for learning and for behaving in a way that fosters learning.

6. They help learners understand that, although the world may be difficult and may at times appear hostile and mysterious, they can use their minds to solve the problems of living in their school world.

7. They help learners see the relevance of the expected school and classroom behavior to behavioral expectations in real-life settings.

Problems affecting the class as a whole, as well as particular problems affecting individual members, are eligible for discussion, although the teacher and class should establish ground rules governing the introduction of an individual problem that is not directly school related. The group discussion should always be directed toward solving the problem; the solution should never include punishment or fault finding. If class meetings are held frequently, participants will become aware that many problems are not amenable to quick solution: Some have no single best solution, and some have a best solution that is only a "lesser evil." If problem identification is an open group process, there is little danger that problems with a clear solution will be the only ones chosen for discussion.

Following is a list of some questions that, singularly or in combination, might serve as topics for a class meeting:

1. What is responsibility?

2. What are some examples of occasions when you felt you exhibited responsible behavior?

3. Describe an action you have taken that you are proud of.

4. What is right?

5. What is wrong?

6. How do you decide what is right and wrong?

7. How can you help someone who is having difficulty following the rules?

8. How can someone help you?

9. Describe something someone else did that made you feel proud of him or her.

10. What does freedom mean?

11. What is a friend?

12. What would you like to change about yourself?

13. What would you not like to have to change about yourself?

14. What motivates you to do your best?

15. Who understands you?

16. How do you feel about yourself?

17. How do you think others see you?

18. Whom do you understand?

19. What is conflict?

20. What do you usually do when you find yourself
    in conflict with a peer? With an adult?

21. What do you want when you are in conflict
    with another person?

22. Does what you do when you are in a conflict with
    another person help you get what you want?

The class meeting is a forum for reviewing school rules and the reasons behind them, discussing the consequences of not following the rules, helping an individual or the group determine alternative behaviors to replace unacceptable ones, suggesting strategies to help an individual deal with someone who is creating a problem for him or her, and exploring a variety of ways to meet expectations. The class meeting can be a forum for generating expectations for the classroom. In addition, the meeting is a time for activities that foster an understanding of basic needs and conflict. For example, learners might brainstorm four lists enumerating the things they do to meet their needs for belonging, power, freedom, and fun. When learners realize that they are controlled not by external events but instead by the desire to satisfy certain internal needs, they begin to make more effective choices to get these needs met. In *Peer Mediation: Conflict Resolution in Schools* (Schrumpf, Crawford, & Usadel, 1991), the authors state:

> Even though all people are driven by the same four
> needs, each person's wants—or pictures—are unique.
> It is impossible for two people to have the same picture
> album because it is impossible for two people to live
> exactly the same life. If a person wishes to understand
> conflict and perceive it positively, the knowledge that no
> two people can have exactly the same wants is central.
> If two individuals wish to satisfy their need to belong
> through a friendship, they must learn to share their com-
> monalities and respect and value their differences. . . .
> Diagnosing the source of a conflict can help define a
> problem, and a definition of the problem is the starting

point in any attempt to find a solution. Almost every conflict involves an endeavor by the disputants to meet the basic psychological needs for belonging, power, freedom and fun. (pp. 6–7)

Life Rules

In the school for quality learning, the focus should be on life rules rather than on classroom rules. The lead-manager teacher orchestrates a discussion of behavior expected in the "real world" that allows people to succeed and to get their needs satisfied. For example, when adults are responsible, prompt, prepared, participate, and show respect, their chances for success and satisfaction increase. Once these life rules are identified, the teacher facilitates discussions and activities designed to enable the class to translate each rule into a desired classroom behavior (see Table 16.2).

Life rules are rarely rigid. Rules need to be flexible to accommodate genuine mitigating circumstances. For example, in real life, there are probably few absolute deadlines: Generally, a deadline can be extended so a quality result will be obtained. Even the Internal Revenue Service allows filing extensions to taxpayers who meet minimum requirements. The life rules of the school and the classroom must also be reasonably flexible. The goal is to

Table 16.2   Life Rules Translated Into Classroom Behaviors

Life rules	Classroom behaviors
Be prompt.	Meet deadlines.
Be prepared.	Have materials. Listen for instructions. Follow directions.
Participate.	Be a part of discussion. Complete work. Stay engaged.
Show respect.	Honor self and others. Value property.
Be responsible.	Accept ownership. Plan more effective behavior.

help learners understand the value of life rules. People of all ages tend to follow rules that enable them to get along and be safe. For example, games require rules that let all players play in the same manner to achieve a meaningful outcome; traffic signs enable drivers to travel with greater safety and a minimum of fear. The real reason that a driver stops at a stop sign is not the possible consequence of getting a ticket but the belief that stopping is in the driver's best interest and the interest of others. A consequence in and of itself will not change a behavior. A consequence only works when learners find value in the relationship with the person asking them to do something or when they see value in what they are being asked to do.

By providing regular and meaningful opportunities for learners to understand responsibility education and quality behavior, largely through whole-class activities such as the class meeting, the lead-manager teacher enables them to formulate a picture of quality behavior that can become a part of their quality world. For many learners, these group opportunities are sufficient to internalize quality behaviors. Others will need additional attention and support from the teacher to understand the expectations and to learn the behaviors that are consistent with those expectations. These learners need varying degrees of assistance through the discipline program to become aware that internalizing quality behaviors will be personally need satisfying. The following two components of the noncoercive discipline program provide two different ways to help learners take effective control of their behavior in two distinct problem areas. C.A.R.E. time is used when a student is not producing quality work or following work guidelines, and time-out is used with the student who is disrupting the learning environment of others.

C.A.R.E. Time

C.A.R.E. (communication about responsibility education) time is a brief period for the teacher and the learner to communicate about completion of work and engagement in classroom activities. This communication can be woven into the natural interactions of teacher and learner within the classroom setting, or it can occur at a scheduled time during or outside the school day. The reality therapy process described in chapter 3 is used during C.A.R.E. communication. The primary purpose of C.A.R.E. time is to help learners focus on how they are acting, thinking, and feeling and on what they want; to help learners evaluate whether their chosen behaviors are helping them get their needs met effectively; and to help learners develop and commit to plans for effective, quality behavior. The teacher can accomplish this by posing questions such as the following:

1. What are you doing? Focus on total behaviors—that is, how the learner is thinking, acting, and feeling. Help the learner understand that all total behaviors are chosen.

2. What do you want? Focus on the learner's present picture and expand it to the learner's quality world—the way he or she wants life to be.

3. Is (*present behavior*) going to get you what you want? Focus on getting the learner to evaluate his or her behavior. What can you do to get what you want? Focus on developing a plan that has a good chance to succeed.

The following dialogue between a teacher and a learner illustrates how C.A.R.E. time can be used.

Teacher:	Diana, have you finished the book report?
Diana:	No.
Teacher:	What are you doing?
Diana:	I'm listening to Tonya and Jason talk.
Teacher:	Is listening to Tonya and Jason right now helping you finish your book report that's due today?
Diana:	No.
Teacher:	What do you want?
Diana:	What do you mean?
Teacher:	Do you want to be a successful learner, a learner who does quality work?
Diana:	Yes.
Teacher:	Remember the life rule to be prompt. Is not finishing assignments on time going to help you be a successful person?
Diana:	No, I guess not.
Teacher:	Do you want to be a successful person?
Diana:	Yes.

> Teacher: What can you do to get what you want?
>
> Diana: I can go to the reading center and finish my report now.
>
> Teacher: Will you do that?
>
> Diana: Yes.

It is important to keep in mind that completion of work is usually a matter of relevance. The learner who fails to complete work often sees no purpose in completing the work other than the avoidance of unpleasant consequences. Thus, work completion becomes a compliant behavior, not a need-fulfilling behavior. When compliance is the reason for completing work, it will rarely be quality work, and it will rarely be done consistently.

In the school for quality learning, the problem with work completion is diminished because the worker has a choice in what to undertake. Even when activities are not of the learner's choice, the completion of those activities will be likely because the learner knows that he or she will have an opportunity to choose other activities later. In the school for quality learning, teachers and learners operate from a relationship of trust. The learner in effect says to himself or herself, "The teacher believes this is important, and the teacher respects me and understands my needs; therefore, I am willing to work hard at something the teacher believes is important." In the school for quality learning the teacher clearly relates the value of the learning activity each time an activity is presented. When there is a problem with work completion, the teacher demonstrates a caring attitude and a willingness to take time to help the learner resolve the problem.

Work completion problems are likely to arise when students fail to meet agreed-upon deadlines. This situation requires feedback and counseling from the teacher. Learners typically miss deadlines because they lack experience with time management and they have not made quality a prime concern. Time management problems usually take one or more of the following forms: (a) the learner underestimates the time required to complete the activity, (b) the learner underestimates the scope of the job—it is more complicated/detailed than he or she thought, or (c) the learner underestimates the quality—he or she does not fully visualize the goal (quality product) until the learning activity is well under way. Self-evaluation and planning during C.A.R.E. time will help the learner become a more efficient time manager.

In the school for quality learning, either the teacher or the learner may request C.A.R.E. time. Students need to know that frustration is part of learning and that it is permissible and advisable to request a conference with the teacher for help in addressing the problem.

Time-Out

The primary purpose of time-out is to temporarily remove the learner from a situation where he or she is disrupting the learning environment of others. It is not intended as punishment. Self-evaluation is the only way to promote long-term change in learner behavior. Time-out, when used properly, will encourage the learner to self-evaluate and make better behavioral choices. In the school for quality learning, the process follows a sports analogy. As in sports, school time-out is used to break momentum, evaluate the situation, and formulate a plan. The message should be "Something is out of sync, and we need to work it out." The plan that the learner develops in time-out emphasizes the positive behavior that he or she is willing to engage in when the learning activity is resumed—for example, "I will do my work and not disrupt others who are working" or "I'll keep my hands and feet to myself."

Time-out is an effective strategy only when the learner and the teacher perceive it as a favorable method for working out problems. If this is to happen, both the classroom atmosphere and the time-out must be positive and noncoercive. Time-out is in essence an opportunity for the learner to evaluate his or her behaviors. It is a process that enables the learner to determine that he or she is responsible for behavioral choices. In addition, time-out gives the learner a chance to develop the skills for making more effective behavioral choices.

The time-out location in the school for quality learning is comfortable and conducive to problem solving. It may be an area of a classroom or another, separate place in the school. When taking time-out, the learner needs a place to become calm, think about the situation, and develop a plan to return to classroom activities. The duration of the time-out is up to the learner. The teacher may set a minimum time to avoid further disruption of classroom activities, but ideally the learner returns to the group when he or she has an acceptable plan of action. The idea is to keep the learner in class and engaged in learning activities, not to interrupt his or her education. Time-out is, in a sense, a last resort. When a behavior problem occurs in the classroom, the teacher first attempts to work it out with the learner, using an in-class intervention.

In-Class Intervention

When a learner disrupts the class, the teacher may issue a command or ask questions to encourage the learner to evaluate his or her behavior. The command approach often invites resistance or confrontation; the question approach is preferable because it focuses the learner's attention on the behavior. The teacher can ask one question and continue with other classroom activities, perhaps without waiting for a verbal response. The intent is to have the learner answer the question for himself or herself. It is very difficult for the learner to avoid thinking about the question. The number and types of questions the teacher asks are determined by the severity of behavior, the activity under way, the learner involved, and so on. The tone must always be noncoercive. The following specific statements and questions are helpful.

1. To identify the expected and/or target behavior:
   "Please find a space to work on your own," "Please do your work quietly," or, preferably, "What are you doing?"

2. If the learner continues the unacceptable behavior:
   "What is the rule about *(specific behavior being challenged)*?" "Are you following our rule about this?" or "Is what you're doing against the rules?"

3. If the learner still does not stop the unacceptable behavior:
   "Are you choosing time-out?" or "Do you know what you need to do to stay in this classroom?" and "Will you do it?"

If the disruptive behavior continues after two or three interventions, it is best to talk briefly with the learner in private. If that isn't possible, the learner should go to the classroom time-out area. To end the time-out and return to classroom activities, the learner must formulate an action plan. The plan may be verbal or written, as the teacher prefers.

Verbal plan. The learner unobtrusively signals the teacher that he or she has a plan and would like to rejoin the group. As soon as possible the teacher goes to the time-out area and asks what the plan is. If the plan is acceptable, the learner returns to the classroom activities; if not, the learner stays in time-out to develop another plan. If possible, the teacher should talk with the learner about the plan. It is especially useful to relate the learner's plan—acceptable or unacceptable—to the behavior that triggered the time-out. A good way to do this is by asking questions—often the same questions the teacher asked before sending the learner to time-out.

Written plan. If the teacher prefers to use written plans, forms for these plans are kept in the time-out area. (Figure 16.1 shows a sample planning form.) The learner must complete the plan before signaling the teacher and returning to classroom activities. The teacher should approve the plan and, if possible, discuss it briefly with the learner. If a learner has trouble completing a plan, the teacher should help by raising the same questions used for C.A.R.E. time: "What do you want?" and "Is what you are doing helping you get what you want?"

Figure 16.1   Sample Planning Form for Time-Out Use

S.T.A.R. PLAN
(SUCCESS THROUGH ACTING RESPONSIBLY)

My behavior (What am I doing?)

_____

_____

_____

_____

My plan (I will . . .)

_____

_____

_____

_____

Name _____ Date _____

Out-of-Class Intervention

When a learner disrupts classroom activities while in the time-out area or fails to follow the plan developed in time-out, he or she may need to take time-out outside the classroom. If possible, the teacher should first discuss behavioral choices with the learner and ask if he or she is choosing time-out outside the classroom. If the unacceptable behavior still does not cease, the learner should be sent to the out-of-class time-out area.

The out-of-class time-out area is supervised by an adult who will encourage the learner to discuss what is happening, find an alternative to the problem behavior, and return to the classroom as soon as possible. The following dialogue between a time-out supervisor and a learner illustrates the use of reality therapy to help the learner change his behavior.

Supervisor: Sam, I understand there was a problem in class. Let's see if we can work it out.

Sam: Nobody ever listens to me.

Supervisor: I'll listen. Tell me what you were doing in class.

Sam: Allyn and Stefonce were teasing me about my haircut, and they made me mad. Mrs. Banks sent me here, and it's not my fault.

Supervisor: Allyn and Stefonce were making fun of your haircut, and you're mad at them. What did you do while they were teasing you?

Sam: I yelled at them. Mrs. Banks asked me if I was choosing time-out when I started yelling . . . they didn't stop laughing when she said that, so I just kept on yelling. She wouldn't listen to me. She said I was disrupting the class. It's not my fault.

Supervisor: Do you have a right to be happy and to be treated with compassion in the classroom?

Sam: Yes.

Supervisor: What's the responsibility that goes with that right?

Sam: Not to tease others or hurt anyone's feelings.

Supervisor: Do you have a right to hear and be heard in the classroom?

Sam: Yes.

Supervisor: What's the responsibility that goes with the right to hear and be heard?

Sam: Not to yell or scream or disturb others.

Supervisor: What were you doing?

Sam: I was yelling.

Supervisor: What do you want?

Sam: I want Mrs. Banks to make Stefonce and Allyn stop making fun of my hair.

Supervisor: You want Allyn and Stefonce to stop teasing you. Was it the teasing that got you in trouble, or was it what you chose to do when they teased you that got you in trouble?

Sam: They made me mad.

Supervisor: What did you choose to do when you got mad?

Sam: I yelled at them.

Supervisor: Did choosing to yell make them stop teasing you?

Sam: No, they laughed and kept on teasing me.

Supervisor: What do you really want?

Sam: I want to be in class with my friends. I don't want to be teased about my hair.

Supervisor: You want to be in class with your friends. You don't want to be teased about your hair. Is yelling helping you get what you want?

Sam: No.

Supervisor: What will help you get what you want?

Sam: I don't know.

Supervisor: Will yelling help you stay in class?

Sam: No.

Supervisor: What might help?

Sam: I don't know. Maybe not yelling?

Supervisor: Is that something you could do?

Sam: I suppose.

Supervisor: Do you want to be friends with Allyn and Stefonce?

Sam: Yes, if they stop teasing me.

Supervisor: If they tease you again, is there something other than yelling that you could choose to do?

Sam: I could walk away and talk to Mrs. Banks.

Supervisor: If you walked away and talked to Mrs. Banks, there are some different things she could do to help you solve the problem.

Sam: Like what?

Supervisor: She could call a class meeting and discuss the right to be happy and treated with compassion by others in the classroom and the responsibility to treat others with compassion. She could refer the three of you to mediation so you could work out your problem face-to-face without disrupting the classroom. Do either of those sound like plans that could help in the future?

Sam: Yes.

Supervisor: There is also something else that you might do instead of yelling.

Sam: There is? I can't think of anything.

Supervisor: You could tell Allyn and Stefonce how you feel. Say, "I want you to stop teasing. It hurts my feelings. You could remind them of the Rights and Responsibilities."

Sam: What if that doesn't work? I think they'd laugh at me if I said that to them.

Supervisor: What do you want your plan to be?

Sam: I won't yell and disrupt the class. I will ask for Mrs. Banks to help when I get mad.

Supervisor: Do you think this plan will work?

Sam: Yes.

Supervisor: Will you do it?

Sam: Yes.

The duration of time-out will vary for each learner. There is no benefit in holding a learner for a set length of time. Such a practice tends to breed resentment, anger, and a desire for revenge. A secondary school student may be kept for the remainder of the class period because he or she has already disrupted the classroom several times and returning may only create a further disruption. In an elementary school with self-contained classrooms, the learner is allowed to rejoin the class when he or she has developed a satisfactory plan.

In most schools there is a schoolwide time-out room, although it is probably not labeled as such. A learner who exhibits unacceptable behavior is usually referred through the disciplinary chain of command (counselor, principal, etc.). This system can rather easily be adapted to the time-out practices described here. We recommend that the learner be required to have an acceptable written plan before returning to class. A plan sheet similar to the in-class form can be used, and the time-out supervisor can help the learner develop the plan. A conference with the classroom teacher is also called for—not to punish the learner but to ensure that the plan has been thought through and that the learner has evaluated the previous behavior. This conference also reestablishes the teacher's and the learner's shared responsibility to preserve the learning environment and to strive for quality.

Mediation

Mediation is a method for negotiating disputes and finding resolutions that combines the needs of the parties instead of compromising those needs. It is a way for students to deal with differences without coercion. Mediation works well to resolve conflict in schools because through it students gain power. The more students become empowered to resolve their differences peacefully, the more responsibly they behave. (Schrumpf et al., 1991, p. 11)

Mediation is a step-by-step process that requires flexibility and spontaneity to respond to each situation. The mediator is pro-active—that is, the mediator is responsible for creating and maintaining an atmosphere that fosters mutual problem solving. Mediation may be conducted by the teacher in the classroom, by the time-out supervisor, by the principal, by a counselor, and so forth, or it may be conducted by trained peer mediators. Briefly, as Schrumpf et al. (1991) outline them, the steps in mediation are as follows:

1. Open the session: Establish the ground rules.

2. Gather information: Listen to both sides of the story.

3. Focus on common interests: Determine and summarize shared or compatible interests.

4. Create options for common interests: Brainstorm possible solutions.

5. Evaluate options and choose solutions: Decide what can be done to solve the problem.

6. Write the agreement: Write what each disputant agrees to do to solve the problem.

Mediation, like reality therapy, attempts to create a supportive environment in which individuals can begin to make changes in their behavior. Mediation promotes a positive classroom environment in which students learn a peaceful, need-fulfilling way to resolve conflict and achieve mutual respect through clear and direct communication. Table 16.3 outlines the steps for bringing about change through reality therapy and mediation.

CONCLUSION

It is absolutely essential for the lead-manager teacher to create a positive counseling environment in the classroom for quality learning. Learners need a friendly, supportive atmosphere to engage productively in self-evaluation and to risk trying new behaviors. A relationship of mutual appreciation and trust between the teacher and each learner is required for the development of quality behavior and quality learning. This important relationship is tested most critically in the classroom's responsibility education program. The success of each learner in achieving quality depends above all on the absence of coercion. The lead-manager

Table 16.3   Steps for Change in Reality Therapy and Mediation

	Reality therapy	**Mediation**
Actions that create a supportive counseling environment	Be friendly and listen to the learner's story.	State the ground rules:
		• The mediator remains neutral.
	Avoid discussing feelings and physiology as separate from total behaviors—relate feelings and physiology to current actions and thoughts.	• Everything said is kept confidential.
		• Each person talks without being interrupted.
		• Both learners will cooperate and do their best to find resolution.
	Do not allow the learner to focus on the past unless the events can be related to the present situation.	Get a commitment to the rules.
		Gather information:
		• Have learners tell their stories.
	Accept no excuses for irresponsible behavior.	• Summarize/clarify perceptions.
		Turn the focus to the present and future.
	Avoid punishing or criticizing the learner, or protecting him or her from the natural consequences of the behavior.	Avoid blaming and criticizing; separate the people from the problem.
Procedures that lead to change	Focus on the learner's total behaviors and help the learner realize that these behaviors are chosen.	Focus on interests, not positions.
		Determine learners' interests by asking, "What do you really want?" and "Did your (*behavior*) get you what you wanted?"
	Ask the learner what he or she wants now. Then expand this to the direction he or she would like to go. If the learner does not know, focus on the current chosen behaviors.	Interests define the problem. The most powerful interests are basic human needs.
	Ask the learner to evaluate: "Does your present behavior have a reasonable chance of getting you what you want? Will it take you in the direction you want to go?"	Have the learners evaluate their positions by asking, "What will happen if you do not find a resolution?"
		Create options for resolution by brainstorming solutions that meet the interests of both learners.
	Plan a new behavior through which the learner is more likely to meet his or her needs.	Evaluate options and decide what each learner is willing and able to do. Get a commitment to do it.
	Evaluate the plan to see if it has a good chance of success. Get a commitment from the learner to act on the plan.	Write the agreement. Remind learners that they may use mediation again in the future.
	Write the plan. Do not give up on the learner's ability to succeed.	

teacher's most important challenge is to consistently relate to learners noncoercively. Meeting this challenge is fundamental to the success of the school for quality learning. All of the crucial decisions outlined in the previous chapters can be nullified unless each learner fully accepts the responsibility to develop quality behavior. Only the teacher who abandons coercion can help students realize this goal. As Haim Ginott (1972) observes:

> I've come to a frightening conclusion that I am the decisive element in the classroom. It's my personal approach that creates the climate. It's my daily mood that makes the weather. As a teacher, I possess a tremendous power to make a child's life miserable or joyous. I can be a tool of torture or an instrument of inspiration. I can humiliate or humor, hurt or heal. In all situations, it is my response that decides whether a crisis will be escalated or de-escalated and a child humanized or dehumanized. (pp. 15–16)

CHAPTER 17

Learner Development: Assessment and Evaluation

Sweeping transformations in existing educational practices, including organization, decision making, curriculum, teaching strategies, and so on, have been advocated as prerequisites to the development of a school for quality learning. Perhaps the most critical and broadest of those transformations concerns evaluation of learning and of the learner. With the exception of the use of punishment to gain compliance (see chapter 16), evaluation is the current practice most antithetical to the development of quality. In fact, evaluation is a misnomer for the competitive, comparative system employed to judge and label learner achievement. The grading system, be it the typical A through F system, a numerical system, or a system of satisfactory-unsatisfactory ratings, is a summative way of comparing learners to one another. Such comparisons are contradictory to the philosophy of individualized learning. The grading system in education is a glaring example of bad practice according to Deming's (1986) Point 3 (cease dependence on mass inspection) and it is a case of the third deadly disease (evaluation by performance, merit rating, or annual review). It is also contrary to what Deming advises in Point 11 (eliminate numerical quotas) and Point 12 (remove barriers to pride of workmanship). Most important, current grading practices flagrantly contradict Deming's Point 8 (drive out fear). The grading system is the ultimate tool of the boss-manager teacher; grading is coercive.

Glasser (1969) argues that schools have inherent practices that limit success and increase failure among students. He maintains that

> the school practice that most produces failure in students is grading. . . . The only acceptable grades are good ones, and these good grades divide the school successes from school failures. Grades are so important that they become a substitute for education itself. . . . Grades have become moral equivalents. A good grade is correlated with good behavior, a bad grade with bad behavior, a correlation that unfortunately is very high. . . . Grades are the currency of education. The highest grades are worth the most in terms of honors and entrance into better schools (or programs) at every level. But, because grades are primarily measures of a student's ability to remember designated facts rather than to think, grades are often unable to indicate those who can do the most in the world. . . . A student has two choices: concentrate on grades and give up thinking; or concentrate on thinking and give up grades. (pp. 59–62)

Glasser further concludes, on the basis of extensive interviews with students over the years concerning the issue of grades, that students "believe that the line between passing and failing in our grading system lies just below 'B'; that is, the student who gets mostly 'C's' is essentially a failure in school because the only real passing grades are 'B' and 'A'" (p. 63).

An additional difficulty with the existing system, according to Glasser (1969), is that grades tend to become permanent labels:

> Another sinister attribute of grades is that they are limiting and damning for life. In a world that sometimes judges people by their records rather than by themselves, a student with low grades has little chance to advance to higher education. . . . Although we know that people do change, that people mature at different rates, that temporary personal problems can cause failure not attributable to inability to learn or think, the grade remains and cannot be wiped out. . . . As long as we label people

failures at some time in their lives and then damn them for the rest of their lives for this failure through grades, we will perpetuate misery, frustration, and delinquency. (pp. 63–64)

Moreover, grades actually encourage cheating. When grades become the currency of the system, those who are greedy for the available riches will do whatever is necessary to obtain good ones, including cheating and deceiving. Although grades purportedly raise academic standards, there is good evidence that just the opposite is true. Grades actually constrain learning: The learner who wishes to succeed will spend considerable mental energy trying to determine what will be the basis of the grade and will spend little effort trying to learn anything not directly related to the grade. In practice, grading systems usually incorporate numerical quotas—a certain percentage of students may receive A's, a certain percentage B's, and so on. The use of grades is thus antithetical to Deming's Point 11 (eliminate numerical quotas).

Grades as used in most secondary schools actually limit the development of talent. Learners with talent, especially in areas such as music, drama, and athletics, have little opportunity to express that talent unless they earn adequate grades. They are not permitted to participate in extracurricular activities unless they show acceptable grades in academic areas that may be only remotely related to their talents. This practice restricts students' opportunities for need fulfillment. If a learner were allowed to succeed in an area of interest and talent, that success might create a sense of belonging and power that could lead to increased success in academic and other areas. Glasser states that the current grading system is not logically defensible. He theorizes that "most teachers hate [grades]. They believe they are harmful to education because they take time away from teaching; they believe they are inaccurate; and they believe they reduce the warm, human involvement possible and necessary between teacher and student" (1969, p. 68).

The grading system certainly has a long history. It is without doubt the most entrenched convention in education. Its survival is an interesting paradox. Few educators overtly defend current practice; instead, they attribute the use of grades to factors beyond their control. One argument is that parents desire grades. On the surface, this may appear persuasive. But we must ask, Do parents really desire grades, or do they not know of an alternative? Parents understand grades—as much as one can understand an illogical system—because grades are part of their own school experience. They probably also encountered the use of grades beyond the school setting as they sought to enter higher education, vocational training, military service, or the job market. But would parents opt for grades if offered an alternative such as a report detailing their child's strengths and weaknesses as a learner, the effort that the child is expending, and the child's demonstrated learning outcomes? Wouldn't they opt for a reporting process that offered them suggestions for helping their child become a better learner?

Defenders of the grading system often argue that competition is fundamental to our society and that participating in a competitive system early on prepares the learner for the realities of life. This argument is based on several myths about competition: that competition is part of human nature and is an inevitable fact of life; that competition motivates one to do one's best; that without competition one would cease to be productive; that competition builds character and is good for self-confidence; that competition in the form of contests is the best way to have fun. Competition in the learning environment, as in any endeavor, creates winners and losers. It also suppresses learners' inclination to work cooperatively. On the other hand, when learners are encouraged to cooperate, combining their talents and energies so that as many as possible can achieve the desired result, the system becomes a win/win instead of a win/lose system. Learning by all individuals is the outcome of a win/win system; in the win/lose system, grades, not learning, become the outcome.

Grades are necessary in school, argue some, because colleges and potential employers require them. This is similar to the argument that parents want grades. Is there an alternative that would provide a college or a prospective employer better, more reliable information? Some educators—perhaps the more honest ones—maintain that grades are necessary because, if it weren't for grades, students wouldn't listen or exert any effort in school. This view reflects the use of grades to force irrelevant activities on students. This is the position of the boss manager who subscribes to the theory X view of the learner (McGregor, 1961; see chapter 6).

The foregoing arguments for the grading system may have been persuasive under the industrial worldview, but they do not fit with our information- and knowledge-based worldview. Competitive structures must be replaced with collaborative ones. The desired outcomes of the school for quality learning cannot be realized in a system in which the most important dimension of the learning activity, evaluation, is handled in a manner that completely contradicts the philosophy. It is highly unlikely that a school that retains grades, regardless of changes in the way they are awarded or defined, can develop an evaluation system that contributes to the full involvement in quality learning of each learner.

In chapters 14, 15, and 16, we listed nine decisions the teacher should make to begin developing the classroom for quality learning. The final, most critical decision relates to evaluation.

DECISION 10. The teacher should establish a plan for evaluating learning and individual learners. The aim should be to increase learners' involvement in the critical evaluation dimension of the learning activity and help them understand the nature of quality in both the process and the products of learning.

The lead-manager teacher recognizes that designing an evaluation system means addressing two distinct but not entirely separate issues. Evaluating learning—or, more precisely, evaluating the learning activities and helping the learners understand the nature of quality—may be primarily a group or whole-class activity. On the other hand, evaluating the individual learner's process and assessing the quality of the individual learner's product is primarily a private matter.

GROUP EVALUATION

To function productively in an individualized learning program, students need to understand themselves and the learning process. An excellent vehicle for developing this understanding is the learning process seminar. It is similar to the social-problem-solving class meeting described in chapter 16, but it focuses on learning and learning behaviors rather than social behaviors. At times it is possible to integrate the social-problem-solving class meeting and the learning process seminar into a single session.

The learning process seminar brings the students and the teacher together as a community of learners to share their feelings and their understandings about the learning activities in progress. It lets them take time out from those activities and focus on what has happened, discuss what is happening, theorize about what might happen, and reflect on how it all affects the attitudes, behaviors, and knowledge of each person involved. The seminar is a sort of laboratory in human dynamics. It allows for the development of communication skills and the building of interpersonal relationships. Examining behavior and trying out new behaviors are encouraged; ideas and theories are tested; quality is demonstrated and diagnosed.

A successful learning process seminar depends on certain conditions that ensure involvement and relevance. The teacher establishes the following conditions:

1. The group may range in size from a few learners and the teacher to the entire class. All group members are expected to participate actively in the discussion. The discussion should be open-ended and focus on learning rather than doing. From the perspective of evaluation, the question, What did you do? is of little value. Instead, the questions, What did you learn and How did you learn it? help the learner assess quality.

2. Equality in communication must be established. No group member has special privileges, especially not the teacher. Each member is important, and all may give and receive feedback as they test ideas or behaviors.

3. Trust must be established within the group, and judgment must be suspended during the seminar. Feedback is the rule, but only the recipient should make judgments about that feedback outside the group, especially when those judgments concern evaluation of the learner or the learner's product.

4. Honesty in communication and feedback is vital. The purpose of the seminar is to help all participants develop as fully as possible. People need to know where they are now in order to grow.

5. The rule of focus should be followed so that each idea is treated fully and each person has full opportunity to expose ideas and behaviors to the group. The rule of focus requires that the person revealing the idea or behavior be the one to determine when the discussion may take a different direction. Others who wish to contribute do so by helping that person clarify or better understand the idea or behavior under discussion.

Following are some questions that might guide a learning process seminar:

1. What do you consider when you decide what to learn?

2. How do you know you have learned something?

3. What have you learned?

4. How did you learn it?

5. What do you expect from school?

6. What do you enjoy learning?

7. What is easy for you to learn?

8. What is difficult?

9. What information sources have you found useful? Useless?

10. How do you solve problems?

11. What problems do you want to solve?

12. How do you decide if you have done a good job?

13. What do you think the learning facilitator should be doing?

14. What kind of feedback is important to you?

15. What are all the different ways you can think of to get information?

16. What is a hypothesis? A generalization?

17. How do you form a hypothesis?

18. How can a hypothesis be tested?

19. How do you form a generalization?

20. What organizing strategies do you use to help yourself learn?

21. What are all the different ways you can show someone else what you have learned?

22. If you needed help, where would you go?

23. Who would you ask to help?

24. Whom could you help and under what conditions would you help that person?

25. What frustrates you in your attempts to learn?

26. How do you know something is your best effort?

Discussion of these questions gives learners the opportunity to broaden their repertoires of learning strategies and to find out how others define quality. The seminar can effectively establish expectations for both the learning process and the learning product. Individuals may identify other learners with whom they might fruitfully collaborate. Learners can give and receive assistance with learning problems, processes, or evaluations. Hearing how others respond to a question gives each learner better insight into the multiple criteria that can be applied to learning and the range of possible judgments. Some of the questions raised in the learning process seminar are also appropriate for the lead-manager teacher to raise with individuals to facilitate their evaluation of their own learning.

INDIVIDUAL EVALUATION

The second aspect of evaluation involves the individual learner and the quality of the learner's process and product. Traditionally, individual evaluation has relied heavily on the objective test. Glasser (1969) asserts that an

> educational practice that helps produce mediocre educa-
> tion is objective testing. . . . Objective tests, except in rare
> instances, are passed by memorizing facts and regurgi-
> tating them correctly, a process that eliminates thinking
> by its total emphasis on the answer. A requirement to
> obtain correct answers gives little encouragement to
> learners to think independently. School is often thought
> of as a place where there are right answers to relatively
> simple questions of fact. We should change this image
> by improving the questions to ask for answers involving
> thinking. . . . Objective tests, which by their nature deal
> only with the known, frustrate effort toward more
> thinking in school. . . . Objective tests discourage
> research, discourage thoughtful reading, discourage
> listening to anything but fact. . . . Many objective tests
> require little more of the student than memorizing the
> jargon of the particular subject, thus emphasizing words
> rather than the ideas behind them. (pp. 69–70)

In practice, the objective test usually signifies the end of the learning activity. The learner is judged (graded) on the basis of test performance. If the performance is poor, the learner receives a low grade or fails and is then expected to go on to the next learning activity. Objective tests might be at least minimally useful if the results were used to show the learner which material needed further study or even if the teacher used the results to determine what needed to be retaught. That is seldom the case, however, and the close marriage of test scores to grades at best renders objective tests nearly useless and very probably makes them counterproductive in terms of quality learning.

Objective tests, especially standardized achievement tests, are not really designed to assess what has been learned. They are usually administered under unnatural conditions and actually assess how well the learner can perform under those conditions. Nearly all tests are closed-book examinations based on the assumption that knowledge remembered is superior to knowledge looked up. Nearly all tests are strictly time monitored. Time-restricted tests place a premium on speed of recollection rather than on quality production. Typical objective test conditions create psychological barriers to performance by increasing the test taker's anxiety or, at least, by doing nothing to reduce that anxiety.

The lead-manager teacher will depend very little on objective tests to assess learner performance. This is not to say that paper-and-pencil assessment instruments (of which objective tests are only one example) have no place in the school for quality learning. They may provide an effective way to judge the mastery of subject matter and (in the case of subjective tests) the development of thinking skills. However, paper-and-pencil tests will not be the exclusive—or probably even the predominant—method for assessing learning. Performance assessments based on the teacher's observation of the learner or the learner's product and on direct personal communication between teacher and learner will be very important. The teacher needs a full range of assessment options—paper-and-pencil instruments, observational assessments, and personal communication with the learners individually and as a group—to gather the data required for good decisions about the learning environment, learning activities, and individual learners. Formal and informal assessment is crucial for each learner; it enables the teacher to effectively question the learner during the evaluation process. Moreover, the teacher must possess quality assessment techniques to adequately facilitate learner self-evaluation.

To offer proof of quality learning, the learner must perform an exemplary task, exhibit an exemplary product, or give an exemplary explanation of something that cannot be demonstrated or displayed. The lead-manager teacher involves each learner in a self-evaluation process designed to achieve two outcomes: (a) to assess the quality of the product dimension of the learning activity and (b) to obtain feedback that will lead to improved problem definition, improved process selection, and a higher quality product in future learning activities. Individual learners should be involved in continually evaluating their efforts and outcomes.

Obviously, the best way to promote this self-evaluation is through frequent face-to-face interaction between the learner and the teacher. Because each teacher will be responsible for several learners, evaluation conferences will probably be less frequent than desired. It is important to establish learner-managed evaluation activities that will make the evaluation conferences as meaningful and efficient as possible.

Each learner should maintain a learning activity log that would provide a written record of the learner's activities between conferences with the teacher and would also require the learner to analyze his or her activities and process. Figure 17.1 shows a sample learning activity log.

Prior to each conference, the learner should also be asked to select an agreed-upon number of learning products to share with the teacher. Examples of those products might be the learner's best piece of writing, best problem solution, best product, and best verbal demonstration of something learned. The learner is really building a portfolio. At intervals, the learner might be asked to choose any item from the portfolio and improve upon it.

Figure 17.1   Sample Learning Activity Log

LEARNING ACTIVITY LOG

Learning activity (Problem attempted)	Learning process (What I did; it was useful/useless)	I learned that . . .

Products of learning activities are nearly unlimited. A reenactment, a speech, a monologue, a newscast, a role-play, a skit, a panel discussion, a game show, a diorama, an expressive reading, a play, a video, an original comic strip, a poster, a scale model, a survey, a flowchart, a graph, a computer program, a three-dimensional display or model, a knowledge cube, a collection, a scrapbook, a collage, a bulletin board, and an experiment are examples of concrete products that a learner or group of learners might offer to exhibit proficiency in a learning activity. The lead-manager teacher encourages variety and originality in the creation of learning products and encourages learners to share them because such products are themselves a learning resource for others. However, evidence of learning and growth toward quality also takes intangible forms. Attitudinal changes, improved verbal descriptions and discussion of activities, signs of self-directive behavior or self-discipline, emergence of leadership qualities, broadening of interests, greater self-awareness, identification of personal goals, and deepening commitment to beliefs and concerns are also clear signals that a learner is growing and pursuing quality.

The learner comes to each evaluation conference with quality samples and a record of learning activities pursued since the last conference. The learner has already applied some evaluation criteria to the activities and has made some judgments. Learners should be encouraged to obtain feedback from others besides the teacher—from peers, other resource persons, experts, family members, and so on—and to use this feedback in choosing quality samples to share with the teacher. The lead-manager teacher attempts to clarify the presentation and challenge the learner with questions. Sample questions, in no specific order, are presented here:

1. Why did you choose this sample?

2. What makes you proud of this?

3. Why do you think this worked for you?

4. What did not work?

5. Where do you see yourself going with this idea?

6. Do you want to pursue it?

7. Are you on the right track?

8. Do you have a plan?

9. Do you need to change plans? Can you?

10. What other things do you want to learn?

11. Did anything surprise you?

12. If you were to do anything here over again, do you think you could do better?

13. Do you want to do anything over?

14. Would you like to submit this to someone else for an opinion? Who?

Group learning activities can be evaluated in the same manner, with the teacher-learner conference including all those involved rather than an individual student.

THE ISSUE OF STANDARDIZED TESTING

Standardized achievement testing will undoubtedly be an issue to be confronted in the school for quality learning. These tests are useless in assessing individual learning and do little to enlighten the teacher about the overall performance of the class. Earlier in this chapter we noted the detrimental effects of standardized tests and especially the detrimental effects of exhortations to improve performance on these tests. Standardized test items are usually kept secret, hidden from learners and teachers; this practice contradicts the most basic conditions required for learning. All assertions made about objective tests earlier in this chapter are doubly true for standardized achievement tests. By constraining curriculum and frustrating teachers and learners, standardized achievement tests undermine rather than foster school improvement. Rather than promoting accountability, standardized tests place control and authority in the hands of an unregulated testing industry.

The lead-manager principal and teachers will not allow tests to drive the curriculum or to limit the learners' and the teachers' choice of learning activities. The lead-manager teacher will not teach to the test, understanding that test performance has nothing to do with quality learning. However, because testing is a fact of life and standardized tests are likely to affect learners in future endeavors—for instance, admission to postsecondary institutions or programs—the opportunity for learners to develop test-taking skills is a responsibility the teacher might well accept. Simply helping to develop strategies for reducing anxiety may improve performance on standardized tests considerably. Such strategies include, among others, answering all questions you know first, not spending time on questions you cannot answer quickly, and guessing rather than leaving a question unanswered. Explaining that no test taker is expected to answer all questions correctly may also reduce learner anxiety and improve performance.

Even the most ardent proponents of national standards and accountability differentiate between tests and exams. They argue that American students take too many tests (indicators of skills unrelated to the curriculum) but too few exams (assessments for which students can prepare). Ruth Mitchell (1992) asserts that "a verbal confusion is muddying the debate about a national system of standards and assessments. The words 'test' and 'assessment' are being used as if they were synonymous" (p. 34). Mitchell holds that the two terms reflect two radically different models of education; the terms, she maintains, must be clarified if any debate about national standards and assessments is to be meaningful.

According to Mitchell (1992),

> tests are machine scored, usually multiple choice and norm referenced. Their essence is speed, cheapness, and psychometric respectability. Assessments . . . are not machine scored, and vary in length and in what they require students to do. Their essence is the active production of response by the student. (p. 34)

Tests, in Mitchell's view, are compatible with a "factory" model of education in which students are passive recipients of discrete bits of information and a premium is placed on the ability to memorize and to recognize "right" and "wrong" answers. Tests are used to track students and to determine access to learning opportunities. Assessments, by contrast, are open-ended and require the active application of knowledge and skills to meaningful problems. They imply a "community of learners" model in which each individual is challenged to develop intellectually, socially, and emotionally. Mitchell states that "using tests to measure progress in schools where change is taking place is wrong-headed. So too is the claim that accountability requires a different kind of measurement than classroom assessment" (p. 34). Finally, she concludes that

> Adopting a national system of standards and assessments—not a national test—implies a national endorsement of the "community of learners" model. Performance assessment should be seen in the context of the model: It is by no means a panacea and should not be regarded

as more than a useful instrument. It is one of many
factors (for example, cooperative learning, whole language, active learning, the community as classroom, the
student as worker) that undermines the factory model
and provokes that asking of fundamental questions about
the purposes of education. (p. 35)

It is debatable whether a national system of standards and assessments can lead to improvement in our educational system, as
proponents argue that it will. The question in the school for quality learning is, Will such a system of national standards actually
promote quality, or will such a system produce an averaging effect, with poor performers showing gains and quality performers
declining? Further, will a national system pay respect to the desired outcomes of the school for quality learning, or will the
national standards be trivial and mundane? Regardless of the
answers to these and related questions, assessment is central to
the evaluation process that will help produce quality learners and
quality learning products.

The evaluation system in the school for quality learning will
usually include three components: exams (curriculum-related
assessments for which teachers help learners prepare by gearing
learning activities to desired knowledge outcomes); portfolios of
student work; and long-term projects. Rather than simply requiring learners to regurgitate facts, as do most teacher-designed objective tests, the exams would feature essays and performances
assessed by the teacher and/or other learners. For example, a
learner might be asked to demonstrate practical literacy skills by
following written instructions and diagrams to assemble a piece
of equipment. A simulated economics game played by a group
might be used to determine how well the learners work together.
Portfolios and projects are longer term efforts. A portfolio, maintained as the record of learner achievement, is a compilation of
the learner's best works, such as lab reports, term papers, creative writing assignments, and problem-solving activities. A project, which might well be done by a group, could entail building a
physical model, investigating an aspect of community life, or
completing a challenging laboratory experiment.

In the school for quality learning, the assessment program
will include a strong element of learner self-evaluation. It will
constitute a record of learner activities and accomplishments and
will provide an ever-rising bench mark in the learner's pursuit of
quality. Progress reports to parents or to other interested parties
will not be summative. Rather, they will be delivered either in a

written narrative or in a personal conference. Ideally, the evaluation report will be prepared by the teacher and the learner together and will be supported by the sample of learning products in the student's portfolio.

CHAPTER 18

Behaviors Beyond Effective Teaching

Research on teaching during the 1970s and 1980s by educational researchers such as Jere Brophy, Madeline Hunter, David Berliner, Jane Stallings, Barak Rosenshine, Lee Shulman, and many others resulted in a compilation of teaching behaviors characteristic of teachers judged effective according to the researchers' criteria. Those behaviors include some that are best called management behaviors and others best characterized as didactic behaviors (a somewhat artificial distinction because classroom management and instruction are intertwined and interdependent).

Following are management behaviors associated with effective teaching.

Establishes a learning environment. Effective teachers establish rapport with their students and provide a pleasant and orderly environment that is conducive to learning. Effective teachers maintain a businesslike—or, more precisely, a learning-like—atmosphere and convey a sense that learning and teaching are important. The classroom is functional, attractive, and orderly, with a warm, accepting climate in which learners are valued and respected. The effective teacher conveys the belief that all students can learn, reinforces their learning efforts, and establishes challenge in lessons while holding varying levels of expectation that allow each learner to experience success.

Establishes a learning routine. Effective teachers maximize time on task by using minimum class time for noninstructional routines. Lessons begin promptly, and the entire class period is devoted to learning. Distractions and unnecessary delays are avoided.

Maintains discipline. Effective teachers clearly define expected behavior. Positive behavior is encouraged and recognized, and negative behavior is controlled. Self-discipline is promoted, and disruptive behavior is corrected constructively. Classroom rules are clearly defined and are understood by all learners. The effective teacher actively monitors learner behavior during class periods, using positive reinforcement to perpetuate appropriate behavior.

Prepares for instruction. Effective teachers plan carefully and thoroughly for instruction. Their lessons are clear and logical, following a sequential format. Every lesson relates to both short- and long-term objectives that are compatible with the academic goals of the classroom and the school. Information about individual learners is used in selection of activities to meet individual and group needs. Lessons are focused and structured to utilize time efficiently, and all necessary materials and supplies are readily available.

Didactic behaviors characteristic of effective teachers include the following.

Establishes objectives. Effective teachers clearly and logically communicate to learners the purpose of the desired learning and the objectives of the lesson. They ensure that those objectives are consistent with the readiness of the learners. Effective teachers relate current topics and learning objectives to previous ones. Effective teachers also build anticipation by suggesting how current topics relate to future learning. Effective teachers use a variety of strategies and techniques to relate learning objectives to the learners' experiences and to show learners how the learning will be useful in their lives.

Involves learners. Effective teachers use a variety of techniques, such as signaled responses, group response, random recitation, and questioning, to involve all learners actively. They demonstrate the ability to work with individuals, plan questions for specific learners that result in correct responses, and diagnose learning in the course of the lesson. Effective teachers respond positively to questions from learners.

Explains content. Effective teachers display a thorough knowledge of subject matter. They use a variety of teaching methods to reinforce learning. They adopt a multisensory approach to provide variety and to appeal to the various learning modes— visual, auditory, tactile, and kinesthetic. Effective teachers use task analysis to divide complex tasks or concepts into discrete steps or components. Effective teachers present ideas logically and emphasize the importance of the concepts being taught.

Explains directions. Effective teachers give directions that are clear and that relate to the learning objective, whether the directions concern procedures, activities, or equipment. Individual or group assignments are specific and clear. Effective teachers make sure learners understand the organization of lesson content.

Models learning outcomes. Effective teachers demonstrate or arrange for the demonstration of the attainment of desired learning outcomes. They are skilled in conveying lesson content in clear and understandable terms, and they use demonstration where possible to provide a variety of outcome models that are visual, auditory, tactile, and kinesthetic.

Monitors learning. Effective teachers continually monitor learners' behavior to determine whether they are progressing toward the stated objective. Effective teachers check learners' understanding at various levels of the learning activity, from simple recall of basic information presented to analysis, inference, and the like. Learners are routinely asked to elaborate on their responses and, at various stages, to demonstrate proficiency in applying the knowledge acquired on the way to the ultimate learning outcome. Effective teachers question skillfully and give the learner enough time to answer before moving on to another learner or another question. Effective teachers provide frequent feedback to learners.

Adjusts instruction. Effective teachers heed the results of their monitoring and adapt their instructional strategies accordingly. Effective teachers accommodate individuals' different learning styles and learning rates. Effective teachers establish individual expectations to challenge each learner to maximum productivity. Varying levels of critical thinking and decision making can be elicited selectively from different learners. Effective teachers use a variety of evaluation techniques to monitor learning and to determine the instructional adjustments required.

Guides practice. Effective teachers require all learners to practice new learning while under direct teacher supervision. Effective teachers are physically active during practice sessions, moving from learner to learner and giving each immediate feedback or correction. Learners are challenged by teacher questions and are encouraged to ask questions about new learning objectives. Effective teachers group learners with similar needs for practice sessions.

Provides for independent practice. Effective teachers expect learners to practice skills without direct teacher supervision but only after guided practice has shown that the learners understand what is expected.

Establishes closure. Effective teachers summarize and place into context what has been learned in each lesson. They tie the current lesson to prior learning and set the stage for what will be learned next. The "why" of the learning is reiterated.

Richard F. Elmore (1992), commenting on the research on teacher effectiveness, finds that body of research

> based on the compellingly simple idea that teaching
> could be reduced to a few relatively straightforward
> behaviors that are reliably related to student achieve-
> ment. These behaviors are "generic," in the sense that
> they can be applied across different subjects and differ-
> ent groups of students. These effective teaching behav-
> iors were inferred by observing differences among
> teachers who were judged to be more and less effective
> in inducing certain types of learning in students, control-
> ling for student background. Hence, effective teaching
> behaviors were thought to be robust across variations in
> content and student background. (p. 44)

Elmore notes that research on effective teaching followed the same general approach. Further, the prescription for effective teaching and effective schools advanced in that literature does not depart significantly from existing practice:

> When you begin by studying the effects of marginal
> variations in behavior among existing teachers and
> schools, you are constrained by existing conventions—

the prescriptions you produce will be very close to existing practice.

Indeed, the marginal nature of effective teaching and effective schools research explains their popularity with practitioners. The changes they prescribe are relatively easy to understand and relatively unthreatening because they involve relatively small changes in existing practice. (p. 44)

According to Richard S. Prawat (1992), the body of research that came to be known as teacher effectiveness research involved the use of various teacher observation instruments and traditional measures of student achievement as the index to determine what technical skills more effective teachers possessed:

> In an approach elegant in its simplicity, researchers sat in the back of a classroom and noted the specifics of how teachers managed and instructed a class. . . . Across several teacher effectiveness studies, consistent relation- ships emerged: Teachers who were more effective in producing gains in student achievement were well organized, minimized student disruptions by monitoring behavior, and enforced rules in a consistent manner. Effective teachers programmed their instruction to ensure success. They proceeded through the material in small, quickly grasped steps and carefully asked ques- tions that engendered short, correct answers. (p. 10)

Teacher effectiveness research, and to a lesser degree school effectiveness research, exerted and continues to exert a powerful influence. The curricula of many teacher education programs are based on the prescriptions of that research. A large variety of inservice teacher development programs designed to instill effec- tive behaviors are commercially available. Many administrators, because of district or even state requirements, use criteria drawn from the teacher effectiveness research as the basis for teacher evaluations.

Relative to the expectations for the lead-manager teacher in the school for quality learning, teacher effectiveness research has at least three serious shortcomings. First, in that research, teachers were judged effective if their students' achievement levels, as measured primarily by standardized tests, increased as a result of instruction. We have stressed the irrelevance of standardized tests for assessing learning outcomes in the school for quality learning. Second, the narrow criteria of standardized test scores confirm only the learning that occurs in school and only fragmented, measurable pieces of that in-school learning. Third, teacher effectiveness research focused primarily on teachers' didactic behaviors, and training programs that apply the prescriptions of that research are designed to increase teachers' proficiency in didactic behaviors geared to whole-group instruction. In the school for quality learning, the focus is primarily on the teacher as manager of the learners and the learning environment; there is much less need for and emphasis on didactic behaviors.

There is a fourth problem that is not a problem with the research per se but rather a problem created by training programs that draw on the research to prescribe behaviors to be acquired through training. The implication, if not the result, of such training programs was the standardization of a set of teaching behaviors across content areas and across student groups. Because these behaviors did not represent significant change from existing practice, many teachers in the training would assert, "I've been doing that all along" or, perhaps more honestly, "Good teachers have always used these strategies." The training, even if taken seriously, seldom translated into changes in actual classroom behavior. The school for quality learning, by contrast, requires a change in teacher behavior. The behavior of the lead-manager teacher is a significant departure from what the teacher effectiveness research characterizes as ideal. When faced with the responsibilities of the lead-manager teacher, very few teachers will be able to claim truthfully, "I have been doing this for a long time in my classroom."

Current educational research also appears to challenge the prescriptions of the teacher effectiveness research. Prawat (1992) attributes this fact to the growing influence of cognitive psychologists, who—building on Piaget's work—have begun to listen seriously to what young people say, as well as to the influence of educational anthropologists and cultural psychologists, who have highlighted the role of context or community in explaining what young people know:

> Piaget alerted us that "real learning" is not simply the parroting back of information. Real learning involves personal *invention* or *construction*, and the teacher's role in the process is a difficult one. On the one hand, the teacher must honor students' "inventions," or they will not share them. On the other hand, the teacher needs to guide students toward a more mature understanding,

which frequently means challenging student constructions. . . . For classrooms to be centers of intellectual inquiry, students and teachers must feel free to pursue ideas and make mistakes.

Anthropologists and cultural psychologists remind us that context plays a key role in shaping and constraining individual learning. Some of the most interesting work contrasts learning in the classroom with learning in out-of-school contexts; these studies often highlight the shortcomings associated with our traditional, didactic approach to formal education. . . . The learning that people do outside of school frequently surpasses what they can do in the classroom. . . . The suspension of sense-making seems to be less common in out-of-school settings. . . . Meaningful activity is perhaps the most salient feature of out-of-school learning. Out-of-school learning focuses on overall goals and strategies, the "big picture," rather than on isolated details. In the classroom, students are expected to master the details and may never see the big picture. . . . Shared activity is another key feature of out-of-school learning. . . . Collaborative learning tends to be more the norm than the exception. In contrast, the focus in school is almost always on the individual. (pp. 11–12)

Even when the focus of research is on subject matter teaching, the principles and practices that promote student understanding and higher order applications of knowledge seem more expansive than the behaviors suggested by the effectiveness research. Jere Brophy (1992) lists the following elements common to programs that successfully promote understanding and application of the subject matter:

1. The curriculum is designed to equip students with knowledge, skills, values, and dispositions useful both inside and outside of school.

2. Instructional goals underscore developing student expertise within an application context and with emphasis on conceptional understanding and self-regulated use of skills.

3. The curriculum balances breadth with depth by addressing limited content but developing this content sufficiently to foster understanding.

4. The content is organized around a limited set of powerful ideas such as key understandings and principles.

5. The teacher's role is not just to present information but also to support, challenge, and respond to students' learning.

6. The student's role is not just to absorb or copy but to actively make sense and construct meaning.

7. Activities and assignments feature authentic tasks that call for problem solving or critical thinking, not just memory or reproduction.

8. Higher-order thinking skills are not taught as a separate skills curriculum but those skills are developed in the process of teaching subject matter knowledge within application contexts that call for students to relate what they are learning to their lives outside of school by thinking critically or creatively about the information or by using the information to solve problems or make decisions.

9. The teacher creates a social environment in the classroom that could be described as a learning community where dialogue promotes understanding. (p. 6)

Gaea Leinhardt (1992) states that research during the last decade on the nature of learning on such topics as authentic activity, apprenticeship learning, case-based research, conceptual change, constructivism, distributed knowledge, narrative/episodic knowledge structure, and socially shared cognition embraces three fundamental constructs that have consequence for teaching: (a) the multiple forms of knowledge, (b) the role of prior knowledge, and (c) the social nature of knowledge and its application:

First, the recognition that there are multiple kinds of knowledge suggests that neither teaching simple hierarchies of actions nor simply having students work with hands-on material in an unfocused way will result in the deep, conceptual kind of learning that we hope students gain.

Second, the recognition that students bring prior knowledge to new learning suggests that teachers need to make this knowledge explicit, then build upon it or, if necessary, challenge it.

Third, the recognition of the social nature of knowledge and learning suggests that when students talk to each other, they rehearse the terminology, notational systems, and manner of reasoning in a particular domain, thus reducing the individual burden of complete mastery of material while keeping the vision of the entire task in view. By building upon the social nature of learning, we may be able to solve some of the problems of mechanistic and fragile knowledge that seem to have plagued our educational system. (p. 24)

These three constructs have important implications for transforming the practices of teaching and learning in classrooms and schools.

Elmore (1992) concludes that

the research on effective teaching and effective schools held out the promise that student learning could be improved by marginal changes in teachers' behavior and school structure. The implicit message of this research was a reassuring one: Model your actions on practices already proven to be successful in real classrooms and schools.

Current research on teaching and learning has opened up a new set of challenges for educational researchers, practitioners, and policymakers. It suggests that teaching practice and school organization should be based on a whole new conception of how students learn. The implicit message is considerably less reassuring: Model your actions on practices that promote conceptual understanding. These practices, by definition, are more likely to require changes in teaching and organization that are far from marginal.

Closing the gap between teaching practice and school structure in the future will require a new kind of thinking. Traditionally, we have acted as if a more or less standard set of structural solutions to the regularities of schooling would suffice for all students in all schools, or at least for most students, and for the rest we could develop "special" programs with somewhat different structural features. The consequence of this approach is that we have held structure more or less constant, and insisted that variations among students and teaching practices accommodate the structure. Now, research on teaching and learning suggests a very different attitude toward structure.

This new attitude is that structure should permit teaching practices that are consistent with the objective of developing conceptual understanding. . . . Rather than school structure driving practice, teaching practice will drive structure. (pp. 47–48)

Part 2 of this book outlined a school management plan that provides each individual classroom teacher maximum flexibility to organize a learning environment and to employ teaching behaviors that will afford each learner full opportunity to engage in quality learning. Part 3 has outlined a classroom management plan that provides each individual learner maximum flexibility to realize the outcomes of the school for quality learning. The fulfillment of the school's mission depends upon extraordinary accomplishments by the principal and by each teacher in all dimensions of this plan.

The job responsibilities of the lead-manager teacher vary considerably from the expectations of the effective teacher set forth in the literature. In some respects, the difference is only in degree or emphasis, but in many other respects the difference represents significant qualitative change—a new philosophy. These differences require the lead-manager teacher to cultivate and refine specific attitudes and behaviors. Some of these attitudes and behaviors are very different from those generally expected of teachers; some differ only in degree, but that difference is nonetheless crucial. The following attitudes and behaviors beyond effective teaching characterize the lead-manager teacher.

Understanding of quality. The lead-manager teacher must have an internalized and intuitive understanding of the psychological framework of quality. The teacher knows and uses reality therapy and understands control theory as it applies to school life and to learning. The teacher thoroughly understands the learners' needs and wants and can generate multiple strategies to help individual learners understand their own needs and wants.

View of power. The lead-manager teacher, like everyone, has a need for power. The position of teacher in the school for quality learning, more than in other schools, is a position of acknowledged power. The teacher enjoys considerable autonomy in fulfilling the important responsibility of developing a classroom environment that will offer quality learning opportunities to every learner. The lead-manager teacher interprets power as the freedom to exercise that responsibility with a minimum of bureaucratic or managerial constraints rather than the ability and status to dictate to others—especially the learners—what they will or will not do. The lead-manager teacher manages the classroom and the learners without coercion, developing and using the skills of persuasion, reason, and challenge to help learners grow.

Collaboration. The lead-manager teacher needs to address collaboration at two distinct levels. First, the teacher must form working partnerships with a wide variety of colleagues within the school for quality learning. These partnerships are necessary for the curriculum integration advocated in chapter 14 and the support strategies outlined in chapter 10. The goal of this collaboration is to provide quality learning opportunities for each learner. Second, the teacher must create opportunities for and insist upon collaboration among learners. The lead-manager teacher implements cooperative learning activities that require collaboration and promote interdependence (see chapter 15), thus proactively teaching the skills of cooperation and conflict resolution. The lead-manager teacher fosters a community-of-learners atmosphere that evokes the feeling that "we are all in this together" and requires learners to help one another actively. Collaboration is the rule; competition is minimized or eliminated. All learners strive to be the best they can be and to do the best they can do. The teacher builds a collaborative atmosphere by promoting the following simple notions among the students:

1. If one learner in the group can do something, everyone can learn to do it.

2. Learners working together can accomplish greater results than learners working independently.

3. If you can do something another cannot, you can help that other person reach the same level of success if you provide encouragement and assistance, and exercise patience.

Accountability. The lead-manager teacher holds himself or herself fully accountable for outcomes in the school for quality learning. This accountability is not directed toward system or management demands for performance but rather toward each individual learner. The teacher addresses two major questions related to accountability:

1. Is every learner being served by the classroom program?

2. Is every learner engaged in quality learning?

Affirmative answers to both questions represent the ultimate fulfillment of teacher responsibility. The lead-manager teacher pursues this aim vigorously, neither accepting nor offering excuses for failure.

Questioning. The lead-manager teacher has highly developed and diverse questioning skills. Questioning is essential in helping and challenging learners in all aspects of learning and in their self-evaluations of behavior and learning. Highly developed questioning skills allow the teacher to influence learner behavior without coercion. The lead-manager teacher not only questions skillfully; he or she consistently demonstrates that, in the pursuit of quality, questions are appreciated more than answers.

Equality of attention. The lead-manager teacher accepts that individual needs and wants vary considerably and that each learner is unique. In accepting the challenge to engage each one in quality learning, the teacher listens equally to all learners, acknowledging both the message and the sender. High expectations are held for and communicated to each learner. The lead-manager teacher rejects practices, conscious or unconscious, that predict outcomes or that presuppose conditions that limit productivity. Such practices give rise to educational myths like "Gifted students will survive and thrive without teacher attention"; "Girls are less capable than boys in science, math, and physical activities"; "Slower learners should be expected to do less work and exert less effort, and therefore they should be rewarded for marginal or even wrong answers"; and "Compliant learners deserve more opportunity for independence than do noncompliant learners." The lead-manager teacher refrains from stating minimum expectations because such expectations have no relationship to quality and, in fact, may diminish quality.

Consistency. The lead-manager teacher's personal behavior is essential for communicating high expectations and modeling desirable behaviors in the classroom. The teacher strives continually to maintain consistency between his or her verbal messages and overt actions. The lead-manager teacher is an active learner, engaged in the pursuit of quality learning through self-evaluation; this engagement should be obvious to the student learners.

Mediation. The lead-manager teacher knows that, in a people-dominated environment like a classroom, conflict is inevitable. The teacher must understand conflict and be well versed in conflict resolution strategies. The lead-manager teacher views conflict as an opportunity for the conflicting parties to grow. The teacher will be required to mediate disputes between learners and will likewise experience conflicts with other staff members that must be resolved if the school for quality learning is to realize its goals. The lead-manager teacher must help learners understand the nature of conflict and develop conflict resolution skills.

Avoidance of adversarial confrontation. The lead-manager teacher avoids adversarial confrontation with learners in the understanding that such confrontation—pitting an adult against a child—is coercive and is thus counter to the mission of the school for quality learning. Lead-manager teachers keep rules to a minimum: They know that when a teacher is put in the position of enforcing a rule, he or she becomes the adversary of the rule breaker.

People orientation. The lead-manager teacher is goal and task oriented, focused on the mission of the school for quality learning: to engage each learner fully in the pursuit and production of quality. Despite this strong focus, the teacher strives to remain accessible to any learner in the classroom. The lead-manager teacher understands that the development of a personal, caring relationship with each learner is required for the development of the school for quality learning. There is no professional role more important than that of friend.

Support. The lead-manager teacher, in the knowledge that each learner is doing the best that he or she knows how to do, skillfully accepts the performance and supports the performer. The teacher learns to use nonconfrontational questioning to challenge each learner to choose and develop higher quality behaviors. In instances of clearly unacceptable behavior, the lead-manager teacher distinguishes between the behavior and the person, demonstrating acceptance of the person while asking him or her to choose a more acceptable behavior.

Facilitation of discussion. The lead-manager teacher uses open-ended classroom discussions or meetings for a variety of purposes. To ensure successful discussions, the teacher establishes ground rules for a supportive environment that encourages the kind of risk-taking required for behavior examination and change and focuses learner participation on the stated purpose of the activity. The lead-manager teacher creates a seating arrangement that encourages exchanges among participants (a circle), assumes a nonjudgmental position with no moralizing, shows warmth and enthusiasm to let the learners know that the teacher is interested in and involved in the discussion, and sets and enforces ground rules early and as needed. The rule of focus prevails: While one person speaks, all others listen. The teacher carefully prepares for discussion by generating a series of stimulating questions to be used as a backup if the discussion among learners does not flow smoothly. The lead-manager teacher is comfortable remaining silent when the discussion is continuing on its own momentum. The teacher ends meetings on a high note so participants will be eager to return to future discussions.

Facilitation of learning. The lead-manager teacher moves from the traditional role expectations of subject matter expert, regulator and director of learning, developer of academic talent, and enforcer of information to the facilitative role expectations of information resource person, learning consultant and manager of learning resources, developer of multiple talents, and assistant in learners' self-evaluation. The teacher serves as a resource person for each learner when the teacher's knowledge and skills are appropriate and the learner is comfortable with the relationship. For certain learning activities, the teacher suggests linkages between learners and other potential resources. By functioning as a linkage agent when appropriate, the teacher decreases learners' dependence on him or her and broadens their collaborative arena. The teacher also helps the learners define learning problems and design realistic learning strategies. By helping students focus their efforts in this way, the teacher helps learners succeed and achieve quality rather than becoming overwhelmed and discouraged. The lead-manager teacher challenges and supports the learners by assuming a variety of interactive roles such as coach, advisor, colleague, instructor, counselor, evaluator, and so on.

Risk taking. The lead-manager teacher is a risk taker and understands that any behavior change involves risk. The teacher designs activities that require both the teacher and the learners to experiment with ideas and behaviors. The teacher constantly engages in self-evaluation, a process essential to survival and growth in a helping profession. The lead-manager teacher challenges each learner to strive for quality as visualized by the learner through self-evaluation.

Vision. The lead-manager teacher maintains an unobstructed view of the school's mission and clearly understands the function of the classroom in the accomplishment of that mission. The teacher is a problem finder and solver and fully understands the classroom as a social system. The lead-manager teacher helps each learner develop his or her personal vision of quality and ensures that each experiences the success needed to fix that vision firmly in the learner's personal quality world.

Trust. The lead-manager teacher possesses and demonstrates faith in each learner. The teacher believes that, within a system of responsibility education and a supportive climate, all learners will consistently do the best they can do to meet their needs and to-fulfill their responsibilities. The lead-manager teacher trusts all learners to strive to be the best they can be. To not trust is to not expect quality.

Part 2 of this book described the lead-manager principal and detailed a management strategy for a school that frees the teacher from bureaucratic and management constraints so he or she can make decisions and organize the classroom environment to facilitate learning. Part 3 has outlined the responsibilities that the lead-manager teacher accepts when granted those freedoms. The expectations for both the lead-manager principal and the lead-manager teacher require great dedication, focus, and commitment. In the school for quality learning there is no room for the minimalist principal or teacher, no room for the principal or teacher whose needs are so great that the needs of others go unrecognized and thus unmet. In the school for quality learning, teaching is truly the hardest job of all. It is worth it; the rewards are astonishing.

When our vision of the school for quality learning materializes into actual practice, all who participate—the principal, the teacher as worker and as manager, the learner, and so on—can experience what psychologist Mihaly Csikszentmihalyi (1990) calls "flow." Flow is what overburdened principals and teachers live for, and it truly feels good. Csikszentmihalyi describes flow as a moment when a task or problem challenges you just enough but not beyond your capabilities. Learners can certainly experience that moment as well. When that condition exists, one enters an altered mental state of concentration and clarity, working at the top of one's creative abilities (but not over the top, which would cause anxiety). One might say that flow is the Zen of working—a transcendental moment in the exercise of given responsibilities. Csikszentmihalyi equates flow with that elusive quality, happiness, and he thinks that work—the right kind of work under the right work conditions—is a way to find it. Not surprisingly, control is one of the keys.

Csikszentmihalyi maintains that flow exists when we are in control of our psychic energy, and everything we do adds to consciousness. This, he says, feels wonderful. He describes the flow experience this way:

> Concentration is so intense that there is no attention left over to think about anything irrelevant, or to worry about problems. Self-consciousness disappears and the sense of time becomes distorted. An activity that produces such experiences is so gratifying that people are willing to do it for its own sake, with little concern for what they will get out of it, even when it is difficult, or dangerous. (p. 71)

Imagine an entire school populated by learners and teachers and other who frequently experience flow. This is the school for quality learning.

Appendixes

The questions and activities that follow are designed to help a school principal and staff as they collectively design the transformations necessary to move their school toward quality learning. The order of these questions and activities is significant. Understanding the psychological foundation of quality learning precedes all other considerations; developing a system of lead management for the school precedes developing a system of lead management for the classroom. The questions and activities are organized into two distinct phases, reflected by the respective content of Appendix A and Appendix B.

Appendix A: Questions and Activities for the Understanding Transformation Stage

These activities are designed to help school staff develop a common understanding of the school relative to the information presented in this book. Activities are designed for total staff involvement; that involvement is critical to the development of a common knowledge base upon which the group can design the appropriate transformations toward becoming a school for quality learning.

Appendix B: Questions and Activities for the Transformation Action Stage

These activities are designed to involve school staff in designing the transformations necessary to move toward becoming a school for quality learning. The activities in this appendix should not be undertaken until the Understanding Transformation Stage activities have been addressed for all 18 chapters. Transformation Action Stage activities should then be accomplished in the order presented.

Appendix C: Assessment Scales

Finally, Appendix C presents two assessment scales, one for principals and one for teachers, to assess the degree to which each is able to implement lead-management principles.

Questions and Activities for the Understanding Transformation Stage

Chapter 1

1. Which of your students do quality work? Why? Is there a difference between succeeding and quality learning?

2. What are the attributes of a successful student in your school?

3. List students who are successful both by their definition and yours. Which of these students are doing the best they can do?

4. List the other students you have. What are they doing? Are there students who are successful but who are not doing the best they can do? What needs to change in order for them to do quality work?

5. Are there students who are not succeeding but who are doing the best they can do? What needs to change in order for them to do quality work?

6. What attributes of the school or system allow students to be successful and not do the best they can do? To do the best they can do and not be successful?

7. What is the financial impact of failure and underachievement on your school budget?

Chapter 2

Identify two or three present practices in your school that would need to change in order to bring your school in line with each of Deming's (1986) 14 points. (See Worksheet 1 at the back of this appendix.)

Chapter 3

1. List practices in your school that support staff in meeting their basic needs, then list practices in your school that thwart staff in meeting their basic needs. (See Worksheet 2.)

2. List practices in your school that support students in meeting their basic needs, then list practices in your school that thwart students in meeting their basic needs. (See Worksheet 3.)

3. Describe the total behavior of quality learning by listing as many verbs as you can that end in "ing" for each component of the total behavior. (See Worksheet 4.)

4. Describe worker behavior (as it relates to both teachers and students) in your school in terms of total behavior by listing as many verbs as you can that end in "ing." (See Worksheet 5.)

5. Identify which of the behaviors listed in the previous activity are a result of Deming management and which are a result of boss management (refer to Table 3.1 in the text).

Chapter 4

Using the philosophy on school and learning described in pages 57–59 of the text, discuss the following questions.

- How is your school a good place for adults and children? How is it not?

- Which management practices in your school are lead management and which management practices are boss management? Develop a list. (See Worksheet 6.)

Chapter 5

1. List major decisions required to operate the school. Who presently makes these? Who is responsible for implementing these decisions?

2. Participate in the group decision-making activity on page 68.

Chapter 6

1. In randomly assigned groups of four, compare your present system of personnel evaluation to the basic beliefs about human nature examined on pages 84–85. What needs to change in your present system in order to operationally embrace these beliefs? Have the small groups share the changes identified with the larger group. Ask each individual in the larger group to complete the following statement: "As a result of this activity, I learned (or relearned) that I . . ." Share these statements in the group.

2. How do you determine whether you have met your goals for the day? Week? Year?

Chapter 7

1. With a learning partner, respond to the questions listed on pages 94–95.

2. Following the partner activity, ask each individual to complete one or more of the following statements, then share these statements in the larger group.

   - "As a result of this activity, I learned (or relearned) that I . . ."

   - "I am proud that I . . ."

   - "I wish that I . . ."

Chapter 8

1. Examine the present discipline policy of your school and reconstruct it in the form of rights and responsibilities.

2. Consider whether there is any part of your present discipline policy that does not fit a rights and responsibilities format. Is that part necessary? If yes, what is the justification?

Chapter 9

1. List parent choices in your present school organization.

2. Which parents currently influence school practices and policies?

3. In what areas of operation and decision making do you believe parents would like more of a voice?

Chapter 10

1. Which staff members in your school are not now fully included?

2. List major system changes that are required in order to fully include those staff members not now fully included.

3. Which learners in your school are not now fully included?

4. List major system changes that are required in order to fully include those learners not now fully included.

Chapter 11

1. Why is change difficult?

2. Construct a pyramid model of your school system and label the parts of your pyramid with the individuals or groups of individuals who constitute each layer.

3. Construct a pyramid model of your own school and label the parts of your pyramid with the individuals or groups of individuals who constitute each layer.

4. What are the forces in your school system that resist transformation? Within your school?

Chapter 12

1. To the principal: Which of the specific attitudes or behaviors of the lead-manager principal do you expect to be the most challenging as you strive to- ward becoming a lead-manager principal?

2. To teachers: Which of the specific attitudes or behaviors of the lead-manager principal do you expect to be the most challenging to you as a teacher? As your principal strives to become a lead manager, which of the specific attitudes or

behaviors of the lead-manager principal do you expect to be the most challenging for you to reconcile in your relationship with your principal?

Chapter 13

1. What learner talents are presently fostered in your school, and how is each fostered?

2. What learner outcomes are required of successful learners in your school? What outcomes are required of all learners?

3. List one example of a current practice in your school that is an embodiment of each of Carl Rogers's (1969) notions about learning (see pages 155–156).

4. Which practices in your classroom are lead management and which are boss management? Develop a list.

Chapter 14

1. How would your school be different if it were organized around what was worth learning as identified by the learners, in collaboration with learning facilitators, instead of around what is now prescribed as that which ought to be taught?

2. List at least one example of a current practice in your school that verifies each of Postman and Weingartner's (1969) outcomes (see page 161).

Chapter 15

1. What are quality learners in your school like?

2. How would your normal day-to-day behavior be different if you were consistently exhibiting the learning facilitation behaviors listed on pages 175–176?

3. What learning activities currently in use are either designed as cooperative learning approaches or would lend themselves to a cooperative learning approach?

Chapter 16

1. Examine your current behavior management practices directed toward students and categorize them as punishment or discipline.

2. Examine the present discipline policy of your classroom and reconstruct it in the form of rights and responsibilities.

3. Consider whether there is any part of your present policy that does not fit a rights and responsibilities format. Is that part necessary? If yes, what is the justification?

4. In triads, answer the questions on pages 191–192 first from the point of view of teachers, then from the point of view of students. Share your thoughts with the larger group.

Chapter 17

1. Individually consider the question, What does the grade of A mean in my classroom? Share the answer within the entire staff group.

2. In random groups of four, discuss how students are currently involved in the evaluation of their learning efforts and products. Think of some specific ways that student involvement in evaluation could be increased. Ask each small group to share their most interesting ideas with the larger group.

3. List the assessments presently used in your school and classroom. Who determined that each of those assessments would be used? What information is generated by each assessment? How is the information generated used by the classroom teacher? By the learner?

Chapter 18

Which of the specific attitudes or behaviors of the lead-manager teacher do you expect to be the most challenging as you strive toward becoming a lead-manager teacher?

WORKSHEET 1   Chapter 2

Identify two or three present practices in your school that would need to change in order to bring your school in line with each of Deming's 14 points.

1. Create constancy of purpose for improvement of product and service.
   a. _____
   b. _____
   c. _____

2. Adopt the new philosophy.
   a. _____
   b. _____
   c. _____

3. Cease dependence on mass inspection.
   a. _____
   b. _____
   c. _____

4. End the practice of awarding business on price tag alone.
   a. _____
   b. _____
   c. _____

5. Improve constantly and forever the system of production and service.
   a. _____
   b. _____
   c. _____

6. Institute training.
   a. _____
   b. _____
   c. _____

7. Institute leadership.
   a. _____
   b. _____
   c. _____

8. Drive out fear.

    a. _____

    b. _____

    c. _____

9. Break down barriers between staff areas.

    a. _____

    b. _____

    c. _____

10. Eliminate slogans, exhortations, and targets for the work force.

    a. _____

    b. _____

    c. _____

11. Eliminate numerical quotas.

    a. _____

    b. _____

    c. _____

12. Remove barriers to pride of workmanship.

    a. _____

    b. _____

    c. _____

13. Institute a vigorous program of education and self-improvement.

    a. _____

    b. _____

    c. _____

14. Take action to accomplish the transformation.

    a. _____

    b. _____

    c. _____

WORKSHEET 2   Chapter 3

List practices in your school that support staff in meeting their basic needs, then list practices in your school that thwart staff in meeting their basic needs.

	Supports	Thwarts
Belonging		
Power		
Freedom		
Fun		

WORKSHEET 3   Chapter 3

List practices in your school that support students in meeting their basic needs, then list practices in your school that thwart students in meeting their basic needs.

	Supports	Thwarts
Belonging		
Power		
Freedom		
Fun		

WORKSHEET 4   Chapter 3

Describe the total behavior of quality learning by listing as many verbs as you can that end in "ing" for each component of the total behavior.

Total behavior of quality learning

Doing	
Thinking	
Feeling	
Physiology	

WORKSHEET 5   Chapter 3

Describe worker behavior (as it relates to both teachers and students) in your school in terms of total behavior by listing as many verbs as you can that end in "ing."

Teacher as worker	Student as worker

WORKSHEET 6   Chapter 4

Which management practices in your school are lead management and which management practices are boss management? Develop a list.

Lead-management practices	Boss-management practices

Questions and Activities for the Transformation Action Stage

Chapter 5

1. Develop a decision-making model for your school by answering the questions on pages 72–73.

2. Use the decision-making model developed to formulate a mission statement for your school based on Deming's (1986) principles.

Chapter 6

1. Develop a philosophy statement and a plan of personnel evaluation for your school.

2. Select a professional growth goal, choose major strategies for accomplishing that goal, establish a time line for accomplishing the goal, and determine a plan to judge your efforts toward the goal and the outcomes of those efforts.

Chapter 7

Design a plan for selecting new staff members that will identify candidates who represent cultural and intellectual diversity and who are committed to the ideals of the school for quality learning.

Chapter 8

Outline the ideal school responsibility education program and brainstorm ways faculty can help learners understand and integrate the program into their lives.

Chapter 9

How can your school be reorganized in order to provide parents real choices?

Chapter 10

1. Select a specific staff position not now fully included and design a program that fully includes that staff position.

2. Do staff positions exist that are not critical to the purpose of engaging each learner in quality learning? If yes, redefine these positions.

3. Choose a specific learner and design a system of support that will guarantee that the learner will engage in quality learning.

Chapter 11

1. Choose one of the forces identified as an impediment to change and design a strategy to neutralize the resistance offered by that force. Design a strategy to convert that force to a force for change.

2. Do the same for other impeding forces that you find influencing your goal to develop a school for quality learning.

Chapter 12

As the principal, complete the Lead-Manager Principal Assessment Scale in Appendix C as you believe the staff of your building will rate you (your "perceived real"). Have teachers complete the Lead-Manager Principal Assessment Scale anonymously, then compile the results (your "real"). Are there discrepancies between your "perceived real" and your "real" that concern you? Are there behaviors you need to change in order to move toward becoming a lead-manager principal? Establish targets for accomplishing those changes. *Note:* If you find this exercise threatening, you are likely a boss manager.

Chapter 13

Develop a listing of general outcomes that will be the goals for learners in your school.

Chapter 14

Choose a unit or a curricular area and make the three decisions called for in chapter 14 on page 169.

Chapter 15

Using the same unit or curricular area selected in the activity for chapter 14, make the decisions called for in chapter 15 on pages 181–182.

Chapter 16

1. Design a C.A.R.E. time program for your classroom.

2. Outline the ideal classroom responsibility education program and brainstorm ways that teachers can help learners to understand and integrate the program into their lives.

Chapter 17

1. Design a learning process seminar for your classroom by selecting a topic and outlining questions to stimulate discussion.

2. Design a learning activity log for a unit of study in your classroom and design a conference format for working with individual students using the learning activity log as a central feature of the interaction.

Chapter 18

1. As the classroom teacher, complete the Lead-Manager
    Teacher Assessment Scale (See Appendix C) as you be-
    lieve your students will rate you (your "perceived real").
    Have each student anonymously complete the Lead-
    Manager Teacher Assessment Scale. Compile the results
    (your "real"). Compare your "perceived real" to your "real."
    Are there discrepancies that concern you? Are there be-
    haviors that you need to change in order to move toward
    becoming a lead-manager teacher? Establish targets for
    accomplishing those changes. *Note:* If you find this exer-
    cise threatening, you are likely a boss manager.

2. Design, for the staff of your school, a staff development
    program to facilitate the transformation to lead-manager
    teachers.

APPENDIX C

Assessment Scales

LEAD-MANAGER PRINCIPAL ASSESSMENT SCALE

For each of the following statements, circle the number that best describes what you think about the principal being rated.

Principal's name

My principal . . .	Strongly disagree				Strongly agree
1. Understands my needs and wants	1	2	3	4	5
2. Relates to me on a personal level	1	2	3	4	5
3. Recognizes my strengths	1	2	3	4	5
4. Has high expectations of me	1	2	3	4	5
5. Solicits my ideas	1	2	3	4	5
6. Tells me what I should do	1	2	3	4	5
7. Listens to me	1	2	3	4	5
8. Deals with my concerns in a timely fashion	1	2	3	4	5
9. Challenges me through questioning	1	2	3	4	5
10. Is consistent	1	2	3	4	5
11. Does not accept criticism	1	2	3	4	5
12. Settles disputes fairly	1	2	3	4	5
13. Avoids conflicts	1	2	3	4	5
14. Is supportive	1	2	3	4	5
15. Is accessible to me	1	2	3	4	5
16. Has "favorites" on the staff	1	2	3	4	5
17. Communicates clearly	1	2	3	4	5
18. Recognizes my accomplishments	1	2	3	4	5
19. Is able to assist me to develop instructional strategies	1	2	3	4	5
20. Is knowledgeable about resources	1	2	3	4	5
21. Allows me to try new ideas	1	2	3	4	5
22. Is confrontational	1	2	3	4	5
23. Has a vision toward improvement	1	2	3	4	5
24. Shares power	1	2	3	4	5
25. Relates effectively to parents	1	2	3	4	5
26. Deals effectively with student behavior	1	2	3	4	5
27. Solves problems	1	2	3	4	5
28. Makes time for people issues	1	2	3	4	5
29. Is fair	1	2	3	4	5
30. Is well organized	1	2	3	4	5

LEAD-MANAGER TEACHER ASSESSMENT SCALE

For each of the following statements, circle the number that best describes what you think about the teacher being rated.

Teacher's name

My teacher . . .	Mostly true	True half the time	Mostly false
1. Understands my needs	1	2	3
2. Seems to know what I want in school	1	2	3
3. Knows when I do my best work	1	2	3
4. Expects too much from me	1	2	3
5. Treats me fairly	1	2	3
6. Allows me to make important choices	1	2	3
7. Challenges me to do my best work	1	2	3
8. Tells me what to do	1	2	3
9. Insists that I cooperate with other students	1	2	3
10. Allows me to help other students	1	2	3
11. Encourages other students to help me	1	2	3
12. Insists that I do my best work	1	2	3
13. Does not accept excuses from me	1	2	3
14. Lets me know when he or she is proud of my behavior or my work	1	2	3
15. Thinks I am capable	1	2	3
16. Asks lots of questions	1	2	3
17. Lets me get by with poor work	1	2	3
18. Has "favorite" students in my class	1	2	3
19. Thinks my opinions are important	1	2	3
20. Expects me to recognize good work	1	2	3
21. Is consistent	1	2	3
22. Gets mad often	1	2	3
23. Helps students resolve conflicts	1	2	3
24. Listens to me when I have a problem	1	2	3
25. Likes me	1	2	3
26. Encourages me to try new things	1	2	3
27. Helps me when I have a problem	1	2	3
28. Provides opportunities for students to discuss their ideas and opinions	1	2	3
29. Cares about me	1	2	3
30. Helps me feel OK when I have trouble accomplishing a task	1	2	3
31. Insists that I do quality work	1	2	3
32. Encourages me not to give up	1	2	3
33. Trusts me	1	2	3
34. Learns new things and shares them with the class	1	2	3
35. Likes students	1	2	3

References and Bibliography

Aguayo, R. (1990). *Dr. Deming: The American who taught the Japanese about quality.* New York: Carol Publishing Group.

Aronson, E. (1978). *The jigsaw classroom.* Beverly Hills, CA: Sage.

Beane, J. (1991). The middle school: The natural home of integrated curriculum. *Educational Leadership, 49*(2), 9–13.

Bodine, R. J. (n.d.). *Leal School staff handbook.* Unpublished manuscript, Urbana, IL.

Bodine, R. J. (n.d.). *Leal School parent/student handbook.* Unpublished manuscript, Urbana, IL.

Brophy, J. (1992). Probing the subtleties of subject-matter teaching. *Educational Leadership, 49*(7), 4–8.

Brown v. Board of Education, 347 U. S. 483 (1954).

Covey, S. (1990). *The seven habits of highly effective people.* New York: Fireside/Simon & Schuster.

Crawford, D. K. (n.d.). *Washington School staff handbook.* Unpublished manuscript, Urbana, IL.

Csikszentmihalyi, M. (1990). *Flow: The psychology of optimal experience.* New York: Harper & Row.

Deming, W. E. (1986). *Out of the crisis.* Cambridge: Massachusetts Institute of Technology, Center for Advanced Engineering Study.

Deming, W. E. (1993). *The new economics for industry, government, education.* Cambridge: Massachusetts Institute of Technology, Center for Advanced Engineering Study.

Dolan, W. P. (1991, April). *The pyramid organization.* Paper presented at a seminar sponsored by the American Association of School Administrators, Chicago.

Elmore, R. F. (1992). Why restructuring alone won't improve teaching. *Educational Leadership, 49*(7), 44–48.

Fisher, R., & Brown, S. (1988). *Getting together: Building relationships as we negotiate.* Boston: Houghton Mifflin.

Fisher, R., & Ury, W. (1981). *Getting to yes.* Boston: Houghton Mifflin.

Fogarty, R. (1991a). *The mindful school: How to integrate the curriculum.* Palatine, IL: Skylight.

Fogarty, R. (1991b). Ten ways to integrate curriculum. *Educational Leadership, 49*(2), 61–65.

Gabor, A. (1990). *The man who discovered quality.* New York: Random House.

Ginott, H. (1972). *Teacher and child: A book for parents and teachers.* New York: Macmillan.

Glasser, W. (1965). *Reality therapy.* New York: Harper & Row.

Glasser, W. (1969). *Schools without failure.* New York: Harper & Row.

Glasser, W. (1972). *The identity society.* New York: Harper & Row.

Glasser, W. (1984). *Control theory.* New York: Harper & Row.

Glasser, W. (1986). *Control theory in the classroom.* New York: Harper & Row.

Glasser, W. (1990). *The quality school.* New York: Harper & Row.

Gonder, P. O. (1991). *Caught in the middle.* Arlington, VA: American Association of School Administrators.

Goodlad, J. I. (1991, Fall). Next century's model. *Agenda: America's Schools for the 21st Century,* p. 12.

Herzberg, F., Mausner, B., & Snyderman, B. (1959). *The motivation to work.* New York: Wiley.

Hoglund, R. G. (1991a). The cost of educational mediocrity and failure. *Journal of Reality Therapy, 11*(1), 21–23.

Hoglund, R. G. (1991b). Made in Japan: Deming's management principles. *Journal of Reality Therapy, 10*(2), 20–26.

Johnson, D., & Johnson, R. (1975). *Learning together and alone: Cooperation, competition, and individualization.* Englewood Cliffs, NJ: Prentice-Hall.

Kelley, E. (1980). *Climate development for schools: Principles and practices.* Reston, VA: National Association of Secondary School Principals.

Kozol, J. (1991). *Savage inequalities: Children in America's schools.* New York: Crown.

Leading indicators—Assorted facts and opinions for recent research on American education. (1991, Fall). *Agenda: America's Schools for the 21st Century,* p. 16.

Leading indicators—Assorted facts and opinions for recent research on American education. (1992, Spring). *Agenda: America's Schools for the 21st Century,* p. 8.

Leinhardt, G. (1992). What research on learning tells us about teaching. *Educational Leadership, 49*(7), 20–25.

McGregor, D. (1961). *The human side of enterprise.* New York: McGraw-Hill.

McNeil, L. M. (1986). *Contradictions of control.* New York: Routledge.

Mitchell, R. (1992, August). Verbal confusion. *Teacher Magazine,* pp. 34–35.

Moore, C. (1986). *The mediation process.* San Francisco: Jossey-Bass.

Naisbitt, J., & Aburdene, P. (1990). *Megatrends 2000.* New York: Morrow.

National Association of State Boards of Education. (1988). *Rethinking curriculum: A call for fundamental reform.* Alexandria, VA: Author.

National Association of State Boards of Education. (n.d.). *Today's children, tomorrow's survival. A call to restructure schools.* Alexandria, VA: Author.

National Center for Education Statistics. (1990). *Digest of Education Statistics.* Washington, DC: U. S. Government Printing Office.

National Commission on Excellence in Education. (1983). *A nation at risk: The imperative for educational reform.* Washington, DC: U. S. Government Printing Office.

National Council of Teachers of English. *Position on the teaching of English: Assumptions and practices.* Urbana, IL: Author.

O'Neil, J. (1992). Preparing for the changing workforce. *Educational Leadership, 49*(6), 6–9.

Postman, N., & Weingartner, C. (1969). *Teaching as a subversive activity.* New York: Delacorte.

Prawat, R. S. (1992). From individual difference to learning communities—Our changing focus. *Educational Leadership, 49*(7), 9–13.

Robinson, G. (1985). *Effective schools research: A guide to school improvement* (Concerns in Education Series). Arlington, VA: Educational Research Service.

Rogers, C. (1969). *Freedom to learn.* Columbus, OH: Merrill.

Schrumpf, F., Crawford, D. K., & Usadel, C. (1991). *Peer mediation: conflict resolution in schools* (Program Guide). Champaign, IL: Research Press.

Sharan, Y., & Sharan, S. (1990). Group investigation expands cooperative learning. *Educational Leadership, 47*(4), 17–21.

Slavin, R. (1987). *Cooperative learning: Student teams* (2nd ed.). Washington, DC: National Education Association.

Stainback, W., & Stainback, S. (1990). *Support networks for inclusive schooling.* Baltimore: Brookes.

Walton, M. (1986). *The Deming management method.* New York: Perigee-Putnam.

Index

About the Authors

Donna K. Crawford has a master's degree in education with specialization in the areas of social-emotional disabilities and early childhood education, as well as an advanced certificate of education in administration from the University of Illinois at Urbana-Champaign. Over the last 20 years, she has held the positions of early childhood education teacher, school principal, and assistant director of special education programs in Urbana, Illinois. She is certified in reality therapy and has served as a practicum supervisor for the Institute for Reality Therapy. She has consulted with numerous schools throughout the state of Illinois in the areas of early childhood education, administration, proposal writing, and conflict resolution. Crawford holds certificates in mediation and conflict resolution training from the Justice Center of Atlanta and the Family Mediation Institute. She is currently executive director of the Illinois Institute for Dispute Resolution, which facilitates the development of conflict resolution programs in Illinois schools. Crawford is coauthor of *Peer Mediation: Conflict Resolution in Schools* (Research Press, 1991).

Richard J. Bodine holds an undergraduate degree in the teaching of mathematics and chemistry and has taught math and science at the upper elementary, middle, high school, and junior college levels. He has a master's degree in special education, with specialization in work with gifted children, and an advanced certificate of education in administration from the University of Illinois at Urbana-Champaign. He has been a secondary school administrator and director of special regional education programs. Bodine has consulted with numerous schools throughout the country on gifted education, individualized learning programs, and administrative issues. He has directed several summer teacher training institutes on innovative practices. He has taught graduate level courses in administration, including several semesters of the course on principalship at the University of Illinois. For 20 years, he has been principal of Leal Elementary School in Urbana, Illinois, working with the staff to implement ideas advanced in this book. In 1992 he received the Illinois State Board of Education's "Those Who Excel" award as outstanding administrator.

Robert G. Hoglund holds a master's degree in special education from Arizona State University in Tempe, Arizona. He is the president and founder of the Center for Quality Education, Inc., whose purpose is to promote the integration of reality therapy, control therapy, and quality principles to continually improve our educational system. He is a senior faculty member of the Institute for Reality Therapy and conducts training seminars for schools in Dr. William Glasser's Quality School Consortium.